UTOPIA'S DEBRIS

ALSO BY GARY INDIANA

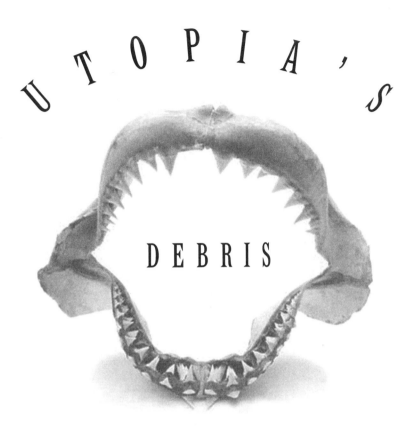

UTOPIA'S

DEBRIS

Selected Essays

GARY INDIANA

BASIC
BOOKS

A Member of the Perseus Books Group
New York

Books published by Basic Books are available at special discounts for bulk purchases in the United States by corporations, institutions, and other organizations. For more information, please contact the Special Markets Department at the Perseus Books Group, 2300 Chestnut Street, Suite 200, Philadelphia, PA 19103, or call (800) 810-4145, ext. 5000, or e-mail special.markets@perseusbooks.com.

Designed by Trish Wilkinson
Set in 11.5-point Adobe Garamond

Library of Congress Cataloging-in-Publication Data

Indiana, Gary.
    Utopia's debris : selected essays / by Gary Indiana.
        p.   cm.
    Consists of articles and essays mainly written between 1996 and 2008.
    ISBN 978-0-465-00248-1 (alk. paper)
    I. Title.

PS3559.N335U86 2008
814'.54—dc22   2008031640

10 9 8 7 6 5 4 3 2 1

For Susan DePalma
Frank Lo Scalzo
Louis Mello
Dena Santoro
Steve Wasserman

There is another point, which I would much rather see determined: whether the world was always so contemptible as it appears to me at present?—If the morals of mankind have not contracted an extraordinary degree of depravity, within these thirty years, then must I be infected with the common vice of old men, difficilis, quarulus, laudator teporis acti; *or, which is more probable, the impetuous pursuits and avocations of youth have formerly hindered me from observing those rotten parts of human nature, which now appear so offensively to my observation.*

TOBIAS SMOLLETT, *HUMPHREY CLINKER*

CONTENTS

— PART IV —
AND THE FOG COMES ROLLING IN

— PART V —
UTOPIA'S DEBRIS

BY WAY OF A PREFACE

THIS BOOK IS a five-part lament, or fugue, interrupted by gales of manic laughter, excoriating sarcasm, and the gape of a gimlet eye—consisting of articles and essays mainly written between 1996 and 2008. I've given individual sections titles that may evoke, for some readers, the persistent state of mind in which they were organized: *Desertshore, The Infernal Evidence, Surrealisms and the Power of Emotion, And the Fog Comes Rolling In*, and, finally, *Utopia's Debris*.

We live in the wreckage of a century I lived through the second half of, a century of false messiahs, twisted ideologies, shipwrecked hopes, pathetic answers. That the debris has implacably dogged us into the 21st century, with its increasingly hollow civic life, its disposable cultures, its massacres and genocides, its magnification of pathologies that no calendrical change can possibly detach from the human situation seems "par for the course," and while abandoning the promiscuous use of the phrase "the incurable in human nature," I have not yet found a more agreeable substitute for it.

To elucidate the title sections: "Desertshore" because all but one of the essays in that section was written in, or about, Los Angeles, the dropping-off point of the westerward expansion the country of my birth wreaked with murderous ruthlessness conflated with idealism; "The Infernal Evidence" because what the essays' subjects either explore or exemplify reflect the skewed relation to sexuality, gender, romantic love, and conventional expectations of happiness that unaccountably dominate human affairs and that so many Americans still take a bath in every morning; "Surrealisms and the Power of Emotion" to indicate that the response of artists and writers and thinking people of all sorts has been, without question, one of extreme skepticism enlivened by giddiness, flights into the fantastic and stunningly incongruous, desperation in comic guises, madness and near-madness that may serve as a cloak for actual sanity; "And the Fog Comes Rolling In"—well, this is a line from a Tom Waits song made famous by Marianne Faithfull, and evokes a thick vapor of uncertainty about what truly lies in front of us, and about how serviceable our understandings of one another, and the world as given, truly are.

I've used the title of this book for its final section, though it's far from my intention to prescribe despair and hopelessness as modes of consciousness. It's by understanding things systemically—whether via the small telling details we find in the novels of Simenon, the political paradox implicit in Barbet Schroeder's *Terror's Advocate*, the often derided and unpopular exhortations to think beyond conventional aporias that Susan Sontag so often declared, or the interweaving triumphs and failures of Brecht and Weill's *The Rise and Fall of the City of Mahagonny* in the closing years of the Weimar Republic and the subsequent time of Nazi ascendancy—that we can, sometimes, at least learn to live with the madness around us, recognize what is different about it than the madness of earlier times, and also recognize what hasn't changed at all.

This is a modest and extremely unrealistic project. It ought to be obvious that the pieces collected in *Utopia's Debris,* in the end, reflect my own tastes, the seductions to which my own sensibilities have surrendered me, and that they do not, alas, primarily group themselves under the sign of eros, but of death. If many of the works and artists examined in these pages heighten a tonic sense of life, more often they have instilled an acute and not entirely uncomfortable reminder of my own mortality, the ephemeral nature of consciousness, and represent the struggle of individuals to wrest from their brief time of existence *something of value*. If that value proves only to be that of affording pleasure to some readers, I think I've done what I set out to do, which was neither to improve the world in a monumental way, nor win any vast esteem from other people for what little I've accomplished, but rather to give some people, whom I may never meet and from whom I expect absolutely nothing, something of the pleasure I got from writing these essays.

Gary Indiana
May 2008

ACKNOWLEDGMENTS

T HE AUTHOR would like to acknowledge a debt of gratitude to the editors of the following publications: *The Los Angeles Times Book Review, The London Review of Books, New York Magazine, Artforum, The Village Voice, Film Comment,* and *Bookforum.*

PART

I

DESERTSHORE

BARBARA KRUGER
The War at Home

War has broken out. Where or how, nobody knows any longer. But the fact remains. By now it is behind each person's head, its mouth agape and panting. War of crimes and insults, of hate-filled eyes, of thoughts exploding from skulls. It is there, reared up over the world, casting its network of electric wires over the earth's surface. Each second, as it rolls on, it uproots all things in its path, reduces them to dust. It strikes indiscriminately with its bristling array of hooks, claws, beaks. Nobody will survive unscathed. Nobody will be spared. That is what war is: the eye of truth.

—J.M.G. LeClezio

TECHNICALLY SPEAKING, "we" know almost nothing about Barbara Kruger. The bits of biography that emerge in scattered fashion from her interviews are carefully circumscribed, illuminating in a general way, withholding in another way. She has pretty much refused to be overly "expressive" about herself-as-artist, and her work, though each example of it is distinctly a signature piece, has something of the impersonal lucidity we find in Marcel Duchamp's work.

Duchamp's subject was art and life, or art-in-life. Kruger's work is about the war at home, in each of us: between good and bad, men and women, black and white, losers and winners, creeps and assholes, all the sociocultural dissonances that make the world so tweaked. It seems to issue from an angrily saturnine clarity about how things go wrong between people, how affection subtly modulates into rage, how the brightest moment can turn to shit on a dime. Less abstract subjects than Duchamp's, let's say. Less parochial in its

3

assumption that the art object is a commodity and a medium of exchange and enough said.

The physicality of Kruger's objects is often surprising because, in a way, their "objectness" seems simply the right thing for that idea in that place at that time, and her ideas translate easily from medium to medium. Transparence is the ideal condition of her work, as in an installation like *Power/ Pleasure/Desire/Disgust,* where virtually everything is a verbally seething skin projected onto architectural volumes—because, in a sense, the condition of consciousness this work recommends is something with sharp, clear lines and a lot of empty space to reflect in.

An art of ideas, in other words, yes, but if conceptual art, say, often reflects a fundamental disjunction between the pleasure the artist took in using materials and the message that comes across, proposes that we locate meaning and pleasure outside the physical, as if the "art" were trapped in expediently attractive containers, and regard aesthetics as a sort of secondary concession to decoratively severe appetites, Kruger in contrast is the least metaphysical and mystifying of artists. An existentialist artist, in a sense. The pleasure in the well-made product, something visually arresting and sometimes horrific, is less distant from our regular menu of pleasures and provocations than a spiral jetty or a field of lightning rods somewhere in New Mexico that we're never going to visit. This work is subtle and blunt at the same time, blunt language with subtle implications, and participates in many strategies of commercial media, since these are, in fact, more persuasive and more authentically gratifying than a lot of contemporary "fine art"—the commercial media comprise the vernacular of our time, and they're what resonate for us in our actual lives. Kruger targets the ego and libido of things, rather than nuances of art history, or intellectual conundrums, though you can read "art issues" into her works as readily as "life issues," and you wouldn't be wrong.

Kruger compresses the telling exchanges of lived experience that betray how skewed our lives are: epigrammatically, slashed across strangely powerful, recuperated iconography. The varying scale of this work has a nice clean "just enough" and sometimes "let's give this icky emotion real grandeur." What I like best are startling incongruities of scale, as in a huge riot of pretty flowers with the simple, small, square kicker in the center: JAM LIFE INTO DEATH. It's the agenda of all advertising and all television, all media all the time.

Kruger's rich raw material is this bizarro world of media that surrounds us and gurgles in our living rooms, that makes our choices for us, shows and tells us what reality's supposed to be, *according to what, we might ask, but fewer and fewer of us do ask, if you want to be clear-minded about it*—a theater of death, where the shadows of the dead—us—flicker in Plato's cave; a theater of unceasing electronic fizz that creates and nurtures the desire to become discorporate, to become a floating, bodyless replica of oneself in a world that's no longer entirely a world, a figure instead of a body, something ME and NOT ME, YOU and NOT YOU in the same collapsed moment.

Mental notes in the housewares department of Wal-Mart. Yes, Wal-Mart. You can get anything you want at Wal-Mart. The fact that you want it means you are already dead. Last Christmas I had an epiphany at Wal-Mart. No, that's a little grand. If you want the epiphanic version, take a look at Kruger's sculpture of Santa Claus molesting a little girl, with Jesus Christ on the verso side, suffering in the extravagant way that Jesus is wont to do. (Incidentally, I wanted to title this, "Why I Am Not A Christian, by Bertrand Russell.") It was two weeks before Christmas. Each department in Wal-Mart had its own Muzak system blaring Christmas carols, and each department manager, apparently, had decided to program a different medley of joyfully moronic carols. And, as you walked through Wal-Mart, these competing festive audios melted together into a completely dissonant, sour, even terrifying melange, as if Stockhausen had decided to do a Christmas album, and you know something, it was perfect, it was almost art, and no one in Wal-Mart seemed to notice they were being subtly encouraged to go home and commit suicide. This has something to do with Barbara Kruger's work, I think. The ruin of certain smug and reassuring representations, the defacement of delusion, with just enough melody left in to seize your attention.

There are moments when some of Kruger's images just paste themselves over reality. It's their precision, their abstemious lack of digressiveness that gives them this force, a concentrated quality, a quality of "here's the issue and here's what it looks like," and people writing about this work have frequently become entangled, tripped all over themselves puzzling out who "I" am and who "we" are and who "you" is, as if the work were "embodied" in the artist and the spectator, the way Jackson Pollock is embedded in his wild and crazy semenoid drips and splatters, but something almost opposite is at work in Kruger's activity, which resists the idea of the self-heroicizing gesture, but more importantly, repudiates the fixing of the subject in the conventional artist/spectator relation.

You don't have to read Lacan to appreciate this work, but Lacan is helpful if you want to take the work in without miring yourself in direct, frontal relation to what it's saying at the moment you're looking at it. For one thing, the moment concretized in a Kruger piece is going to connect with a different moment in your life, in fact the "meaning" you perceive in it is bound to be different when it does fold into your biography—you can save the personal part of your eureka, in other words, for some dark night of the soul, some appropriately hideous moment with a special someone whose mask just fell off. I am always urging people to read Lacan. In a Lacanian sense, I and we and you are floating signifiers of a paradigm, the elements of a model of consciousness in a particular scenario of crisis. "I" is an idea of "I," "you" a construct of "you," as in, this is how "we" manage a crisis, how "we" negotiate sex and money and politics, here's a map of "our" habitual responses, here's a diagram of "our" dynamic, and if you look at it head-on, look at the naked lunch at the end of your fork, you can figure out what's wrong with it, why the mechanisms of transpersonal exchange that dominate our society leave you feeling like a turned trick, why it's killing you softly with its dumb song, because it hurts so good.

Your comfort is my silence. Your money talks. Buy me I'll change your life. These are propositions, albeit more visceral than logical propositions—though they are logical too, and follow the equation of democracy = capitalism = demolition of utopia. The logic of a system in which anybody's loss is someone else's gain. Where commodities substitute emotions, products replace empathy, only the externalized manifests existence, and life no longer lives, its impersonation enacted, instead, upon a labyrinth of screens. It becomes possible to watch life turn into death from the passive spectatorship of the posthumous. It becomes impossible to intervene in time and space, impossible to occupy a concrete reality, impossible to change the movie of virtual chimera and actual absence.

How do we verify a proposition? If you're Wittgenstein you follow the thread to the place where it runs out short of the punctum. If you're Kruger you picture how the proposition seals itself, how it might incarnate as a metaphor, what the shorthand way of showing it is. And often this has

a narrative teaser going on, the suggestion of a B-movie or film noir extension at either end of it, carrying both a sense of its punishing absurdity and
a tacit bow to its seductiveness. Kruger is more the frame-by-frame analysis
of *Laura* or *Where the Sidewalk Ends,* perhaps, than the semiotic autopsy of
Cat People or *I Walked with A Zombie.* But *I Walked with A Zombie, the Musical* wouldn't be an implausible Kruger installation. In a way, she's already
done that.

Much of her iconography is drawn from the 1940s and 1950s, and from
reconstituted later images that carry traces of the slightly *recherché* quality
associated with the 1940s and 1950s, when American imperial clichés were
minted and permeated the visual style of magazines, newspapers, movies,
and early TV. The look is *io ipso* "ironic," because we're all several decades
beyond the look. But all culture has done with what the look signifies is
translate it into more bedazzling, "modern" pictorialism that fools us better
and makes the imaginary payoff even more imaginary. You won't have better sex in a Lexus than you did in your father's Oldsmobile. You might have
better *looking* sex, more *modern* sex, sex in a glistening world where everything's a throbbing penis and everything's a moist vagina and every second
is an orgasm as explosive as a hydrogen bomb, if indeed you were going to
have sex, but the truth is you aren't going to have sex at all, you're just going
to spend a lot of money on a car, and that car isn't even going to be a nipple
ring. That car is going to be the cradle for your cell phone. And you're not
going to be young again, so the car will look great but you're going to look
really old. So what we have, looking at the Oldsmobile, is the memory of
sex—in other words, what sex really is.

*Radio: This is Calypso Debbi (I swear), now you know when you go to Car-
nival in Peru, stock up on water balloons, and skip the manure.*

A lot of people get freaked by Barbara Kruger's art. Uptight around it, de-
fensive, hostile, threatened, as if it were a person telling them things, which
it is, of course, but then a certain number of people never get the joke, and
don't want to get the joke: that they're telling it while it's telling them.

Or it's not their mode of amusement. They'd like a *New Yorker* cartoon
instead. And of course there will always be times when a *New Yorker* cartoon is more welcome than something darker and smarter.

It can be troubling, perplexing, irritating, whatever, when an artist goes
for an extreme purity of diction, as Kruger does, because we often crave a

certain messiness, a bit of throw-away, some superfluous oxygen, an aria of the asshole-ism Kruger has frequently lauded in her writing: Her visual work doesn't provide those types of escape. It's a distillation, a type of essence, and not to get the joke is to miss the only relief it offers. If you get the joke—better still, if you adopt the joke, take it over as your joke, put yourself in whichever "I" or "you" or "us" seems to be winning here, on the side of the angels—the work becomes conversational, even relaxed, an effort to break through the reciprocal deafness that modern life has wreaked on our ears and nervous systems.

The implicit faith of this work is that we can, now and then, find our way out of our delusions and the infantilization our culture prescribes as a placebo utopia, to something like an authentic adulthood, reason, and the golden rule, and that the effort to do this is worth the mental anguish it entails, and could even make us happier, in many ways, than the gladiatorial fantasies we're trained to apply in every social arena. This is the subtext: The conviction that empathy can, in fact, change the world—a little at a time, and not always, and you will only improve things a little bit, anyway, but if you don't even try, the incurably ugly side of human nature has already won the war inside us all.

When he was still LeRoi Jones, Amiri Baraka wrote a novel called The System of Dante's Hell, *where I found the following lines: "And it seemed a world for Aztecs on the bone side of mountains. A world, even strange, sat in that leavening light & we had come in raw from the elements. From the cardboard moonless world of ourselves . . . to whatever. To grasp at straws."*

KINDERGARTEN GOVERNOR

THE 2003 California gubernatorial recall was launched by a group called the People's Advocate, an anti-tax organization founded by the late Paul Gann and Ted Costa, the purported brains behind the 1978 Jarvis Amendment, a.k.a. Proposition 13 (the granddaddy of California referenda, a bonanza for property owners), and the outgoing state Republican chairman, Shawn Steel. In accordance with Article 2, Section 14 of the California Constitution, the People's Advocate, or any recall movement, is obliged to collect signatures equal in number to 12 percent of the last vote for the governor's office, an effort that initially floundered. But in May 2003, Congressman Darrell Issa of San Diego started his own recall effort, with a view to becoming governor himself, bankrolling the petition drive with $1.3 million of his own money, or at least what he claimed was his own money. What had begun as a quixotic twinge of spite from an office behind a Krispy Kreme franchise in Sacramento surged into a surrealist juggernaut, culminating in the ousting of Governor Gray Davis, and the risible election of Arnold Schwarzenegger, action figure, as the custodian of the world's fifth largest economy.

Like Schwarzenegger, Congressman Issa has a piquant history. In the early 1980s, his car-alarm company, which did work for a much larger firm, Joey Adkins's A.C. Custom Electronics, lent Adkins $60,000, then called in the loan. Issa went to court, and wrested possession of Adkins's firm. Three weeks after Issa quadrupled the insurance on parts and equipment in the building, the electronics facility burned to the ground.

In 1973, Issa pleaded guilty to possession of an unregistered firearm, which he tended to brandish at his employees, supposedly in jest. He was arrested twice for grand theft auto. In his unsuccessful 1998 run for the Senate, he claimed that he had been a member of Nixon's security detail during the 1971 World Series. Nixon did not attend the 1971 World Series. After a 2001 trip to the Middle East, Issa, an Arab-American, announced that Hezbollah is not a terrorist organization. Perhaps not; the People's Advocate, however, is.

After securing 1.6 million signatures on the recall petition, thus forcing the special election, Issa tearfully withdrew his candidacy on 7 August 2003, when it became obvious that he lacked the winning charisma of billboard bimbo Angelyne, vertically challenged child star Gary Coleman, self-proclaimed smut peddler Larry Flynt, and 151 other amusing candidates ($3,500 was enough to get your name on the ballot). These included the ultra-right, anti-abortion state senator Tom McClintock, the inestimable Arianna Huffington and the former Baseball League Commissioner Peter Ueberroth. By no coincidence, Arnold Schwarzenegger announced his candidacy—on the Jay Leno *Tonight* show—on the day Issa withdrew.

It was clear from the outset that if a "No on Recall" vote supporting Davis failed to pass by even a slight margin, only a fraction of the votes cast for Davis would be enough to elect one of the alternative candidates. Had Davis himself been allowed to run on the alternative ballot, he might have been elected twice in 11 months, if "universal loathing" for him hadn't become the incessant mantra of virtually every media commentator. In the event, the No vote rolled in at 3,559,400; Schwarzenegger gleaned 3,743,393, winning somewhere in the numeric ballpark in which George W. Bush lost the Presidential election of 2000.

Some independents, including Huffington, dropped out of the race to lend support to the No on Recall movement; Ueberroth faded into the woodwork; numerous Republicans, though not McClintock, left the field to campaign for Schwarzenegger. People running just for the fun of it stayed in.

Cruz Bustamante, Davis's lieutenant governor (and now Schwarzenegger's), became the Democratic front-runner, but there was something askew about slogans like "No on Recall, Yes on Bustamante," suggesting as they did that Bustamante was second-fiddle, even to the allegedly most detested governor in recent California history. Bustamante has slightly more charisma and self-deprecating humor than the aptly named Gray Davis (who resembles an especially depressive funeral director), yet he failed to interest most of the Latino community he comes from.

I lived in Los Angeles through much of the recall drama, and found the supposedly ubiquitous hatred of Davis bewildering: For one thing, nobody I encountered ever expressed such overheated feelings toward the incumbent, and the very notion of Schwarzenegger as governor (or governator, as the tabloids were fond of calling him) provoked incredulous hilarity from movie stars and supermarket check-out clerks alike. On the other hand, face (and, in his case, body) recognition gave considerable momentum to Schwarzenegger's ever-grinning will to power. He had, after all, progressed from steroid-inflated grotesque to box-office legend, thanks to an infallible eye for the main chance. Despite his overthroaty, mangled diction and general clunkiness, he has won the heart of every American male suffering from testosterone psychosis—a sizeable portion of the electorate. It certainly helped that Schwarzenegger movies started playing non-stop on television, often in competing time spots, and that professional sycophants such as Larry King and Oprah Winfrey featured Schwarzenegger on their chat shows, which, being non-political, were exempt from equal-time strictures.

Leaving aside the rather puerile debates staged among the leading contenders (Schwarzenegger skipped the first one; the second, in which he threatened in veiled fashion to push Huffington's head into a toilet, was scripted), the hourly fluctuation of poll figures and the avalanche of pundit blather that filled the newspapers and radio shows (and, at the eleventh hour, television), there were four salient factors that fed into the passage of the recall and Schwarzenegger's landslide election.

First, allegations of his recreational sexual assaults on no fewer than 15 women, along with "revelations" that he had said positive things about Hitler back in his weight-training days, surfaced at exactly the wrong moment for his opponents, five days before the election: Though the *Los Angeles Times* coverage was the result of a three-month investigation, much of the electorate dismissed the disclosures as a desperate partisan effort to derail Schwarzenegger's candidacy. Pundits who knew nothing about it brayed that the *Times* "sat on the story for weeks." Worse, Davis decided to exploit the charges, reminding Californians that he has always run rather unseemly negative campaigns. Additionally, movie stars generally get a free pass on this sort of thing—Schwarzenegger dismissed his habitual tit-and-ass grabbing as pranks that happen on "rowdy movie sets"—whereas professional politicians don't. Besides, as Susan Faludi pointed out, the core of Schwarzenegger's white, male, locker-room constituency *likes* the idea of assaulting and humiliating women, so long as there's no emotion involved—a further reason Clinton got pilloried for his indiscretions (he seemed to care about the women he romanced).

Second, a tripling of automobile registration fees was signed into law by Davis in August and took effect on 1 October. If you live in California, you have to drive a car, and this drastic hike, though passed by the legislature, was perceived as another example of Davis's perfidy. (In a reasonable universe, it could also have been seen as an effort to balance the budget: Individual states, unlike the Federal government, are not allowed to run deficits; and other revenue schemes have been blocked by the "direct democracy" of ballot referendums.)

Third, right-wing chat shows on TV and the radio endlessly cited a California budget deficit of $58 billion (every now and then, this was amended to $35 billion), when a simple check with the California budget office revealed the deficit to have shrunk, during Davis's second term, to a mere $12 billion. When talk-show hosts were corrected on this point, they reverted to the $58 billion figure a few soundbites later.

Fourth, the voters of Orange County, the most retrograde and fascist-minded enclave in the state, turned out in droves for Schwarzenegger, after the polls had nailed the more virulent McClintock as a "loser."

Schwarzenegger won handily by tossing off lines from his movies, vowing to "terminate" this and "terminate" that, and bidding "hasta la vista" to Davis, the deficit, the miserable decline of the state's education system and, hardly least, the energy crisis. Precisely how he planned to terminate all these evils never came into focus, but pundits concluded that Schwarzenegger "held his own" by resolutely saying nothing.

It was quite forgotten by the candidates and the press that the energy crisis was caused by deregulation and the leasing of the state's electricity to Enron and other now-convicted Texas fraudmeisters, a disaster locked into place by Davis's Republican predecessor, Pete Wilson, whose advisers are now clustering around Schwarzenegger like flies in a privy. Davis hardly helped, renewing the corrupt contracts and allowing Texas corporations to sell California's energy back to California at an obscene mark-up. Last year, however, when the full effects of this wholesale looting became evident, Lieutenant Governor Bustamante, with Davis's blessing, filed a suit against

Enron and the other power companies, under the Unfair Business Practices Act, to recover the $9 billion the companies had squeezed from the state. With Schwarzenegger in the Governor's Mansion, this unsettled lawsuit will doubtless be mooted.

Schwarzenegger, as it happens, held a secret meeting on 17 May 2001 with Kenneth Lay of Enron and the convicted stock-swindler Mike Milken. What deals were struck remains a mystery. Governor-elect Schwarzenegger's current plan is to continue the ruinous deregulation process, though he also wants 50 percent of new homes to be equipped with solar heating panels. This kind of qualifier used to be called throwing peanuts to the monkeys, though some benefit may come out of it when the number of new homes outstrips the number of old homes—say, in 2030.

Twenty states allow driving licenses to be issued to undocumented aliens. A clear minority of Californian voters regard this as something akin to creeping Communism, or at least the Welfare State. The number of uninsured, unlicensed drivers who cause accidents in California is epidemic, pushing insurance rates for the ordinary motorist as high as $300 per month. Schwarzenegger wants to rescind the recent law allowing illegals to get licenses, and, further, promises drastically to curtail illegal immigration. This will have a devastating effect on the availability of domestic help, leafblowers, tree trimmers, supermarket clerks, shopping mall security guards and transient agricultural laborers: all those people doing the jobs that native Californians consider beneath them. Guest workers welcomed in good times face deportation hearings when the economy turns sour.

Rescinding the tripled auto registration fees, as Schwarzenegger promises to do, will cost California something in the area of $8 billion—approaching the level of the current budget deficit. Yes, no one wants to pay the new fees. Yes, everyone wants a clean environment, and at the same time wants to drive Sherman tank-sized SUVs that gobble fuel at 9 to 13 miles per gallon. Californians want top education for their kids; they just don't want tax increases to pay for it.

Wanting it all and paying for none of it could pass as the state motto of California. The infamous Proposition 13, passed in 1978, froze property taxes and, more peanuts to the monkeys, "rolled back" rents from their most recent increases. Enterprising landlords simply hiked rents before Proposition 13 passed, then "rolled them back" to what they'd been in the first place.

Since the Jarvis Amendment, the appetite for "direct government" in the form of endless referendums has crippled the ability of the state government to operate in a fiscally responsible fashion, since the voters, year after year, "directly" decide what they will and won't pay for. To recall a governor elected less than a year ago is the ultimate pandering to this demand for instant fixes to systemic problems. Given the rampant cult of celebrity that grants full personhood only to the well-known, the rich, and those whose names have clout at the box office, it was logical that an amiable Cro-Magnon from Austria who plays an indestructible, mush-mouthed cyborg in Hollywood blockbusters would morph into a "strong leader" in the magical thinking of star-struck know-nothings, who crawled out of a Nathanael West novel to the few polling places it was possible to find. (The usual number of California polling locations, 25,000, was reduced for the recall to 15,213.)

In the face of the fait accompli, the propaganda on both sides of the party divide spun out of control. Democrats insisted that the socially libertarian Schwarzenegger would be of no use to Bush and his puritanical cohort, while Republicans predicted an exploitable fissure in California's solid Democratic majority in the next Presidential contest. Less partisan commentators made the apt observation that nobody won in this carnivalesque travesty, except for Enron and the INS.

Once the circus had packed its tents, some interesting facts that might have been more usefully aired before the election began to surface: James Diffley, an economist at Global Insight, told the *New York Times* on 12 October: "California has obvious problems, but the economic performance has been surprisingly good." In the same article, Mike Van Daele, chief executive of Van Daele Communities, a building firm, remarked: "We've never seen it like this in 25 years. Housing prices are appreciating as much as $10,000 to $15,000 a week." And, by some Arnoldophilic sleight-of-hand, the correct, $12 billion figure for the California budget deficit was suddenly cited in virtually every news story, even in media outlets that had drilled the $58 billion fib into the brain of every voter. "Despite the political upheaval, growing budget deficit, the electrical power crisis and the bursting of Silicon Valley's bubble—all of which have created the image of a state deep in recession—California's economy, by many measures, has done better than the rest of the nation's in the last few years," the *New York Times* report concluded.

One can only surmise that the "hatred" of Gray Davis (who was, after all, California's governor "in the last few years"), the inflated deficit figures and the economic fear-mongering that so much of the nation's press whipped up to add "substantive issues" to a special election that was really about celebrity worship and circus acts were simply the latest tweaks in a media oligarchy's implacable manipulation of consciousness, indifferent to its deleterious effect on the remnants of the American democratic system. It's a significant advance in the melding of politics and entertainment: A photogenic straw man gets inserted into office and a cabal of shadowy advisers dictate policy and carry out the dirty work. This formula was polished during Ronald Reagan's first Presidential term, and until recently it had much of America hypnotized by the glove-puppet posturings of George W. Bush. Whether it will work with Arnold Schwarzenegger depends largely on how much puppetry a conniving narcissist is willing to abide. There have been plentiful signs that Schwarzenegger has a few maverick ideas of his own, and it's too soon to assume they're all bad ones.

MURDERING THE DEAD

S HE CAME to Los Angeles during World War II from nowhere special, a pretty girl with big hair and bad teeth who liked to go to bars and nightclubs. She believed in love and romance and lived on hot dogs and Coca-Cola, lavished hours on her makeup in dollar-a-night furnished rooms. A drifter, something of a cipher, she was a person people remembered vaguely but could never quite pull into focus. A good-time gal who didn't really seem to have a good time, demanded a little too much sympathy and hardly ever returned a favor. She sometimes spoke of a husband killed in the war, a baby who died, but these were figments of a waking dream that carried her through sleepless nights. If someone hadn't cut her in half, the world would know precious little about Elizabeth Short.

She had been nicknamed the Black Dahlia, a name so movie-perfect for the era of noir that her murder became symbolic of everything weird and inexplicable festering under the city's gleaming surfaces. Steve Hodel's best-seller, *Black Dahlia Avenger,* is the latest in a long procession of novels and nonfiction books to treat the Dahlia case as Los Angeles's emblematic homicide, a killing affixed to the city the way Jack the Ripper is to Victorian London and the Strangler is to Boston. The Dahlia killing engraved itself into urban mythology; it seemed to say something stark and ugly about the emptiness of glamour and the wages of sin. Short's dead body became a movie star, a cautionary tale and a magnet for a large assortment of pathologies, many of them literary.

The symbolic message of Short's corpse as the killer arranged it at 39th Street and Norton Avenue in Leimert Park in early 1947 could not in itself be less mysterious or more readily aligned with notions of Hollywood as a sausage factory for the young and beautiful. Like the Manson killings, the Hillside Strangler slayings and the Night Stalker spree, the Black Dahlia murder was carried out with its effect on the public very much in mind. The perps in all these cases had something to tell the world, posing the bodies, writing things in blood, sending a garbled telegram about the incurable in human nature.

The classic account is John Gilmore's *Severed,* which achieves the almost impossible feat of turning the very blankness of Elizabeth Short's brief life into a thing of riveting oddity. According to Gilmore, Short had a rare vaginal deformity that made the image of a sexually easy creature of the night nothing more than an image; if we accept this premise, the Dahlia story becomes the dark tale of a hapless mimic whose grasp of adult relations extended only to what they looked like in the movies. There's no reason not to credit Gilmore's fastidious account, in which one drifter kills another, then dies in a flea-pit hotel fire: This cruddy, depressing solution to the mystery is utterly consistent with the pathos of the world the Black Dahlia traveled through on her way to the big nowhere.

For a certain mentality, however, prosaic justice demands that an unusually vicious, legendary murder turn out to have been committed by a truly unlikely, preferably famous individual or, failing that, someone connected to famous people. Hodel, a former homicide detective for the Los Angeles Police Department, manages to implicate several famous personalities in Short's murder. *Black Dahlia Avenger* has the added *frisson* of its author's bizarre discovery, after two entire years of research, that Short's killer was—gasp!—his own father.

Hodel is not the only person in recent years to discover exactly this skeleton in the family closet. In 1995, a book called *Daddy Was the Black Dahlia Killer* revealed that its co-author, Janice Knowlton, a former lounge singer, had discovered through recovered memory that her father murdered Short after Short left an aborted fetus in her father's garage. Horrifically, Knowlton was forced to witness much of the torture and mutilation inflicted on Short and to help him dispose of the remains.

Knowlton's is the kind of book it doesn't do to argue with: Its author seems to have channeled a rich vein of snuff pornography while gazing at healing crystals in some quack's office. Hodel, having been a homicide cop, would seem a more rigorously fact-driven investigator. And yet Hodel's father, like Knowlton's, was named George. What Hodel considers proof is strangely tangled with nebulous memories. Could Steve Hodel be an "alternative personality" of Janice Knowlton?

Let's call this personality Steve and see what he has to say. After an obligatory shock-horror opening that whisks us back to Leimert Park on that dreadful morning in 1947, Steve recounts his own bittersweet and strained relations with his father, Dr. George Hodel, up until his death in 1999. There would be no funeral, as per his will, but Steve flies to San Francisco to console Dad's widow, June. She gives him a small photo album that belonged to his father, unwittingly opening Pandora's Box.

Among the pictures Dad—at one time a professional photographer, among many other things, and an intimate of Man Ray—has kept throughout the years are two of a woman with her eyes closed. Something tries to bubble up from memory. The face is familiar yet unknown. At last it hits him: It's the face of Elizabeth Short.

There are also pictures of Hodel Jr.'s first wife, Kayo, whom we now learn had been, unknown to Steve, one of Dad's mistresses before Steve married her. We later find out that she cheated on Steve and lied about her age (that is to say, lied about her age extremely). Steve now realizes that the love between Kayo and his father was a deep and tumultuous one, rather than a silly fling, and concludes that Kayo married him to wreak revenge on Dad.

To get to Short, Steve seems to have taken a cherished bromide of American prosecutors a bit too much to heart—that is, circumstantial evidence is often more valuable than eyewitness testimony.

He tells us first about his father's extremely rangy life. Dr. Hodel had been, at various times, a concert pianist, a crime reporter, a radio announcer, an artist, finally a surgeon and psychiatrist. In 1947, he and the family were living in the posh Lloyd Wright's Sowden house at Franklin and Normandie avenues, in Steve's account a brooding Gothic pile full of secret rooms straight out of *Vathek*. Dr. Hodel operated a venereal disease clinic downtown, presumably another accursed lair of dark secrets. Among his friends were Henry Miller and John Huston.

The picture Steve paints of his father unavoidably calls to mind those sinister doctors in novels by Raymond Chandler and Jim Thompson, usually found at a starlet's bedside at 3 in the morning brandishing a syringe. There were, at the spooky Lloyd Wright house, orgies. There was, among

Dr. Hodel and his famous friends, an interest in the Marquis de Sade. One of Steve Hodel's older brothers recalls seeing Dr. Hodel write something on a woman's breast in lipstick at a typical get-together. Shortly after the Dahlia slaying, another unsolved homicide became known as "the Lipstick Murder."

At various moments in the book, after depositing such tidbits, Steve announces that he has "proven" something, perhaps meaning something in the realm of the occult. Dr. Hodel, we are told, admired Man Ray, who did a famous portrait of the Marquis de Sade and was a surrealist. The surrealist group once made photo-booth portraits of themselves with their eyes closed to emphasize the belief that dreams and reality are the same.

In the pictures of Short that Steve found in his father's album, her eyes are also closed. Moreover, the way the dismembered Dahlia was posed bears a close resemblance, *qua* Steve, to the figure in Man Ray's photograph "Minotaur." The Marquis de Sade left instructions that he did not want any funeral obsequies or memorial, virtually the same stipulation found in Dr. Hodel's last will and testament.

There is more, much more. Dr. Hodel was—or so Steve claims—the "prime suspect" in the Dahlia police file, though which file, discovered in what year, in whose department and by whom are questions so muddied by Steve's account that any methodical reader would be skeptical. Steve's revelations occur to him by way of "thoughtprints": products of free association. An accomplice of Dr. Hodel's named Frank Sexton is remembered by a witness; photographs and "thoughtprints" summon him as a "swarthy" man. Steve is later made aware of the presence of a swarthy man in some 15 murders, including that of James Ellroy's mother.

The Dahlia body site is only a few miles from the Sowden house. So are a million other things in Los Angeles, but this kind of pataphysical eureka defines this entire book's methodology: The mere physical proximity of one thing to another suggests a relationship—Dr. Hodel lived in Los Angeles, so did Elizabeth Short; an interest in the Marquis de Sade (an interest shared by Simone de Beauvoir, Pierre Klossowski, Maurice Blanchot and many other literary figures) becomes solid proof that Man Ray, Huston and Dr. Hodel were "sadists" and that Dr. Hodel, at least, along with swarthy Frank, had no inhibitions about perpetrating the tortures and mutilations of De Sade's novels in real life; a man claiming to be the Dahlia killer who called a reporter spoke in a refined, sibilant voice; Dr. Hodel had once been a radio announcer and also had such a voice; and so on.

Perhaps aware that his portrait of a libertine, murderous coven in his childhood home is only marginally more plausible than Janice Knowlton's acrobatic feats of memory, Steve eventually rolls his sister, Tamar, onto the proscenium. Tamar, once a freewheeling buddy of Michelle Phillips, is now an older and wiser mom of two daughters, named Fauna 1 and Fauna 2.

As a teen, Tamar told police who picked her up as a runaway that her father had molested her. This resulted in an indictment, a trial, a scandal. After being acquitted, Dr. Hodel fled the country, staying away for most of the following 40 years, leaving Steve in the clutches of his mother, a drunk. Man Ray went back to Paris around the same time.

Like Steve, Tamar is willing to say anything about anybody as long as they are dead. John Huston, Tamar asseverates, tried to rape her when she was 11: He was, she says, exactly like his character in "Chinatown." According to Steve, Dr. Hodel had such powerful goods on the high and mighty because of his VD clinic that Tamar's accusations would never have resulted in formal charges, except for a bureaucratic screw up. Man Ray, he implies, somewhat contradictorily, might also have been snared by the webs of justice had he, too, not been "powerful," but he fled the country just in case. The notion of Man Ray as a person with awesome power over the Los Angeles police and district attorney's office is itself rather ponderous.

What we have here is a wacky parody of a police procedural, with a rich and fascinating subtext of delusion. There is also something plangent and, in an underdog way, tragic about somebody so wounded by a lousy childhood that his father becomes a veritable Minotaur in his adult imagination, a scourge to all women, faceted and diabolical as Fu Manchu. Remember that Oedipus, too, was a kind of detective.

All the same, it isn't nice to drag a lot of famous dead people into your family muck, unless you have witnesses a little more reliable than someone who differentiates her children by numbering them.

It is, finally, and not at all sympathetically, appalling that a homicide detective would sell out his professional integrity to produce this piece of meretricious, revolting twaddle, which amounts to evidence manufacturing, litigation-proof slander and chicanery on a fabulous scale and does absolutely nothing to answer the question: Who killed Elizabeth Short?

PRETTY VACANT

THE DINGBAT is to residential building in Los Angeles what strip malls are to its commercial construction: a space-optimizing method of gouging cash from the urban landscape while replacing its vestiges of eccentric garishness (the Brown Derby, Perino's, the Nicodell, etc.) with a repugnant, omnipresent dwarfism.

The capitalist version of Soviet drabness and uniformity, it shares a hypnotically ugly spirit, given the climate, with the instant decay and intentional banality of Cuba's architectural "socialist realism." (After the revolution, Che and Fidel briefly favored dynamic-looking modernism; El Supremo, however, was far more intent on micromanaging the personal business of his subjects than providing them with anything distinctive to live in, while his Argentinean stunt double of the World Revolution never sustained much interest in anything that didn't involve weaponry and bloodshed. Cuba soon condemned the peninsular extrusions and long stretches of the Malecon seafront to the same fusion of residential design with prison construction already ubiquitous in Eastern Europe.)

A cheap travesty run amok, these one- or two- (sometimes three-) story stucco Dumpsters that nearly everyone lives in at one time or another in LA have an existential emptiness that can be gussied up and dissembled by track lighting and the right sort of throw pillows and furniture, but the spatial insipidity of the dingbat eventually defeats any effort to turn a "unit" into a "home," even when little sparkle lights add the allure of dazzling acne to the façade.

Like strip malls, however, dingbats have persisted and spread through the city so inexorably—a sluggish fungal infection between 1945 and the early '60s, later spreading everywhere like a rent-feeding species of kudzu—that a kind of delectation of their various styles becomes possible. They are, after all, the standard vernacular and often quite as livable as a refurbished mortuary, their units not at all predictably functional or dysfunctional when viewed from outside. It must be said that dingbat functionality is strictly a matter of maintenance (some dingbats are kept up with considerable pride by their proprietors; others are left to rot by management companies fronting for film stars and TV personalities), since the apartment layouts of a dingbat are invariably as boxy and generic as the building shell: studio, one-bedroom, two-bedroom, with unimportant variations in the placement of kitchen and bathroom.

It makes sense that Clive Piercy's *Pretty Vacant* carries no text besides the author's introduction—what is there really to say about these excrescences, except that one either has a perverse fondness for them or a horror of ever living in one?—and that this fat rectangular book, itself suggestive of a stiltless dingbat toy model, consists entirely of exterior black-and-white snapshots, taken by Piercy from his car window. These shrines to mediocrity speak for themselves. Even brand new, they emanate an unmistakable mixture of poorly medicated depression, transience and an occult perception of entrance tables piled high with unpaid parking tickets and kitchen trash buckets topped by bisected credit cards.

Piercy, a graphic designer, offers us something closely akin to Ed Ruscha's serial documentation of Los Angeles boulevards. (Ruscha is thanked in the book's acknowledgments.) His introduction credits the architect Francis Ventre with naming the dingbat. "[T]hey all began life as variations on the modernist stucco box that had effectively replaced, through economic necessity and postwar inventiveness, the Spanish colonial revival style that had dominated up until then," Piercy writes. "Structurally, that's what they consist of: generic boxes on three sides with all of the attention paid to the street façades." The difference-within-sameness revealed in *Pretty Vacant* is the kind associated with the thread patterns of Warhol silk screens; they're all much the same, but if you look carefully, each has its distinct, if ultimately meaningless, fingerprint.

Warhol taught America to embrace and reify its own visual repulsiveness as a new version of beauty, since this endemic preference for ugliness is an irreversible fait accompli in the built environment. If we must live in an ever-expanding human hive, so quantified and electronically tagged that we've become interchangeable consumers and surveillance objects, living in sardine-can cities that will one day achieve Asiatic human density, the little differences between a monstrosity called the Capri and a twin called the Flamingo acquire the cachet of something almost like concepts. Like many things in California, the dingbat represents the triumph of quanta over quality, illustrating the leveling nature of totalitarian democracy. The dingbat owes nothing to utopian city planning or to architecture as an art. These are not Case Study Houses and bear no resemblance to any such seriously considered scheme of "affordable housing." They do owe something to Frank Lloyd Wright: If you took all the upscale nuances out of one of his blockier houses and blanketed the floors with pre-mildewed carpeting, this is what you'd get.

Somewhere in the many writings attributed to Warhol (what persons wrote which ones, you tell me and we'll both know) it's remarked that the queen of England can't buy a better hot dog at a baseball game than you or me. This was meant to illustrate what's great about America, and at certain times of the day it's the kind of thing one occasionally enjoys about the sensory overload of American cities: that just about everybody has to put up with the same environmental importunities. But not everybody experiencing the aging process while stuck in traffic is headed home to a dingbat apartment, and a derelict scrounging up the queen of England's hot dog leftovers under the bleachers is as close to Buckingham Palace as he's ever going to get.

Dingbats are not so much déclassé or redolent of full-time poverty as they are an architecture of gone tomorrow, of three-month leases or month-to-month rentals, in some ways ideal for the dicey professions so many Angelenos follow: illegal hair salons, "therapeutic massage" and a spectrum of feast-or-famine jobs in the entertainment industry. One can move from dingbat to dingbat on an income scale that slides up and down, and the very flimsiness of these buildings, which are usually planted atop stilts, on at least one side, to accommodate a few parking spaces, indicates that their ideal occupancy is a temporary one, that the people inside are waiting to bottom out and segue to a skid row SRO, hoping for the right Richard Neutra to come on the market, or scouring the fringes of better neighborhoods for something in between—a guesthouse in the Hills, a Silver Lake triplex with a long-term lease, a bungalow in Atwater.

This is precisely where dingbats serve a legible social need: as housing for people who want the option of reinvention—or of quick, surreptitious flight, as Alan Arkin and his family do in Tamara Jenkins's 1998 film, *Slums of Beverly Hills*. Jenkins's film is a superb illustration of the pall of melancholia that checks every blandishment of Los Angeles from ever producing an unqualifiedly good time, and the dingbat apartment building freezes the same ineluctable dread in stucco crypto-solidity. The anonymity of the dingbat, given the lavish architectural marvels available in Los Angeles to those who are (or think they are) permanently richer than God, mirrors the anonymity of its occupants. Piercy's affectionate visual documentation, replete with close-ups of the surface details by which their anonymous builders have sought to give them some illusion of personality, evokes the pathos and longing of those not-always-impossible wishes and dreams that draw people to Los Angeles, city of dreams, from the vast spiritual dingbat of America's heartland.

GAVIN LAMBERT (1924–2005)
The Goodbye Person

GAVIN LAMBERT, who died in July 2005, found his subject at an early age, sitting in cinema darkness while giant figures passed before his eyes. The movies offered escape from a drab, middle-class English childhood. In adolescence, a conspiratorial excitement, shared with fellow Cheltenham College student Lindsay Anderson, resulted in their founding of *Sequence* magazine in 1947. Lambert occupied a key role in the Free Cinema movement (which included Tony Richardson and Karel Reisz), becoming editor from 1950 to 1956 of the British Film Institute's *Sight and Sound.*

England in the 1950s wasn't a happy place to be gay, and if America was hardly less oppressive, its entertainment business, sub rosa, was much less regimented. A love affair with Nicholas Ray, who hired him as an assistant, brought Lambert to Los Angeles in 1956, and into a subculture where homosexuality, however heavily veiled, was commonplace.

By that time, oddly, Lambert had already directed a film; *Another Sky,* an hypnotically seductive, yet harshly honest meditation on otherness and the exploitation of the third world by the privileged Westerner, shot on location in Morocco, was a flukish opportunity provided by Sir Aymer Maxwell, "a frustrated impresario" who financed the film, then retired permanently to a Greek island when it got an indifferent reception in Britain.

Although *Another Sky* met with the approval of both Rossellini and Buñuel, Lambert never directed another movie, and apparently never attempted to. Living elsewhere than England seems to have been his overriding priority when he fled with Ray to Hollywood. He quickly adapted to the less flashy, equally dicey job of writing for movies and TV—sometimes credited, sometimes not—while trying to write fiction.

27

The Slide Area was published in 1959. Lambert's first book is at times described as a collection of stories, at times as a novel; the discrepancy is natural, since the book's seven "scenes of Hollywood life" describe a place where connections occur with the randomness of accident. The ones that link Lambert's characters have an especially louche and coincidental quality. Like the trope of six degrees of separation, the peregrinations of *The Slide Area*'s narrator—an unnamed screenwriter we assume to be, more or less, Lambert—depict the restless figures he encounters as moving points on a sprawling psychic map, crossing and recrossing one another's paths.

I say "more or less" because the "I" of *The Slide Area* is an example of that peculiarly modern first-person narrator who is not the principal subject of the narrative, and also the "I" who, like Proust's Marcel, performs as the author's surrogate, while the question of whether they are the same person has almost no speculative importance. Our representations of ourselves are even more selective and partial than our portraiture of other people, and there is by now a whole literature in which writers deliberately muddle the conflation of themselves with "I" by attaching their own names to their fictional constructions. The practice begins with Céline and becomes hilariously refined by Gombrowicz, whose novels invite us to believe that he remained in Poland during World War II, when he was actually marooned in Argentina (*Pornografia*), a deserter when he in fact tried to volunteer for the army (*Trans-Atlantyk*), and so on.

Lambert dissembles himself behind this ambiguous "I" in *The Slide Area* and *The Goodbye People* (1971), novels separated by more than a decade that read like parts of the same biography of Los Angeles. (Lambert's "I" resembles a detective whose curiosity impels him to follow leads, solving mysteries of personality rather than crimes.) With a single exception, all his works of fiction contain allusions to the others: The unforgettable, somewhat bovine Countess Marguerite Osterberg-Steblechi, for example, (whose final "trip around the world," a bizarre simulation engineered by two avaricious Italian nieces, is described in "The End of the Line" in *The Slide Area*) is resurrected in *Norman's Letter* (1966) and makes cameo appearances in at least two other novels. Figures like Mark Cusden, the sexually insatiable, dissipated former school chum from England whose exasperating narcissism is almost exasperatingly well chronicled in *The Slide Area*'s "Nukuhiva!," turns up as a mainly off-camera minor character in

A Case for the Angels (1968), with the obscure Pacific island Nukuhiva also reappearing as a sort of symbolic endpoint of the incessant "search for the self" that Lambert's characters so often claim, perhaps truthfully, to be undertaking.

In Lambert's novels, people tend to have either a stolid, delusional sense of who they are or want to be, or none at all. *The Slide Area*'s subtitle is artfully misleading in one way, brilliantly apt in another; one of the first writers to emphatically parse the difference between Los Angeles and Hollywood, Lambert populates his books with damaged, alienated people on both sides of the candy-store window, some with their noses pressed against the glass, desperate to get in, others trapped inside, desperate to get out.

The myth-ridden Hollywood of *The Slide Area* is embedded in a city that Lambert depicts as a hubless, pointlessly expanding, but simultaneously crumbling network of suburbs, a chimera floating between desert and ocean. People escaping from the stifling nightmare America of Sherwood Anderson end up in Lambert's Los Angeles, hoping for either transformation or death—it's often hard to tell one wish from the other.

> Her face became almost reverent. "It's a funny thing, I've always believed in myself. I always knew I had to do *something*. My aunts are very religious people, but the worst kind if you know what I mean. They never go to the movies. They were always making me pray and I guess I believed in God because they told me to. Well, I used to wonder how I could attract God's attention. Honestly." She gave herself a little hug. "I felt—well, such a nobody. How could God ever notice me unless I was somebody? That's what I felt."
>
> I watched her face, intent and serious, her hands embracing at the memory of a prayer. "What did you want God to do?" I asked.
>
> "I told you, I wanted Him to notice me."

Emma Slack, the seemingly clueless fourteen-year-old from Galena, Illinois, who speaks in this passage, is one of many losers strewn throughout Lambert's fiction whose stories are first presented as non sequiturs, but later resume, at a later stage of evolution, like tenacious microbes—sometimes imperfectly transformed, yet surviving; Emma Slack becomes Delia Blow, not exactly a screen goddess, but at least the $400-a-week star of *Attack of the Ant Women* and *High School Ghoul.*

Like the ambiguous "I," most of Lambert's important characters could be pinned to real-life models, as Lambert pinned some of them himself, in interviews, long after his books appeared. The director Cliff Harriston was drawn from Nicholas Ray, Joan Crawford was the inspiration for fiftyish glamour queen Julie Forbes, etc. The game of guessing who's really whom in a novel, however, despite its inevitability in cases like Proust (with whole albums of photographs devoted to the writer's familiars, who are thus rendered identical to their fictional incarnations), cheapens the whole enterprise of writing fiction, as if fiction had been invented simply to avoid libel suits.

Lambert was an avid collector of the movie industry's nasty secrets, which he spilled in abundance in biographies of Norma Shearer and Nazimova; in a book on the making of *Gone With the Wind;* in his book-length interview *On Cukor.* But none of his nonfiction has the low altitude of quotidian "movie star" bios, or the envious malice of the trash exposés sometimes attempted by gossip columnists of the Joyce Haber variety.

I knew Lambert personally, and well enough, to be impressed by his generosity, in print, toward certain people he privately couldn't bear; even one individual whom Gavin consistently referred to as "it" (keeping his back turned on "it" for an entire evening when the three of us happened to be at the same Los Angeles party), Gavin mentions in his writings without a hint of disdain. This could, I suppose, be dismissed as self-protective tact, but I think it had more to do with his understanding that his opinion might be true for himself, but was still just an opinion. (He did get a certain amusement from privately sticking pins in certain friends who weren't present—who doesn't?—but was also quick to credit their accomplishments and worthy personal qualities. His sense of fairness was exemplary.)

The Slide Area is remarkably undated, not least for its matter-of-fact presentation of homosexual affairs and casual sex. Throughout his fiction, Lambert exposes the libidinal realities behind the trite rituals of masculinity and the bogus images of marriage and "family values" cherished by the film industry. In a similar spirit, his Hollywood books unfold in the yawning chasm between real life in Los Angeles and the fantasies manufactured by its dominant business. Lambert recognized that the American Dream in the twentieth century had become indistinguishable from its manufacturing center, which sucked in, chewed up, and discarded its dreamers in truly industrial quantities.

The transient character of every aspect of Los Angeles is its only unchanging quality, and is as true today, in the era of rampant Disney'ed architectural grotesquerie and clownish "restoration" of a vanished past, as it was in the long era of decline that encompasses *The Slide Area, Inside Daisy Clover* and *The Goodbye People*—roughly, the mid-'50s through the early '70s.

Inside Daisy Clover (1963) is the first of several novels in which Lambert's first person is explicitly someone else. Neither the book nor the subsequent movie starring Natalie Wood and Robert Redford quite won blockbuster popularity, but both have acquired a legendary aura. Daisy Clover, who begins telling her own story in the sometimes cloying vernacular of a rebellious but basically sweet urchin who haunts the carnival pier between Venice and Santa Monica, starts with nothing except her good looks, a voice, and a slowly-going-gaga, solitaire-addicted mother in a decrepit mobile home. As per the cliché Lambert so often douses with ice water, Daisy is "discovered" by a stoatlike producer and his gelid wife (both of whom, like Raymond Chandler's characters, have richly sordid back stories), and Daisy actually becomes a movie star.

The strength of *Inside Daisy Clover* is its subtle tweaking of the rags-to-riches clichés it traffics in. It seems almost weightless at first, though its opening's bleak poverty-row setting creates an expectation of disillusionment ahead, and unless the reader separates what actually happens from Daisy's charming retelling, some of the book's impact can get diluted. Much of *Daisy Clover* describes horrific loss and disappointment, madness and near-madness, corrupt and awful people preying on the vulnerable; if you subtract Daisy's somewhat contrived, last-minute "comeback" from her rise, breakdown, and fall from industry favor, almost every scene in Joan Didion's later *Play It As It Lays* reads like a Gothicized version of something in *Inside Daisy Clover.*

Daisy's Hollywood is familiar from *The Slide Area,* a few years longer in the tooth, with traces of the same personnel, including spectral appearances by figures like Julie Forbes. Daisy, an amalgam of Judy Garland and Natalie Wood, embodies both the shipwreck of Old Hollywood and the beatnik Hollywood of *Rebel Without a Cause,* New Hollywood's segue into youth culture, hippies, LSD, Woodstock and, inevitably, Tate-LaBianca. *A Case for the Angels* picks up the chronological thread after Lambert's foray back to the '30s in *Norman's Letter,* the story of a dissolute, gay English aristocrat, reputedly based on the life of the notorious addict-dandy Denham Fouts.

Norman's Letter is the first of two significant fictional ventures outside the slide area of Southern California. Written before a long, provisional second expatriation to Tangier that Lambert undertook from roughly the mid-'70s to the mid-'80s—with frequent travels to Paris and London and back to LA by way of New York—*Norman's Letter* is addressed to a deserted Moroccan lover and composed in the voice of a witty prig utterly spoiled by wealth and decadent tastes, who is "inhabited" from time to time by an invented female alter ego, the Arab poetess Oum Salem.

The book's inspired farce has the arch Firbankian campiness found in Gore Vidal's caprices like *Myron, Duluth* and *Kalki.* Its characters are "larger than life" and consequently slightly less than real; but in a biographical sense, *Norman's Letter* can be viewed as Lambert's imaginative staging of an alternative life for himself—not, certainly, one with any close resemblance to title character Norman Lightwood's, which ranges all over '30s Europe, England and the American Southwest, but simply one with its geographical center somewhere other than Los Angeles.

There is a great deal of internal evidence to suggest that "the counterculture" burgeoning all over America in the '60s, particularly its sexually relaxed and hedonistic aspect, strongly appealed to Lambert's optimism, while it also activated his skepticism and contradicted his sense of how human beings are basically wired. This tension is the central conflict in *A Case for the Angels,* which, like the film *Another Sky,* is about a sexually repressed Englishwoman transplanted to a milieu of sexually hypercharged, morally unbuttoned easiness.

A Case for the Angels unfolds entirely within the materially comfortable hills and canyons looming above the sprawl of everyday Los Angeles. Its characters, with few exceptions, are part of the inchoate social and spiritual improvisation of the mid- to late '60s. There is group sex, more or less continuously. There are hallucinogens and downers. The book's protagoness, Dora Poley, has been abandoned, sort of, by her husband, Keith, who prefers orgies to exclusivity, but she is trapped in Keith's world by the unexpected arrival of his mother, an unstoppable Christmas party planned before their separation and a dead dog that a hit-and-run driver dumps on her front lawn.

While Dora ultimately decides, in the vernacular of the day, to go with the flow, Lambert's own unease about where the '60s were leading is perceptible throughout. By the time of *The Goodbye People,* what the Hollywood Hills were actually alive with at the end of that decade had become hideously clear. *The Goodbye People* is curiously akin to parts of James Leo Herlihy's *Season of the Witch,* also published in 1971; set on opposite coasts, both novels describe the crash-and-burn phenomenon that followed the Summer of Love.

> East of Hollywood you reach a dead, flat no man's land. The surrounding hills are far away and often masked in smog. Geologically, the rock strata have dipped down to a wide, level expanse here, and decay has slid into the section too. Paint peels on the jumble of buildings. Neon signs have a letter or two missing. Sidewalks betray ancient cracks and the smog has left a layer of grime upon everything, faces included.

Nearly all roads in *The Goodbye People* lead to some kind of fatal self-abandonment. The bisexual draft dodger living on the skids, the glamorous young widow in search of enlightenment, and the skinny gamine from out of town who wants to make it in the movies no longer inhabit a world bursting with possibilities. The successive lives each of Lambert's characters tries on are predestined to be discarded; nothing fits. Los Angeles now offers the sick, delusional enchantments of a Manson Family or the absolute solitude that an indestructible buffer of wealth can ensure against the insanity of the streets.

In many ways, the span of Lambert's fiction terminates at the end of *The Goodbye People.* Only two novels follow it; Lambert's writing shifts to biography and one-of-a-kind books like *GWTW: The Making of Gone With the Wind* and *The Dangerous Edge,* a brilliant series of essays about practitioners of suspense such as G. K. Chesterton, Wilkie Collins, Georges Simenon, Raymond Chandler, and Alfred Hitchcock.

Lambert's novels all use the first-person narrative device in different ways. *The Slide Area* and *The Goodbye People* both invite the close identification of an unnamed "I" with the author but, more significantly, shift frequently backward and forward in time and foreground a succession of individuals as the temporary subjects of the narrative—this portmanteau effect is rarely used in literature, and even more rarely used effectively. Aside from Proust, whose work contains multiple structures and whose principal work is a single, many-chambered novel, the notable examples include Tolstoy's story "The Forged Coupon," Gide's *Caves du Vatican,* and some of Buñuel's late films. *Norman's Letter* is epistolary and diachronic; *Daisy Clover* consists of what purports to be Daisy's entries in a series of "theme notebooks." *A Case for the Angels* is a straightforward, first-person account arranged in a three-act structure, describing what occurs over a three-day period.

In the Night All Cats Are Grey (1976), written during Lambert's tentative semiexile in Morocco, is probably his least-known novel. It's his most anomalous and ingeniously structured fictional work, utterly direct yet also deceptively so: It has the feeling of an intricately planned book, though I am doubtful that Lambert actually "plotted" it in advance; it's too rich in details and incidents that must have surprised the author as much as they do the reader. Here again is a first-person novel in which no one ever addresses the narrator by name; unique among Lambert's fictions, the taleteller is as much the subject of the book as anyone else, and eventually quite a lot more so.

The book apparently takes place in London in 1974, since the protagonist is thirty and was born in 1944. Yet the narrator's engagement with the outer world is so etiolated and intentionally limited to what is absolutely necessary that he could be living in London at any time after World War II. His London is one where absolutely nothing has ever happened, a city of gray weather and bad food, where it's still possible to live without a telephone or a TV set and carry on a completely inconspicuous, drastically asocial existence.

I should add here that all of Lambert's fiction has loneliness as a conspicuous theme, however frenetic and crowded his characters' social lives often appear to be. The movie star and the beach bum equally suffer from the inability to connect with the people around them. In *Natalie Wood: A Life*— the second of three masterful nonfiction books Lambert produced near the end of his life (and which, along with his other biographies and nonfiction, deserve an entirely separate essay)—Lambert notes that Wood instantly grasped the key aspect of Daisy Clover, i.e., that at every important moment of her life, she's alone, beyond help from anyone else.

From the first seemingly unremarkable incident, when a neighbor lady pretends not to notice a dead vagrant in the gutter near their rooming house, the narrator of *All Cats Are Grey*, by happenstance, arms a trap for himself. Broadly speaking, it's the trap of involvement with other people in his environment. As his whole existence is organized around the avoidance of familiarity, the reader becomes complicit with his strategies for deflecting it, and sympathetic to what appears to be successful resistance to breaches of his privacy. It's possible to read almost to the end of the novel thinking it will end where it begins, with quiet, immutable desperation. But because the real trap is that of narrative itself, the ceaseless generation of form that occurs when any two people come in contact with each other, *All Cats Are Grey* suddenly pulls all its scattered, sad little happenings into a pattern of horrific inevitability—everything, it turns out, *is* connected, but in the ugliest and most destructive way imaginable.

In *Running Time* (1983), Lambert resumes his long-suspended fictional portrait of Hollywood. Instead of bringing everything forward in time, his last novel looks backward to the era before the action of *The Slide Area*, commencing in the glory days of the silent films and continuing through the end of World War II. This uncharacteristically long, consistently engaging, funny, tragic novel resembles a farcical encyclopedia of film history, recapturing the surreality of an industry before it became completely industrialized.

What Hollywood had morphed into after *Jaws*, *The Godfather* and *Star Wars* didn't deserve the sly glorification that even a damning novel would bestow on it. Lambert's books after *Running Time* are nonfiction epitaphs for three friends who had been vital parts of his life: Lindsay Anderson, Natalie Wood, and Ivan Moffatt. He had begun a final novel, about what precisely I don't know, but it would surprise me to learn it was Hollywood—not that he ever hinted otherwise.

Although Gavin Lambert continued to make a modest living as a writer of teleplays and the occasional film after he returned to Los Angeles in the 1980s from North Africa, the LA he found waiting, as he casually told me one evening, was just a more agreeable place to finish up than Morocco. It was a place where he had many friends, a place where many people loved him. But it was no longer exactly the place he had wanted to be, when life was new; as Tangier eventually became for Paul Bowles, Los Angeles was simply the place where Gavin Lambert ended his time when there was no longer any reason to go elsewhere.

PART

II

THE INFERNAL EVIDENCE

EVEN COWBOYS GET THE BLUES

YOU COULD infer from the production notes that Ang Lee's *Brokeback Mountain* would be useful if it came in a spray can: Spritz a little on a fundamentalist and change him into a liberal, or neutralize a whole church basement of rednecks with a full-strength tolerance bomb.

This film is inflected to instill something akin to high moral dudgeon. Its depiction of ordinary Americans trapped in loveless marriages and dead-end jobs, its laconic naturalism, and the . . . well, natural way its two male protagonists find themselves, one boozy night high up the Mountain of Love, riding bareback in a sleeping bag, builds an industrial-strength case for breaking the mold, following your heart, and Daring To Be Different. How can anyone find happiness otherwise? On the other hand, the film makes the explicit point that deviating just a tad from the norm will probably lead you to a brutally violent end at the hands of your neighbors. But maybe if they saw this movie . . . ?

Curiously, neither cowpoke dares to be different enough to avoid bourgeois marriage, serial reproduction, quotidian if unequally remunerative jobs, nauseating in-laws, and lives pissed away in the bohunk wastelands of Middle America. Their difference remains furtive, though one is less bent out of shape by guilt than the other; moreover, *Brokeback Mountain* deals with the same ruinous romantic fixation that Gore Vidal described with far less mawkishness and pathos in his 1948 novel *The City and the Pillar.* Incessantly revisiting the same transient moment of erotic gratification instead of moving on produces a dissociative yearning, not simply illustrative of the repetition compulsion, but an impossible wish for time to freeze, for youth to last forever, for reality to eternally coincide with a Kodak moment that's a gone dead train. So it ceases to be reality and becomes an inability to negotiate reality on one's own terms.

Brokeback Mountain casts the delusional parity of desire and gratification in a tragic light—not that the film itself recognizes the chasm between craving and getting, but perhaps precisely because it doesn't. The perfect orgasm you experienced at age 13 with the cutest, best-hung boy in school may be a lovely memory, but trying to lose your innocence in the same way—and with the same person, no less—throughout the ensuing decades is not, strictly speaking, tragic, or at any rate, less tragic than stupid. It may be that this film intends by the very stifled inanition of its main characters to demonstrate how natural and ordinary homosexual attraction really is. Since it unfolds in a milieu where this attraction is considered highly unnatural and is furthermore persecuted when it reveals itself, however, its protagonists' limp efforts to maintain their sexual connection implies that rotten marriages, unwanted children, and crapulously bigot-ridden little towns are as inescapable as the Gulag Archipelago. The only things that can truly make this so are cowardice and imaginative vacancy. These are not the qualities of tragic heroes, but the weaknesses of ninnies.

The "problem film," Hollywood-style, generically equates sexual intercourse with "love," and often ends with the reconciled lovers implicitly living happily ever after—not the case here, but probably never the case when sex is the only real adhesive between two people, anyway. Even so, *Brokeback Mountain* suggests that the opposite could be true, if only other people could respect all kinds of love, not just the kind they imagine they themselves enjoy. A silly speculation at best, considering that all kinds of love, from Pushkin's passion for women's feet to Caligula's marriage to his horse, have manifested themselves throughout a human history primarily characterized by the irresistible urge of discrete groups of people, very much in love with themselves, to slaughter whatever groups happen to live next door, which would happily slaughter them if they'd thought of it first.

The presiding narrative trope is that of The Decisive Turning Point, the kind of pivotal life moment we actually seldom recognize as such until years after it occurs. One summer of love leaves cowpokes Ennis and Jack in an insoluble quandary. Seasonal workers, they're soon divided by a lot of wide-open space, marriages, families, and in Ennis's case, guilt and ambivalence. In Jack's, a lot of steaming anger, tempered by opportunism: rich father-in-law, hefty bank account, sporadic dick action on the side, a wife who truly understands that running a business is much more involving and fun than fucking her husband.

Probably the best thing about *Brokeback Mountain* is its portraiture of grim, idiotic family gatherings where brewing antagonisms explode into open hostility, and glimpses into shit-kicker country barrooms full of squat, ugly men with stringy beards itching for a brawl: the whole nine yards of ghoulish Americana, for which the film rather perversely demands an over-generous degree of sympathy. It's important, as actors like to tell us in interviews, for even the nastiest or most vapid characters to have something "human" about them, something—why not say it?—lovable. Because let's face it, in the end, you've really got to love everybody.

Four years after the first taste of unholy carnal knowledge, Jack's reappearance rekindles Ennis's kundalini into a veritable bonfire, followed by 20 years of sporadic "fishing trips" where they restage that ever-receding time up on Brokeback Mountain. Ennis divorces. Jack, the less inhibited and hornier of the two, makes furtive excursions to Mexico when his Uranian urges overpower him in Ennis's absence.

What Ennis and Jack both refer to as "this thing," established early, is more or less the same thing that glued Rock Hudson and Jane Wyman together in *Magnificent Obsession,* yet separated them in *All That Heaven Allows*—a socially inappropriate love, rendered acceptable in the former movie by Rock Hudson's dedication and skills as an eye surgeon, but made impossible in the latter by his low station as a gardener. Needless to say, "this thing" activates Neanderthal reactions in the rowdy cultural backwaters of the film, necessitating a tragic conclusion with calculated echoes of the Matthew Shepard murder.

The case has already been made by some critics that Ang Lee's is the first "mainstream" movie with "A-list stars" to deal with a gay male relationship—a weird assertion, given how narrowly "mainstream" would have to be defined for this to be true, and how small the theater audience for mainstream films, however you define them, has become, and how wholly dependent on DVD sales and rentals this putative mainstream currently is. (As far as that goes, Jake Gyllenhaal and Heath Ledger, impressive as they are as Jack and Ennis, respectively, have been fast-tracked "A-list" stars for a very few years, that only seem like a decade or two because of the staggering number of movies they've been crammed into every season, which isn't the same thing as being Barbra Streisand or Warren Beatty.)

I'm not sure what this type of claim is supposed to signify—that Hollywood is on the cutting edge of social progress? That every other movie on this subject has been merely a "festival film" or in some other way unimportant compared to one with saturation booking in a thousand multiplexes? Or could it mean that we prefer to think we're making progress when the clock is running backwards?

Consider *Brokeback Mountain*'s overt pandering to Rousseauian notions of the American West and its insularity, the toughness and self-sufficiency of its tight-lipped, xenophobic denizens, its rituals of faith and patriotism. You could say that simply depicting this hillbilly heaven accurately is itself an unsettling criticism, yet the effect, again, is to make it seem, in many ways, admirable—its unflagging work ethic, its quasi-mystical connection to harvest, soil, livestock, and weather. Along with this idyllic agrarianism, however, comes a fabulous ubiquity of ignorance, self-righteous greed, the elevating atmosphere of a barnyard and an epidemic inability of people to mind their own business. Romanticizing landscape is like mentally erasing the human web to make it easier to be enthralled by minerals. Everybody loves a pretty vista, because they don't have to clean it.

Just as Capote's eastern Kansans referred to western Kansas as "out there," *Brokeback Mountain*'s characters seem to shun the wider world as terra incognita. No one ever refers to the large events of the day, or to places outside his or her immediate ken. Between 1963 and somewhere in the early 1980s, the only evidence of any realm beyond the rodeo circuit and the ranch is the cathode eye in the living room, the slowly mutating look of motor vehicles and supermarket wares, and an occasional reference to the state of the economy.

In effect, two decades of history produce no important impact on the communities and individuals under scrutiny. Attitudes and opinions remain obstinately immobile, without any help from televangelists or Phyllis Schlafly. Even TV, which replaced verbalization in so many American homes during the period spanned, can only emit meaningless images to people who have nothing to say to each other in the first place.

This is depressingly credible. Tight-knit communities, like tight-knit families, manage to stay tight by deflecting any strong sense of connection with larger social configurations—"America," to this mindset, is, or ought to be, a country whose norms are indistinguishable from their own, ergo not such a big place after all.

The insular quality of American life reinforces a stubborn naïveté about sexual matters that's been part of our national character from the outset. The hermetic communities pictured in *Brokeback Mountain* define themselves in terms of what sort of people don't belong in them. From the days of the Massachusetts Bay Colony to the present, American exceptionalism begins on the microcosmic level. In this respect, *Brokeback Mountain* is a pungent slice of an essentially unchanging reality.

What's less credible, despite the months that separate each of Jack and Ennis's reunions, is the unfaltering rock-hard stiffies they give each other on sight. It's not uncommon for two people who love each other to continue for 20 or even 60 years to love each other. Any truly honest adult, however, knows it's rare for people to stay sexually interested in someone they love for much longer than two years. Of course it happens, and good for them if it does, but generalizing this into the normal state of things is like encouraging children to continue believing in Santa Claus after they're enrolled in college. There are people who've been struck not once, but *twice* by lightning and survived it, and it makes the same amount of sense to regard this as typical. If things were otherwise, the world's oldest profession would probably be arms dealing.

On this point, denial mechanisms become mobilized in defense of institutionalized couplehood, not only by liturgical types but their surrogates in Congress, manifested in submental decrees like the Defense of Marriage Act. One wonders if marriage needs defending, or ought to be more lucidly understood as a property arrangement, which any two individuals should be able to enter as a legally binding thing.

The relatively recent repackaging of homosexuality as an arrangement of committed couples takes the highly defective social processing of heterosexuality for granted as an ideal. "We love just like you, and have families just like you," the argument runs. Yes and no. Not everyone wants to be in a family, or a "relationship," or any kind of marriage, and not everyone wants to love whomever he or she happens to be having sex with. It's often easier to do things you enjoy with somebody you merely like, or don't know. As long as Americans deny such realities in favor of puerile, Calvinistic models of adulthood, they will also continue to refuse any responsibility for their country's international lawlessness and indifference to the mass death and suffering produced by its so-called foreign policy.

As the author of *Our Lady of the Assassins,* Fernando Vallejo (in my opinion, the most singular and essential writer of our time), says in Luis Ospina's documentary film *The Supreme Uneasiness,* "Sex is innocent, no matter who or what it's with. Reproduction is another matter. In animals it's blind. For the majority of mankind, even now, it is still blind. People reproduce blindly because they relate the two things." Even Jack and Ennis, who know they don't want any such thing, blindly father children as if it were an uncontrollable biological imperative. It isn't. In fact, you could justifiably argue that homosexuality ought to be encouraged over procreative sex. The world has too many babies being born for no conscionable reason. (Vallejo is perfectly correct in ridiculing the stupidity of people who defend the huge families spawned by parents too poor to take care of themselves, let alone their offspring.)

"Love," an opaque if many splendored thing, isn't much of an antidote for the ignorant attitudes movies like *Brokeback Mountain* seem intended to change. Some people are just shits, as the wise old drag queen told William Burroughs. The more pointlessly fecund our species, the more shits we are likely to have. Rich or poor, gay or straight, transgendered or of interplanetary origin, there is not enough world left to sustain an exponentially metastasizing human population.

Propaganda on behalf of gay couplehood, even intelligent and well-made propaganda, invariably addresses the social question with a defense of "love." "Everybody has a right to love," "if you have love, you should hold on to it," and "a pure and beautiful love story" are a few quotes plucked at random from *Brokeback Mountain*'s press kit.

Yet love, in this context, is simply a euphemism for sex—Ennis and Jack never do shack up in the little ranch Jack dreams about them playing house in, hence never experience the downside of cohabitation; this seems like too much love for too little content. And there's too little sex to make a good argument for needing it eternally from the same person, given that there's one fairly explicit rear entry and otherwise as much steam as Peter Finch's smooch with Murray Head in *Sunday Bloody Sunday* (1971).

As for the idea of *Brokeback Mountain* as a reinvention of the western genre, Andy Warhol went much, much further with *Lonesome Cowboys* back in 1968. Heath Ledger, who plays Ennis, gave the most revealing read on *Brokeback Mountain* in an interview: "I find there's not a lot of mystery left in stories between guys and girls. It's all been done or seen before." The truth is, there's not much mystery left in stories of this kind anyway, no matter who's riding high in the saddle.

THE MADNESS OF THE DAY

THERE IS an appliance in every living room that makes people stupid. This was a widely known fact before the late George W. S. Trow's essay, "Within the Context of No Context" appeared in *The New Yorker* in 1980 (and in book form soon after), but Trow's impressionistic meditation on the world of television, and the world of television's effect on mass culture, fingered the trance effect of the medium's stupidity, and the medium's message, with arresting precision—arresting not least because the essay's form mimicked the fractured pastiche that was, in 1980, only beginning to be called "postmodernism," a condition of things engendered by television that Trow clearly viewed with fascinated disgust.

The essay made waves. It was, among other things, the revenge of *The New Yorker,* as it then was, on a punitive construct *The New Yorker* called "downtown," the retort of a vanishing class to the barbarians at the gate. This was not so much the important thing about the essay as it was its throbbing little imperfection. Like Renata Adler's jeremiads against the avant-garde in *Toward A Radical Middle* (1969), it pitted its imperious adultness against a perceived culture of mushrooming infantilism, and sometimes cited little well-intended things that didn't quite work as powerful, malefic symptoms of regression. It proceeded from assumptions that mostly rang true, and sometimes (just when they began to seem irrefutable) betrayed the careless impatience of hereditary snobbery.

Like Adler before him, Trow had been raised and trained in an upper-middle class whose values were no longer viewed by people outside or even inside that class as desirable or necessary. That class had expected to define the mainstream from generation to generation, and suddenly no longer did, or if it did, the mainstream it defined no longer held any cultural authority. In "Collapsing Dominant," Trow's new introductory essay to the reissue of

WTCONC, the author's candor on this point is blunt and admirable, and, in its way, as subtly irritating as the tone of his original essay.

That said, the meat of Trow's book, in both essays, is impressively fresh. As a diagnostician of American consciousness, Trow brings to his job a playfulness and poetic finesse that demonstrate how much the literary mind can do that ideology can't. He has a genius for parsing the inanities that batter an audience into a demographic, a problem into a product, an idea into a jingle. His subject is the chasm between private feeling and "the grid of two hundred million." *WTCONC* is about agreements and betrayals, unreasonable promises scrawled in vanishing ink into a fraudulent social contract, the art of the con job on a massive scale. "No one, now, minds a con man," Trow writes. "But no one likes a con man who doesn't know what we think we want." What Trow does best is show how what we think we want is invented and projected with less and less reference to anything real. And implied in all this is the desperate emptiness of most American lives, without which television as we know it would never be necessary or desirable.

What are we being sold, and how much are we paying for it? Why are we buying it? What's the implicit exchange? Applying such questions to game shows, talk shows, serial melodrama, celebrity gossip, popular magazines, and "programming" in the broadest sense, Trow sees the original impulse behind such phenomena—the initiating, plausible need—decaying over time, as the context of earlier values (of authority, say, and the principled flouting of authority) crumbles, leaving a foreground of empty forms, which then becomes the background against which ever-emptier forms appear. One apotheosis of this process is a "new cable television channel called TVLand. And on TVLand one will view, as entertainment, Classic Commercials . . . I think people will reinvent their history using specific images from a more organized moment."

The highly disorganized moment we are living in now, which Trow nailed with such prescience seventeen years ago, owes much of its tinny, squalidly masochistic flavor to the erasure of historical consciousness. We no longer know who we are because we no longer know who we were, which makes it rather easy for other people to sell us an identity. This is a core issue in Daniel Harris's *The Rise and Fall of Gay Culture,* a brilliant suite of essays that ranges across many facets of gay culture—from camp, drag, S&M to "lifestyle" magazines, personal ads, pornography, and AIDS kitsch—and which, like Trow's book, injects the historical sense into a seemingly ahistorical present. Trow documents the collapse of a dominant class; Harris delivers an unsentimental eulogy for a vanishing ethnicity, one that's been assimilated into commercial culture at the expense of its defining characteristics.

"Long before homosexuals were accepted by mainstream society," Harris writes, "we had become so financially useful to the business world that our integration as respectable Americans was inevitable, for how could any ethnic group that contributed as heavily as we did to the nation's economy be ostracized forever?" In America's urban areas, at least, this integration is fairly complete. With the help of repetitive propaganda from magazines like *Genre* and *Out,* fashion designers like Calvin Klein, endorsements for understanding and tolerance from Hollywood's "role models," and a publishing subindustry of self-help literature, homosexuals have achieved the middle-class mediocrity, and even the Pavlovian patriotism, typical of successfully assimilated groups. Harris has no great longings for imaginary good old days, but his book has the immense virtue of exposing the unspoken, i.e., what gay people have had to abandon in order to be accepted and absorbed. Not all of it was good; much of it was pathological. But none of it was quite as banal as the current emphasis on gay marriage and monogamy, for example, or "coming out" as the endlessly restaged, central drama in every homosexual's life, or the compulsive mimicry of mainstream tastes and "lifestyle" options promoted by bourgeois gay media. While gay politics has suffered serious recent setbacks, gay culture, in a drastically sanitized form, has won the patronage of corporate America, eager to exploit a vast market of "dual-income no kids" consumer units. Gay culture has, in effect, had its vectors swallowed by the pulsating pudding of disintegrated contexts that Trow describes as "adolescent orthodoxy."

The exchange involved here—and it is an exchange, for which liberationists have avidly lobbied, not a unilateral colonization—requires the suppression from public view of everything that really does, or really did, make the homosexual different from the average American, whether it's male effeminacy, elitist artistic taste, specific sexual practices, or the forming of easy alliances between same-sex persons of radically different classes. The reward is the transformation of the outcast into a welcome, faceless consumer. "The permission given by television is permission to make tiny choices, within the

context of total permission infected with a sense of no permission at all,"
Trow writes. For "television" substitute "corporate benevolence" or "inclu-
sion in the demography of a product's target audience."

Assimilation hurts. Harris's argument is similar to that of Pasolini's
Lutheran Letters, i.e., that the special features of distinct groups fall away as
these groups are homogenized into commercial culture. In the case of gays,
much of what is disappearing came into existence in the first place as defense mechanisms against exclusion—camp, for instance, provided a species
of wit that turned straight culture's artifacts into double entendres, by
which homosexuals devised a rich, densely coded underground culture, that
despite its abjection, had an uncanny quality of difference no longer discernible in contemporary gay life. (Harris makes the point that young gays,
today, have more in common with young heterosexuals than they do with
older gays; what Harris calls "glad-to-be-gay propaganda" is almost exclusively focused on people under forty, and its points of cultural reference are
exactly the same films, music, books, celebrities, consumer products, and
leisure activities promoted by mainstream media.)

The process of hidden-things-becoming-visible that's unfolded since the
late '60s has been one of seasonal identity crises for the "gay community," a
construct that requires quotation marks since part of these crises has always
been a question about which parts of this "gay community" the culture at
large is prepared to assimilate. Another part has been a question of redundancy: At what point do we admit that something is no longer "transgressive," no longer a challenge to the dominant society, no longer interesting?
As the raison d'être of such phenomena as drag evaporates from a culture
where gender roles are no longer strictly codified in clothing and behavior,
getting up in drag becomes an exercise in folkloric kitsch, with no more
subversive content than the costume pageants at Colonial Williamsburg.

Many years ago, Fran Lebowitz said that if you removed the homosexual
influence from American culture, what you'd have left would be *Let's Make A
Deal.* Today, the social oppression that drove so many homosexuals into the
arts is disappearing. As Harris puts it, "When gay men no longer feel degraded and insecure and therefore driven to prove their worth to the heterosexual mainstream, they will cease using culture as a means of achieving social
prestige and, as a consequence, will stop flocking to art schools, the stage, the
concert hall, or the opera house, becoming much more conventional in their

aspirations and gravitating to less creative jobs in the business sector." While none of us exactly long for the oppressions of the past that brought us everything from Ronald Firbank to Lypsinka, the passing of this culture cedes ever more ground to the philistinism and mediocrity of the consciousness industry. In their different ways, Trow and Harris sound the alarm that *Let's Make A Deal* is quickly becoming all we have.

TESTOSTERONE EXPRESS

THE MEN'S magazines surveyed in Adam Parfrey's *It's a Man's World* enjoyed their glory days during the first long leg of the Cold War. Their evolution, reflected in the feverishly vivid illustrations Parfrey has assembled, is readily linked to notions of masculinity that seemed firmly in place throughout World War II and embattled ever after. The decay of certainty, the sense of ideological threat that accompanied the postwar economic boom, the mutation of the GI into the man in the gray flannel suit summoned a nostalgia for an unambiguous manliness expressed in violent action and a longing for coherent adversaries in a world in which enemies were increasingly faceless and prosperity had a curious resemblance to zombie-ism.

The staples of publications like *Argosy, Peril, Sir, Fury, Male, Men Today, All Man, Real Men, Men in Conflict, Man's Adventure* and dozens of similar titles—sadistic Nazis, menacing wildlife, headhunting natives of voodoo islands, marauding Apaches, killer Communists—express in lurid, living color the deep wish for a morally and sexually black-and-white world. Masculinity is defined by the testing ordeal. The protagonist is typically pitted in grossly unequal, unfair combat against implacable, monstrous enemies. The comic book cousins of these magazines show evil reliably vanquished by superhuman heroes. The men's magazines emphasized unceasing struggle against an inexhaustible variety of threats and the possibility of unhappy or incomplete outcomes: Perils are so myriad and multifarious that the price of security is eternal vigilance, eternal grimacing, scowling, cowering, and shredded wardrobes.

The extreme depictions of danger the pulps trafficked in carry a freight of dread more evocative of moral twilight than triumphalism. The pictorial style on view here is virtually the same melodramatic rendering of "the dark side" associated with film noir and the early paperback novel. The iconography is

one of pure immanence. The moment most often captured on these magazine covers is one in which the menaced subject has already slogged through a
snake-infested swamp, been tortured in a Nazi prison camp, washed up on
the shores of a cannibal island and now, in torn or shredded clothing, sopping
wet or desiccated after crawling through a desert, faces decapitation, consumption by vicious marine life, amputation by hacksaw, attack by alligators,
weasels, ferrets, Indian arrows or samurai cutlasses, sexual exhaustion by Nazi
libertines, cigar torture at the hands of Fidel Castro and sometimes—not
often—incineration by H-bomb.

The yearning for an ennobling mythos embodied in this canon of popular art had a furtive aspect. These were not the magazines that went on the
coffee table, and the fact that they were "gendered," just as *Redbook* and
other women's magazines were, assimilated them into the loose orbit of
soft-core pornography. In their time, testosterone was perceived as such a
volatile and vulgar quantity that home and family life were designed to
"contain" it, siphoning chaotic energies into productive, uniform channels.
Yet it was well understood, in the suburban dream homes of the 1950s, that
the male essence was prone to spillage and explosion; the rituals of postwar
marriage included the male's periodic defection from the nest, in the form
of cocktail party brawls or fishing and hunting trips.

For many decades now, popular and political culture has promoted a
fantasy of the 1950s as a long idyllic moment when family life, gender roles
and moral values were fixed in utopian perfection. Yet it is clear from the
subliterature surveyed by *It's a Man's World* that at least half the gender
equation was deeply troubled by the restraints of domestic life and felt most
energized and fully alive imagining situations of mortal peril and physical
combat, ones that included supine and often half-dead female bodies in urgent need of rescue or whip-wielding vixens to be overpowered and tamed.
A restive, neurotic quality slips into the mix in publications like *Dare, Exposed, Crime Confessions* and the like, in which the men's adventure sensibility is brought to bear on contemporary life in America. The same tropes of
deadly exotic menace, applied to the landscape of middle-class domesticity,
reveal the social schizophrenia of an idealized era.

Along with their characteristic obsession with sex as a pointedly under-
described, lavishly prefigured mating of hunters and gatherers, the men's
magazines devoted to subjects closer to home than saber-toothed tiger at-

tacks or "Teen Terrors of the Tamiami Trail" suggest the suffocating, panic-stricken undercurrent of American conformity, in features like "What Are Your Homosexual Tendencies?" and "How to Tell if Your Girlfriend Is a Lesbian." The racial tensions rolling under the era's apple pie crust erupt in both the *Photoplay* type of Hollywood item ("Joan Fontaine and Her Negro Screen Lover Court Racial Explosion!") and more directly libidinal, generic articles ("The Interracial Sex Experimenters"), whose illustrations stimulated the miscegenative impulses the articles decried or condemned.

It's a Man's World features several interviews with, and reminiscences by, the people who labored on the pulp magazines in their glory days, including Bruce Jay Friedman and Mario Puzo. The world of the pulps was simply a venue where some writers could make a decent, if frantic living, rather than a deliberate engine of ideology or politics; the magazines' fortunes rose and fell according to the public mood; their stories usually had some loose relationship to documentary reality and arguably a stronger relationship to cinema than literature. Often a powerful illustration became the occasion for a story rather than the other way around. Speed of production was everything. There was a wealth of retrograde, stereotypical bromides embedded in the pulps, and the impetus was simply to entertain the escapist fantasies of a grimly stratified, imaginatively constipated, lethally conformist era, continually recycling whichever stock villains, deadly threats, sexual innuendoes and combat paraphernalia had proved their appeal at the newsstand.

The writers themselves attest to having no idea who the readers of these magazines were, though they sold in huge quantities; the decline of the men's adventure pulp appears to have been steady throughout the 1960s, its audience eroded by hybrid high-lowbrow offerings like *Playboy*, reaching a nadir during the Vietnam War, which none of the pulps rendered in an appealing way.

It's a Man's World deserves a companion survey of the contemporaneous "middlebrow" literature of disaster: novels such as *Alas! Babylon, On the Beach, A Canticle for Leibowitz* and other works in which the nuclear threat was terrifyingly manifested as fait accompli. When we recall the role of paranoia in the construction of normality during the Cold War, the men's adventure magazine becomes an artifact of considerable charm, providing scenarios of the individual fighting formidable but legible adversaries against daunting but not impossible odds. If the pulps looked back to a just war of improving sacrifice or an earlier time of struggle against nature, the nuclear fiction of the period looked to a future of moral relativism, ecological catastrophe, political incoherence and the all too plausible extinction of everything.

HOMICIDE CAN BE SUCH A DRAG

*B*AD EDUCATION extends the formal exploration of recent Pedro Almodóvar films like *Flower of My Secret, All About My Mother* and *Talk to Her,* stories dealing with "identity crises" in the most extravagant terms. Almodóvar's comedies have always gone to dark extremes of farcical melodrama; they operate with a kind of acrobatic weightlessness, their characters resembling unstable chemical substances trapped in human containers, spilling out in foaming torrents when shaken. They appear, too, to leak into one another and borrow each other's form.

I had not paid close attention to what Almodóvar was up to during what I call his "Hollywood" period: Not that he "went Hollywood," but the films that start with *Women on the Verge of a Nervous Breakdown* (1988) didn't much snare my attention and were so widely well received that I felt sure there was something wrong with them. With *Flower of My Secret* (1995), though, Almodóvar's immense cunning hit home: a writer successful as someone else, under another name, writing books that in no way coincide with her emotional constitution, decides to write entirely different books, assuming an identity in every way opposed to her inauthentic "self"—every writer is someone else at heart. And, too, with *Flower of My Secret* begins a discourse on identity that reaches into the scientific or medical realm.

It has become entirely usual in recent years for AIDS to feature as a narrative element in Almodóvar's films, and the nature of a retrovirus has some metaphorical bearing on the characters Almodóvar invents: They enact an infernal argument with themselves, a conflict about what is "me" and "not me." The confusion of the self with another becomes literalized in the "theater" of organ donation in *Flower of My Secret* and the theater-that-becomes-real in *All About My Mother* (1999); the latter film takes the internal oscillations of identity to bizarre extremes, wherein the father figure is, in one sense, also a mother, engendering a sequence of identical children.

Within the "secret" of *All About My Mother* we see an unfolding and a neutralization of class distinctions, of the bourgeois realm revealing a submerged history of subproletarian existence, the mother-becomes-pseudowhore, the patriarchal role feminized, the maternal role conflated with a sort of feminized patriarchy. Something else is also at work, in the intense physicality of Almodóvar's people. They may suggest in general outline creatures out of Evelyn Waugh or Ronald Firbank, but their extreme vulnerability introduces modes of discomfort more readily associated with "realism"—one especially thinks of the Penélope Cruz character in *All About My Mother,* who, as a pregnant, HIV-positive nun, is doubly fragile, carrying a child that may be seropositive.

In *Talk to Her* (2002), Almodóvar achieves what would appear to be the ultimate destination of the "me, not-me" conundrum: a film about characters who are technically dead, whom the narrative "keeps alive" in the same way that the nurse Benigno keeps the comatose Alicia alive; Benigno's refusal to recognize that Alicia is "not Alicia"—like the stubborn actors in the organ donation videos of the earlier films who refuse to understand the difference between brain death and "life"—opens a space of infinite suggestion, where a life story can occur in a breath. This space is one the viewer apprehends viscerally, which is to say, Almodóvar brings us uncomfortably close to our own deaths. The self-abandoning risks his characters take by assuming the full consequence of their wishes are an excoriating commentary on the varicolored, one-dimensional conformity of ordinary modern life; even at the nadir of "the lower depths," Almodóvar locates more authentic human will, more genuine feeling, than can ever be found in the bourgeois world. His work doesn't despise that world; instead it tries to open it to deadened feeling, to indicate what is essential to life and to expose its empty formalities and discriminations.

Some kind of histrionic genius is at work in these acrostic narratives, which start from impossible premises and steadily raise the ante of unlikeliness; Almodóvar's exaggerations have affinities to Molière as well as boulevard comedy, and emit the veracity of metaphors beyond the reach of logic. Almodóvar's position is eminently sane and human—the permutations of identity, whether willful reinvention of gender, or Manuela's deliberate return to a painful earlier version of herself in *All About My Mother,* or Victor's drastic "rehabilitation" in pursuit of an immutable obsession in *Live Flesh* (1997), are bracing assertions of existential freedom in the daily confrontation with necessity. Perhaps the most admirable figures in these films are those incredibly resilient, antic transvestites who invariably prove to be better "men" than the macho characters so often willing to use them for sexual relief.

Almodóvar has recast the Spanish picaresque in contemporary terms, as Buñuel did in his later films. *Bad Education* has roots in *The Saragossa Manuscript* and similar epics of digression featuring stories within stories. Its main thread is the kind of interrupted tale the picaresque renders in pleats and fragments.

As schoolchildren, Enrique and Ignacio enjoyed a special friendship that ended when Father Manolo, infatuated with Ignacio, had Enrique expelled. The film opens as Enrique (Fele Martínez), now a successful film director, rummages through sensational news items looking for a usable story. A handsome youth appears in the office, none other than Ignacio (Gael García Bernal), whom Enrique hasn't seen in 16 years. Ignacio has become an actor and prefers to be called Angel. He gives Enrique a story he's written, "The Visit," based on their experiences at school.

"The Visit" more or less faithfully mirrors the repressive environment of the school, the boys' escapes to the local cinema, their clandestine bond, and the malignant attentions of Father Manolo (Daniel Giménez Cacho). Ignacio has also written of his later life as Zahara, a transvestite junkie attached to a burlesque company, reencountering Enrique as an anonymous trick and attempting to blackmail Father Manolo—who, with the help of another priest, manages to dispose of him.

Enrique wants to film the story. Ignacio insists on playing the role of Zahara. Enrique explains that Ignacio isn't the right physical type. Ignacio angrily withdraws his offer of the story. Enrique then begins looking into the later parts of "The Visit" and learns that the Ignacio he knew at school is dead; "Angel" is Ignacio's brother Juan.

Bad Education becomes progressively more complicated, as Angel sculpts himself into Zahara and becomes Enrique's lover and star, maintaining the fiction that he is Ignacio; ultimately Father Manolo, now defrocked, with a family, reenters the story to reveal how Ignacio died.

Nothing here is at all what it seems. *Bad Education* is particularly un-rewarding to synopsize, since its textures owe so much to the performances of Gael García Bernal, Francisco Boira as the "other" Ignacio, Lluís Homar, and Daniel Giménez Cacho; Bernal plays three remarkably distinct cha-racters or personalities, with a smoldering conviction that verges on the psychotic.

Some of this film's basic elements revisit Almodóvar's early works like *Law of Desire* (1985), where there's also a film director, an ambiguous love object, and a freight of transpersonal exchanges that defy the broad conven-tions of its narrative setup. As Enrique, Fele Martínez has a general resem-blance to that earlier director, and a similarly persistent curiosity; he's considerably more ruthless and is quick to sense Angel's predatory nature, and, it must be said, Enrique's personality reflects the artist in the ostensibly mature phase of egotism wherein life becomes the sacrificial material for creative work and only secondarily what is lived.

Enrique's ego immunizes him against the abject and dreary trajectory "The Visit" has imagined for him as a fictional secondary character in Igna-cio's drama. If he allows Angel to manipulate him, this is entirely in the in-terests of his own project, while Angel's purpose remains ambiguous. As director, Enrique holds all the cards, even if he doesn't have all the puzzle pieces. Yet *Bad Education*'s central mystery is not his, nor is it the mystery of his creative process—though it does, miraculously, provide a guided tour of Almodóvar's.

The mystery is this: What does Angel/Juan/Zahara want? Is he Barbara Stanwyck in *Double Indemnity? Bad Education* may very well be *The Re-venger's Tragedy,* and a little bit *All About Eve,* but it's a given that all Angel's manipulation can accomplish is a film by Enrique, who will, in the course of making it, learn what really happened to Ignacio, which then becomes the revelatory climax of a film by Almodóvar.

Angel/Juan "becomes" Ignacio, "becomes" Zahara, and the question re-mains: Why? To dissemble a crime or assimilate his victim? To accomplish his revenge on "Mr. Berenguer" (Lluís Homar), formerly Father Manolo? As Enrique's lover, Angel completes a story broken in mid-sentence 16 years earlier, and arguably incarnates Ignacio, effects the gratification of someone else's desire. His seduction of Berenguer, likewise, rewrites the incomplete narrative of Ignacio and Father Manolo. Angel's impersonation has the aura of a criminal act, and he assumes it, it appears, as an essential ingredient of an actual crime.

Bad Education answers "why" with further equivocation. Angel inhabits the film like some process of oxidation. He is its Iago, the pure embodiment of amoral desire. In this he seems hardly different from Ignacio after Ignacio has become Zahara. The victimizer Father Manolo becomes the victim Berenguer; ultimately, the wreckage of several multiple identities has piled up, so to speak, on the set of *The Visit*. In the end, no one is entirely to blame for the nasty lessons life has taught him, and everyone is trapped in the institutional madness of church, state, capitalism and cinema.

ABOUT MARY WORONOV

SOME FORMS of literary expression resemble a controlled mimicry of de-monic possession. Mary Woronov's writing proceeds with the crackling intensity of a witch's sabbath, rendering everyday life as an incitement to suicide, human contact as a kind of forcible self-immolation, shooting sparks like live cinders crackling off a bonfire. The women she writes about are loaded with rage the way pistols are loaded with bullets. And yet, and yet. It is the self-doubting, second-guessing, easily deflated and deflected rage of the Abject Woman, by turns rejecting and embracing her suffocat-ing role. Woronov's women are tapped into forces more powerful and anni-hilating than the ugly circumstances they're trapped in. They have a pact with the natural world, especially its most virulent elements. They have an understanding with death. This allows them to live. They may triumph by changing form. They even win by destroying themselves. They hold their powers in check until all options are exhausted. They then fling themselves into the whirlwind.

Woronov is well known as an actress in avant-garde films and Hollywood B movies. In her Warhol-era memoir, *Swimming Underground*, Woronov is not simply, prosaically, the Mary Woronov who helped burn *Chelsea Girls* into memory and toured as a whip dancer with the Velvet Underground. Far from trying to out-cool the rest of the Factory gang or enlarge her niche, Woronov focuses on peripheral weirdness beyond the spotlight's glare. She cops to her own naïveté, her decidedly uncool sexual fears and in-experience, and, quite candidly, her marginality to the Warhol enterprise. And, I should add, its marginality to her enterprise.

Two of Woronov's recent novels, *Snake* and *Niagara*, share some dicey narra-tive strategies. The most jarring—the initial withholding of key information—is one most writers are well advised to avoid, but Woronov carries it off, as the delayed revelation, in both books, appears when the tracking of a plot line has become secondary to the metamorphosis of the heroine's sense of herself, her history, ultimately her fate.

In *Snake,* Woronov's Sandra willfully stumbles into ever-murkier zones of underground Los Angeles. Her quest has no defined object. She's unable to draw boundaries, not for lack of strength, but owing to a sense of unreality and the abitrariness of any action. She drifts into s/m orgies and massive drug ingestion. At one skanky bacchanal, she witnesses the murder of her inescapable, loathed boyfriend by a drug runner, Luke, who abducts her to a survivalist encampment in Idaho, pausing in Las Vegas en route for a paranoid breakdown.

Paring away the appurtenances and rituals of "romance" and the illusory stability of the urban hive, *Snake* refines Luke and Sandra's liaison down to atavistic, cold simplicity, illustrating the defective, violent and futile—and, sporadically, tender and empathetic—habits of sexual connection between men and women. Italicized flash-forward scenes indicate that events haven't unfolded precisely the way Sandra remembers them. Woronov leaves open to doubt which parts of either narrative might be considered real. This ambiguity gives *Snake* its coiled texture of lingering mystery. Opacity splashes this very dark book with a quivering light. The flash-forwards, set in a mental clinic, are hauntingly blurred, like oversaturated, unsteady dream images.

Mary Woronov and Jean Rhys may seem an improbable pairing, but Woronov and Rhys share a fluid gift for framing the external world through the eyes of anguished, disintegrating women. The situations they depict differ, but their characters inhabit similarly despairing, unnervingly circumscribed lives they're powerless to change. A ruminative, restless evocation of destroyed wishes and increasingly puny joys marks the narrator's incremental spiritual shrinkage in the novels of both authors. The private, useless satisfactions their heroines derive from mercilessly clear perceptions are their revenge on the predatory society that defeats them. *Niagara*'s recurring evocation of the sound of water, the susurration and surging tumult of the falls, brings Rhys consciously, though at first unaccountably, to mind. Niagara Falls and suicide are ancient friends, like Rhys's women and their self-annihilating inability to hide their bitterness and exhaustion.

Both Rhys and Woronov avoid all literary garnish and filigree, strip their sentences of everything but what they plainly say and track the toxic progress of emotion as it spreads from a wound, a kiss, a kindness, a betrayal, until it poisons the entire universe. Rhys's heroines live in a world that destroys them all over again every day; so do Woronov's. They hope for things, but not for very much. They basically expect nothing from their lives, and usually get it.

A significant difference is that Rhys's inconsolable despair can be confused with self-pity, though her novels actually indict self-pity as another cause of self-defeat. Woronov never risks this misapprehension, building into her protagonists a capacity for brusque indifference to affection and the distress of others, a ruthless refusal to distract themselves from staring into the void. Rhys knows what her characters don't: that love and two dollars will get you a ride uptown on a bus. Woronov's characters know it as well as she does.

Narrated by Mei Li, known as Molly to all but her immediate family, *Niagara* opens in San Bernardino years after she and her high school boyfriend, Bobby, married and left Buffalo. Molly's brother, Kenny (Bobby's closest school friend), was fiercely and jealously loved by their otherwise cold, cash-fixated Chinese mother, and ridiculed as effeminate by their alcoholic father, a Vietnam burnout. When Molly and Kenny graduated high school, Kenny proved his "manliness" by rolling over the falls in a barrel. His body was never recovered.

Bobby runs a car dealership. He cheats. Molly drinks. Molly drinks all day—like Jean Rhys's Parisian vedettes, not to strain the comparison. Her father dies. She goes to the funeral in Buffalo. She learns some unpleasant secrets about the past. Her mother, whose mind is abandoning reality, announces that she's moving to Florida. Soon afterward, the former dragon lady, senile and toothless, has to be placed in "managed care."

Molly's first account of her childhood withholds some critical information. Some of it she doesn't know herself, but she does knowingly hide one vital detail until the middle of the book. The veracity of her memory is undermined by later conversations with her mother in Florida, with her husband, and with another, unexpected source. What Molly believes about herself is turned inside out as *Niagara* proceeds. Even the secret she keeps later proves to mean the opposite of what she imagined.

Niagara uncovers a story draped in illusion veils, one layer at a time. Purported fact crumbles under a second fact, the second under a third. One of the novel's trickiest turns is brilliantly effective: Woronov reveals the most shattering secret—one that overturns every assumption—so offhandedly the reader attaches no significance to it for several subsequent chapters, as if the narrative had conjured a fast-dissolving mirage.

Niagara's self-consuming structure masters the art of literary risk-taking, but its larger audacity and brilliance emanate from Woronov's portrait of Molly. Like the hopeless, obdurate, quixotic, brutally unsentimental but appetitive, self-conscious women of Rhys's novels, Molly is a downfall child with a deeply frightening impulse to find out what there is in this world to care about, if anything, and to understand herself without special pleading. What she ultimately understands produces her obliteration. When we reach the final page, we can't tell at all where Molly is going. We might guess it's nowhere pleasant, but we won't really ever know.

DANIEL SCHMID'S *LA PALOMA*

A CASINO IN the south of France. A suicide at the roulette table. A magician fanning a hand of cards. A hermaphrodite in a laurel wreath and toga reclines on a Recamier couch, with back titles: *La Force de l'Imagination.* An ancient party, her hard face vibrant against the theater curtains, sings without emotion: "You came along, from out of nowhere . . . wonderful dreams, wonderful schemes from nowhere . . . made every hour, sweet as a flower to me!" And then, through the crimson velvets of desire, Viola appears, the chimerical essence of *fatale.*

An epicene young man named Peter, alone at a table with his glass of champagne, falls in love with the mysterious singer. She has tuberculosis. They marry. A honeymoon at various spas, where she is cured. On a train to the races, he looks up from his newspaper and says, matter-of-factly: Eva Perón is dead. Oh yes, Viola sighs.

At Peter's family château in Switzerland, boredom sets in.

She has an affair with his best friend, who refuses to run away with her. She becomes spectral, withdrawn. A year later she is dead. The two men read her will together. Viola poisoned herself, slowly. She wishes to be exhumed, her remains to be put in an urn in the family crypt, in accordance with tradition. They dig her up. The poison she took preserved her body exactly as it was in life. The widower is forced, then, to slash her corpse into small pieces. We are whisked back to the casino, where he still sits with his champagne, watching her sing: "Shanghai, Shanghai, longing for you, all the day through . . . Shanghai, Shanghai, how could I know? I would miss you so. . . ."

In the blink of an eye, a magnificent and terrible romance has blossomed and died: what we would call a great love. When you want someone crazily, whether it's based on his looks, the way he behaves, his smell, whatever, and the person is one you cannot, finally, have, even if you come to possess him for a time psychologically or physically (but especially if you don't), you can fill the world with this desire: enough, at least, that when it ends you have a story with a legible arc, one that will feature myriad exalting and pathetic details.

La Paloma is a story every human person lives at least once. If I return again and again to this early film of Daniel Schmid, it's because I have lived this story a few times, irrationally, against my better judgment. I recognize the delirium of the process this film describes as identical from person to person. The warp of an obsession, the way it grabs its victims out of the current, so that any conversation becomes a pretext to discuss the Loved One, is boring. Only the details are intriguing: the small scar below his right ear, for example. For the lover it's a question not of interest but of necessity.

La Paloma contains the voluptuous plenum of romantic madness as well as the deflating revelation that losing yourself in another person is always a story that happens in a champagne glass, in the blink of an eye.

It's possible to be a citizen of this age, to approach all human problems in entirely existential terms, and still succumb to the feverish solipsism of desire. As the advice of perfection, one can say that desire is bad, pleasure good. Certainly yearning becomes an unattractive state when it becomes utterly unreasonable; having said this, I must add that the person who has seamlessly rationalized desire into wishing only for what he can definitely have is, in a sense, already dead.

La Paloma is essentially the same story as Gus Van Sant's *Mala Noche* (1986) or Paul Vecchiali's *Drugstore Romance* (1983), or my novel *Horse Crazy:* a story that mimics conventions of 19th-century opera, in which the heroine is inevitably sacrificed in the fifth act, and the hero is left with a story to tell. These recent works are compromised by modernity, contemporary consciousness; one doesn't die for love anymore, except in fantasy, and soon emotion itself will seem a ridiculous extravagance, a relic like *Tosca*.

Eva Perón is dead. Outside is the bitter truth of events, mortality, duty, wars, our bodies in the world, systems that control our choices. Inside are feelings: the craving for maternal warmth, our childhood dreams and wishes that we cling to and fight for at the expense of all else.

I like Daniel Schmid's idea that we are all private radio stations transmitting on our own frequencies, sometimes audible to each other, sometimes not. Personally, few blue-ribbon cultural products occupy my consciousness with anything like the force of my own imagination or experience, and those that do, like *La Paloma,* seldom belong to the upper reaches of any established canon. I am indifferent to any argument that a "greater" work should affect me more profoundly, or that there exists a legitimate authority to declare one thing "major" and another "minor." In the end we have only our experiences, and we feel them with the particularity of monadic creatures.

Why this film and not another? The intense perfection of its metaphor, possibly; something gorgeous in its refusal to coalesce around a conclusion that is less than hallucinatory; the sublimity of Ingrid Caven, whose voice and persona have always evoked for me the most sardonic and melancholy reflections.

Romance involves us in abjection and absurdity. Beyond a point we have no choice about it. We do violence to ourselves by pursuing it and equal violence by squashing our feelings. It's a souvenir of the last century, and not the worst one. The protagonist of *La Paloma* is a dull man who becomes interesting through his infatuation. For one moment in his life he is truly alive. I can't answer the question of whether his fixation is "worth it," and because I can't answer it, *La Paloma* continues to haunt me as the paradigm of certain disappointments.

WILLIAM SEWARD BURROUGHS
(1914–1997)

WILLIAM S. BURROUGHS'S work tends to affect people like a Rorschach test. It separates cultural conservatives from avant-gardists, social reactionaries from libertarians. Or, to use one of Burroughs's favorite distinctions, members of the Johnson Family from the Shits. Johnsons have a live-and-let-live, mind-their-own-business mentality. Shits have an uncontrollable need to pass judgment on, and to be RIGHT about, everything. In today's censorious climate, police work dominates the pages of the book reviews: This writer has the wrong attitude and must be done away with.

Burroughs has always elicited a testy response from the cultural establishment. While early support for *Naked Lunch* from such mandarins as Mary McCarthy and John Ciardi has been matched over the years by encomiums from many of our best writers and by a substantial body of excellent academic criticism, the overall literary world's recognition of Burroughs has been grudging more often than not. Perhaps Burroughs's achievement represents a threat to the well-mannered, conventionally crafted, middle-class novel. It could be as simple as that, but what Burroughs's work actually says is much more menacing to received ideas than his formal eccentricity.

Burroughs expanded the content of fiction, giving artistic form to extremes of contemporary abjection. *Naked Lunch* opened a path into the world of the addict, the homosexual, the social outlaw. From this despised and largely unmentionable territory Burroughs extracted a presiding metaphor of Control. *Naked Lunch* deals with the control of consciousness and behavior through addiction—to sex, power, money, drugs, even to control itself. When themes of this nature, which ultimately have to do with politics, lie at the heart of a writer's work, appreciation is often checked by the timidity of those who prefer not to think about such issues, the implications of which are uncontrollable and inherent in all aspects of contemporary life.

Burroughs liberated writing from linear structure and ossified form. He opened the novel to chance operations, using the "cut-up" and "fold-in" techniques he had developed with Brion Gysin and Ian Sommerville. Earlier writers like Conrad sometimes bring the same characters from one novel to the next. Burroughs recycles phrases, "routines," descriptions and characters through successive works as if they were musical figures or colors in a paint box. His novels suggest an artful arrangement of blocks of prose rather than linear compositions. *Naked Lunch* and the successive books mined from the thousand-some pages Burroughs produced while in and out of heroin addiction in the 1950s—*Nova Express, The Soft Machine, The Ticket That Exploded* (and, recently exhumed, *Interzone*)—compose, in advance of postmodern theory, the first truly postmodern literary texts. Eliminating classical armature and syntax, these books embrace the fragmentary, the "incomplete," the deconstructive.

No doubt the unconventional approach taken by this work inspires nightmares of literary anarchy—what if everyone started writing this way or started writing about what Burroughs writes about? This two-pronged assault on traditional fiction came as the third and arguably furthest-sweeping wave of the Beat movement after Ginsberg's *Howl* and Kerouac's *On the Road.* These set a generation in motion and helped spawn the '60s counterculture. Burroughs deserves consideration apart from the Beats, but there is no doubt that *Naked Lunch* seemed, on publication, the literary apotheosis of that movement. One obvious difference between *Naked Lunch* and Beat literature is what Mary McCarthy called Burroughs's aerial perspective. Long exiled from the United States—in Mexico, Peru, France and Morocco— Burroughs takes a long, jaundiced, global view of things. His evocation of America, though suffused with a gelid sort of nostalgia for the sexual dawn of adolescence, lacks entirely the provincial romanticism found in much Beat writing. (Problematically, much of Burroughs's work does share the Beats' extreme gynophobia; one can only defend his remarks about women in *The Job* by noting the misanthropy in his writing overall.)

In any event, Burroughs's absence from the United States during much of the Beat era and the subsequent hippie movement encourages us to link him with British Pop Art as well as the Velvet Underground, with Godard's

Alpha 60 as well as *Wild in the Streets*. At this distance, it's tricky to separate quintessentially "Burroughsian" ideas from ideas that were generally in the wind in the '60s. Widespread disgust with and revolt against the gray Cold War conformity of the 1950s was certainly fueled by the Beats and a constellation of associated writers and artists. Strategies of transcendence and escape flowed from such disparate sources as Marxist theory and LSD. Linguistics, along with comparative anthropology, became a countercultural preoccupation. Nonverbal communication loomed as a great undiscovered continent; the nature of the prelinguistic brain was much speculated about. These crypto-scientific interests of the radical young, which existed alongside a vogue for Eastern mysticism and magical operations, coincided with Burroughs's artistic and personal quest for a "breakthrough in the gray room." A radical interrogation of language permeates his books. As we can see from variously reproduced pages from Burroughs's scrapbooks, his word-and-image experiments closely parallel certain contemporaneous artifacts like Eduoardo Paolozzi's silkscreen series *Moonstrips Empire News* (itself inspired by Wittgenstein's *Philosophical Investigations*), and slightly later work by Joseph Kosuth. (Burroughs has collaborated, both visually and verbally, with Robert Rauschenberg, David Hockney, George Condo, Philip Taaffe and Keith Haring; in recent years he's been enjoying a second career as a painter.)

Burroughs has always written for the Space Age. His work addresses readers who want OUT of present slave-planet conditions. His theory of language as a virus is closely connected to an (ambivalent) repudiation of Western consciousness in favor of "the savage mind." (This theme, a favorite of '60s culture, is deftly conveyed in Barbet Schroeder's film *The Valley Obscured by Clouds*.) In the tense-scrambled, oneiric narratives of *Nova Express* and *The Ticket That Exploded*, Burroughs invokes the synchronic, telepathic mind of the aboriginal, linking the hieroglyphic "Mayan control calendar" with the image manipulation of contemporary mass media. Other texts, exploring the mind-altering possibilities of Korzybski's general semantics and the Scientology E-meter, read like manuals for dismantling prerecorded consciousness. Burroughs's basic project is psychoanalytic: to discard imprints, received ideas, the residue of psychic wounds, all forms of false consciousness. Since he pictures liberation as a state of tranquility and "mineral silence" rather than one of religious or sexual ecstasy, this goal seems close to Freud's ambition to replace neurotic unhappiness with ordinary unhappiness.

Being a novelist instead of a theoretician, Burroughs invariably paints the catastrophic possibilities inherent in any scheme of liberation. His pointed refusal to endorse "the garden of delights" of the psychedelic movement, though widely ignored at the time, reflects the stubborn complexity of a born realist. A strain of solid common sense serves as a bracket around writing uncommonly open to the apocalyptic imagination. It's difficult to pinpoint the precise amount of put-on in the dozens of texts Burroughs contributed, in the '60s and '70s, to English and American underground newspapers, describing methods for instigating riots and disrupting the urban infrastructure. The chill-blooded revolutionary stance is seldom struck without irony; prescriptions for poisoning water supplies or launching biological warfare often turn up later as "routines" in Burroughs's fictions like *The Wild Boys* and *Blade Runner: A Movie.* Nevertheless, it's worth remembering that between roughly 1967 and 1973, the mood of much of the West was apocalyptic; authentic populist movements really did threaten the control mechanisms of the media-military-industrial complex for the first and only time since World War II. Burroughs's writings were part of a seminal, restive cultural mix that included Herbert Marcuse, N. O. Brown, Frantz Fanon, Claude Levi-Strauss and Marshall McLuhan—which in turn influenced musicians such as John Cage and LaMonte Young; diverse artists including R. J. Kitaj, Robert Rauschenberg, Yoko Ono and Jasper Johns; numerous theater directors such as Jean-Claude van Italie, Joseph Chaikin, and Julian Beck; innumerable writers; and filmmakers Nicolas Roeg, Vera Chytilova, Alessandro Jodorowski, the Godard of *One Plus One* and *Weekend* and the Pasolini of *Pigpen,* to name only a few.

Burroughs has remained an influential figure throughout the last two decades, partly on the strength of later novels like *Exterminator!, Port of Saints, Cities of the Red Night, The Place of Dead Roads* and *The Western Lands,* in which earlier experimental procedures have been integrated into more traditionally coherent narratives. Another part of Burroughs's appeal, especially to younger readers, is the prophetic aura of his books. *Naked Lunch,* for example, refers ahead twenty years to liposuction ("stomach tucks"), autoerotic asphyxia and a fatal AIDS-like viral epidemic. Some of his writing is uncanny in this respect. Some of it simply identifies problems that recur and magnify themselves historically: for example, drug hysteria, a relatively minor tool of social repression in the 1940s and 1950s, today a major implement of state terror. The "purple-assed baboon" routine, used in "Roosevelt After Inauguration" to satirize Roosevelt's attempt to pack the Supreme Court, also anticipates the neoconservative take-over of the American judiciary in the 1980s and 1990s.

The culture has absorbed many of Burroughs's ideas so thoroughly that their source is now obscured. A conspiratorial view of government didn't originate with Burroughs, but he was the first American novelist to make justified paranoia a major literary theme. The idea of sinister forces controlling the world of appearances is commonplace in post-Watergate, post-Iran Contra America, but it was considered bizarre and unseemly when Burroughs invented the Nova Mob.

The pitch-black humor and rejection of humanism in Burroughs's works were naturally embraced by the punk movement, notably by Patti Smith. In the distinctly unpsychedelic and junk-ridden milieu of downtown Manhattan in the late '70s, Burroughs was elder statesman, guru, and cautionary presence all in one. It would be foolish to claim that the strong antijunk message of *Naked Lunch* ever dissuaded a single junkie, or indeed was ever intended to. Both the courtroom transcripts from the 1966 Boston obscenity trial and Burroughs's "Deposition: Testimony Concerning a Sickness" that preface all later editions of *Naked Lunch* serve exactly the same satirical purpose as the frontispiece disclaimers and pledges of high moral altitude that accompany any picaresque novel out to shock, from Defoe's *Roxana* to Nabokov's *Lolita*. In the '70s *Naked Lunch* was to junkies what *Alice in Wonderland* and *The Hobbit* were to acidheads in the '60s. In other words, a completely accurate guide to what you could expect if you got addicted to heroin. In the days before AIDS, many people wanted, for reasons of their own, to go through hell and (maybe) live to tell about it. Burroughs's writings were useful in the sense that reading them kept you from being too deluded about what you were doing.

The extravagant homoeroticism of *The Wild Boys* and *Cities of the Red Night* echoes in the films of Derek Jarman, which also employ the aleatory cutting techniques of Burroughs's fiction. The device of anachronism in *Cities of the Red Night*—a formally tidy variant of the "time travel" produced by scrambled texts in earlier works—crops up in Jarman's *Caravaggio*, Rudy Wurlitzer and Alex Cox's film *Walker* and a recent novel by William Gibson and Bruce Sterling, *The Difference Engine*. Burroughs's literary influence on

Kathy Acker, Dennis Cooper, David Wojnarowicz and myself is as various as we are and probably something for others to elucidate.

Repetitive variations of the cut-up method using tape recorders and film, investigated by Burroughs in collaboration with Ian Sommerville and Antony Balch, have been adapted in music by Philip Glass, Gavin Bryers (the looping in *The Sinking of the Titanic,* in particular) and Glenn Branca (*Symphony #2*), among others; groups like the Insect Trust, Steely Dan, Hüsker Dü and Throbbing Gristle have named themselves out of *Naked Lunch* and/or applied Burroughs's techniques of composition. Burroughs has made numerous recordings combining readings of his work with experimental music, including the highly successful *Dead City Radio,* as well as other recordings made in collaboration with Giorno Poetry Systems. He recently collaborated with Robert Wilson and Tom Waits on *The Black Rider,* a music drama. Though imperfectly realized, the picture book projects *Ah Pook Is Here* and *The Book of Breeething* were sufficiently well known to have informed the recent outgrowth of "graphic novels"—grown-up comic books by serious writers such as Clive Barker and Michael Moorcock, intended to catch the short, primarily visual attention span of the TV-and-Nintendo generation.

The question of how Burroughs's themes, characters and ideas might be communicated to a wider audience remains complicated in 1991. Because certain important aspects of the work—explicit homoerotica and homoerotic violence, defecatory fantasies, etc.—are not only controversial but banned from mainstream film and from television, Burroughs's mythology for the Space Age has "entered the mainstream" at an oblique angle. Religious hysteria surrounding the depiction of sexuality and bodily functions is a depressing, near-universal fact of life today. However, it would be insultingly reductive to suggest that Burroughs's achievement consists entirely in his exemplary frankness about sucking and fucking. His invention of alternative worlds, of creatures like the Mugwumps, the Green Boys, and the Nova Mob, and archetypal characters like Bradley the Buyer, A. J. the After-Birth Tycoon, Hamburger Mary and Dr. Benway represents a protean effort of imagination. Some of Burroughs's complex insights into the social dynamics of addiction—and a good deal of Burroughsian humor—were incorporated into Gus Van Sant's *Drugstore Cowboy,* a film that features Burroughs as a defrocked junkie priest. Though Ridley Scott adopted the title rather than the story of Burroughs's *Blade Runner,* the movie's cast of renegade androids and its bosky, evocative ambiance—Piranesian architectural and human ruins outscaled by the monolithic "Mayan pyramids" of the corporate future—belong to Burroughs's fictional world, as does the device of Scott's *Alien,* i.e., a parasite that eventually consumes and assimilates its host organism. Among major filmmakers, it's undoubtedly David Cronenberg, now director of the movie *Naked Lunch,* whose imagination most closely parallels Burroughs's own. The lethal telepathic practices of *Scanners,* TV-induced brain tumors and "organic" video cassettes in *Videodrome,* fatal symbiosis between twins in *Dead Ringers* and even—especially—the disembodied gall bladder that swims up between Barbara Steele's legs in *The Parasite Murders* correspond to the queasily visceral marriages of flesh and technology pioneered by *Naked Lunch, The Soft Machine* and *Nova Express.* More pertinent still is the crisply detached "paranoid realism" practiced by both artists: the sense that every human interaction contains the possibility of homicide. Or, as the title of Alan Ansen's 1959 essay on Burroughs put it, "Anyone Who Can Pick Up a Frying Pan Owns Death."

THAT AWFUL MESS AT
THE GOVERNOR'S MANSION

"**M**Y TRUTH is that I am a gay American."
Governor Jim McGreevey of New Jersey, his wife eerily smiling at his side, his bewildered parents supportively hovering nearby, dropped this particular bombshell in the course of his resignation speech at the Trenton State House, also confessing to "an adult consensual affair with another man."

It was a strange moment in a strange life, a kind of life that had always been strange when it was commonplace and stranger still on 12 August 2004, when it seemed an anachronism. Gay men and lesbians who had married straight partners, or each other, in an effort to hide from their own identities had become even rarer than "white marriages" involving men and women candidly gay among themselves and selected friends who seek protective covering, or a mingling of finances, or the social and economic perks that accompany legal matrimony in matters of taxes, insurance policy coverage and the like.

Appearing "normal" to people who consider being gay abnormal hasn't been a difficult trick in the gender-scrambled urban cultures of America in recent years; gender stereotypes that dictated every aspect of self-presentation in the 1950s have been progressively erased from popular culture and the life of what we habitually imagine to be the American mainstream. No marriage ever coincided with the smugly cynical ludicrousness of the Ozzie and Harriet thing, and the image of family perfection presented in shows like *Leave It To Beaver* and *My Three Sons* was likewise all image and no reality. The effort of credulous audiences to approximate these perpetually chuckling, cheery, red-white-and-blue lobotomy jobs was the conspicuous deformity of American families in the era of Howdy Doody and the Red Scare. But while sexually bogus marriages of that Golden Age were transparent to homosexuals, they still usefully deflect any suspicion the average home-makers of the heartland might otherwise entertain about that funny couple next door.

Maybe Jim McGreevey fooled himself into two marriages and fooled other people all the way to the Trenton State House, though it emerged soon after he threw in the proverbial towel that his sexuality wasn't the best-kept secret in New Jersey, nor, if media samplings around the state were credible, the big public dealbreaker McGreevey himself considered it to be, if indeed the deal he was breaking was the one he berated himself over in his speech. A legible majority of New Jerseyans interviewed in the press said McGreevey's homosexuality didn't matter to them, and didn't disqualify him from being governor.

In fact, if it had just been a matter of announcing his sexual preference, Jim McGreevey's press conference could have stopped way short of resigna-tion. A week poking around in various New Jersey cities and towns, how-ever, proved ample time to consider that Jim McGreevey's sense of wind direction was simply a few fortuitous beats quicker than the average voter's. Virtually everyone with a stronger sense of politics indicated a distinct pos-sibility that this weirdly stiff, somehow distasteful coming out party was itself the beard for a smart, preventative move—deftly aborting an impend-ing revelation of direct links between McGreevey, the malfeasance and cor-ruption of various campaign donors, and beneficiaries of appointments and state contracts during McGreevey's abbreviated tenure.

Certainly the talking heads whose musings fill so many television hours were not prepared, in August 2004, to characterize McGreevey's, or any-body's, homosexuality as "wrong" in itself: The value-free word of choice, in this case, was "shocker," in the sense of shaking hands with a joy buzzer rather than feeling scandalized. The sheer awkwardness of reporting the story as a story, when so often in recent times the same disclosure has flopped as a narrative with legs, evoked the McCarthy era's glum, ugly atmosphere—which produced the obverse, desired impression of McGreevey's victimiza-tion by his own Catholic rectitude. (If you can't oppress yourself, what sort of Catholic can you be?) This neutralized an entirely different set of questions than a less sympathy-extorting perception would have—namely, that a gay governor could be just another slick, standard-issue New Jersey politician who happened to suck dick on the side.

As multi-untalented cable "pundits" debated whether McGreevey's people had offered hush money to the governor's presumed consensual male partner, an Israeli national named Golan Cipel, or if Cipel and his attorney had or had not attempted to blackmail McGreevey, Americans drinking this in from the media cooler felt eerily transported into a Douglas Sirk melodrama, circa 1957.

While it's also true that it felt even more 1957 a few weeks later, when debating Presidential candidates were asked by the usual 40-watt moderators if they "thought homosexuality was a choice"—a question that might have been more usefully framed by asking if their picture of a nice world included it as an acceptable option.

If there was a "message" embedded in any TV cablegram that didn't emit from an Evangelical ministry, it was the eternal-wisdom-du-jour that American society had gotten beyond "the gay issue." As it had, so to speak, moved past "the Jew issue" or "the non-Caucasian issue." This may have had some qualified truth to it, but American society as it is no longer holds any allure for the career politician; we have a ruling class determined to use any kind of trivia it can hammer into the highly porous brains of the lower classes to distract them from unpleasant reality, freshening up their conditioned practice of scapegoating themselves in response to crises, rather than develop any aptitude for cold, unemotional analysis.

America's educational system dispensed with the learning process long ago: If you can pay to get in, any college or university will issue your job certification papers after the requisite period of sleepwalking through various buildings owned by the institution. The reputations our highly regarded schools earned between their founding and the year America went off the gold standard has magically persisted long after any justification for it disappeared. Thus many credit-accruing "subjects" that would have been confined to campus clubs, or less abstractly explored in the back seat of a Pontiac, when college admission had rigorous criteria, enable a person who can't spell "cat" to emerge with a graduate degree in "gender studies," "deconstructivism" or the piquantly amorphous "theory" of subjects its specialists never had to learn before theorizing them down to the ground. Many become heads of departments after their pedigrees are formalized, still uncertain how to spell "cat."

"The gay issue," no longer much of an issue itself, morphed into the still-flammable, irrelevant issue of "gay marriage"—a burningly urgent necessity to its advocates, who probably blew the McGreevey autumn's election for the Democrats; for its opponents, a phenomenon more lethal to the Republic than global warming or any other matter crucial to the general good. So much more menacing than our sad country's industrious sale of weapons to both sides of any conflict, to countries where human rights enjoy the status of mosquitoes—to anyone, in fact, pulling out the stops to coerce sales orders from countries that don't even want them—that the incumbent President-appointee perceived a need as essential as oxygen for a constitutional amendment barring this atrocity from ever occurring. Or, where it had already occurred, denying it ever had and erasing it from state laws and memory itself, in the manner customarily applied to American atrocities of any kind.

Marriage, correctly understood as a property and inheritance arrangement, only became tangled up with "love" in the 19th century. It has never been "sacred" except in a ceremonial sense, when ritually enacted in a liturgical setting. Moreover, it doesn't acquire "legality" when some pedophile in a Roman collar or some other kind of liturgical drag mumbles vows and litanies to the "bride" and "groom." It's only legally binding with a state-issued license.

When American infant mortality was more common than not, the Catholic church helped the state ensure a steady work force by commanding the poorest of immigrants to churn out as many as fifteen or twenty babies. Most died, but enough survived to supply a reliable number of slaves for textile mills and other labor-dependent industries. "Love and marriage" today is an artificially glued-together commodity supporting other commodities—for example, deBeers Diamonds, a consortium claiming to have effectively purified its inventory of blood diamonds with careful screening; the methods by which diamonds move from Africa to Belgium reveal the absurdity of this utterly cynical assertion.

Love that is enforced by the state or any religion is hardly "eternal," but a tool of economic exploitation. Sexual love has an average two-year lifespan, so getting married to "legalize" what the state has no business sticking its nose in, namely whether married people fuck each other or not, has now made not having sex with a spouse punishable with a five-year prison term and a $500,000 fine—try marrying to emigrate in or out of the bastion of liberty we live in. Thanks to the fools in Congress who voted in the Patriot

Act, unless your marriage looks convincing as a love-besotted fuckfest, you can land in the slammer and be driven into bankruptcy at the same time.

The complete separation of church from state is a central tenet of the founding document of the United States of America. The state has awarded itself the right to parse every fraction of sexual difference or sameness, and in reality it has already legalized marriage between persons of the same sex, one of whom has undergone medical gender reassignment surgery; a logical argument for dispensing with this requirement could be made on the simple legal grounds that it discriminates against people who can't afford a sex change operation. But in a genuine democracy, as opposed to a totalitarian one, the state should also be separated from the private arrangements between its citizens altogether: Get rid of marriage and have any couple of any kind contract to share property, legally inhabit the same rental property even if one party dies, and so on. Otherwise, Americans aren't citizens at all, but subjects.

Shortly after the McGreevey tempest-in-a-urinal, as America's television blabbermouths were still congratulating themselves and the country on America's enlightened indifference to anyone's sexual orientation, 11 states plopped initiatives against gay marriage on their ballots. The Republican side of the Property Party began to feature a brand of innuendo that had, in previous election years, produced campaign spots showing black fingers reaching for welfare checks from a white hand across a desk, and the inky outline of Willie Horton issuing from a revolving door.

Lest anyone forget that something formally called the Know Nothing Party was once a formidable force in American politics, the "anti-gay marriage" initiatives were, collectively, endorsed by just short of 60 million voters. At least 3 percent more than half of that half of eligible Americans who showed up to vote in the 2004 Presidential election viewed the cementing of marriage as an immutable "sacred bond between a man and a woman" into the country's crumbling foundations. Vastly more imperative than terminating a world-toxic military folly in Iraq, or anything else of actual, immediate menace. Code phrase: "moral values."

"Morals" derives from the Latin *mores* and means simply "rules of behavior." Behaviors regulated by law and behaviors dictated by religion are sometimes coincidentally the same but hardly identical, and sometimes antithetical—regarding, let's say, the consumption of shellfish or acceptable methods of contraception. The state protects the seafood industry's freedom to do its business, likewise the prophylactic and pharmaceutical industries' right to produce contraceptives without regard to Jewish or Catholic dogma. It protects my right to buy and eat clams and your right to buy a condom and use it. In law if not in reality, behavior that inflicts no tangible harm on others is either expressly allowed by the state or acknowledged to be none of the state's business.

It would take an extremely determined optimist to imagine many of the Red State Majoritarians have ever read the U.S. Constitution or know what any of it says, except for the Second Amendment in the Bill of Rights, which they interpret as the right to maintain a military facility in one's basement. It's more probable that like most people, they don't really give a shit what it says in the Constitution as long as they can do their own thing. Which, oddly enough, is more or less what the Constitution is meant to guarantee. The hard part, what we might call the fine print, is the guarantee that other people unlike them can do their own things, too.

How odd to consider the unmanly methods by which our nation now conducts war, to use "unmanly" in an old-fashioned way, how "pansy" to blast whole neighborhoods of civilians out of existence, from an untouchable distance, to get that one little speck of an "insurgent" hiding out in a mosque, in light of an apparently widespread conviction that the "moral values" the majority hold dear are anything anybody should respect, just because the majority voted for them.

With all its absurdities and stupidities, America's pop culture is infinitely more progressive than its politics—intellectually, spiritually, sensually and, as far as that's concerned, morally. What politicians claim to consider appalling, most 13 year olds find barely worth mentioning. Pop culture has its own mores and "values," and its indifference to the Puritanical masochism of the Jesus-toxic few makes it a source of unending resentment, and a much easier target to hit than Osama bin Laden. The social loop that connects the destruction of a social safety net and the construction of an amply funded, Christian Fundamentalist network of services formerly provided by the government translated into votes, votes for demolishing the thinning wall between church and state, in Election 2004.

Votes, in effect, to restore the social ugliness of the 1950s and early '60s, a time when getting an abortion meant risking your life, and guys like Jim McGreevey were driven to an early closet. Worse for him, he locked himself in his closet more inescapably during the same years when ever-growing numbers of Americans were coming out of theirs, with less and less embarrassment and fear.

Whether or not George Bush, who has failed at everything he's ever done besides win or steal elections, will succeed in delivering to its corporate owners an America where gays and abortion and other phobias become invisible to the average Joe, his stay-at-home spouse, and their three adorable little replicas, consider that the 1,000-Year Reich fell short by 988 years. And what happened to Jim McGreevey has always happened to many people in the Land of Liberty: gay, straight, bisexual and otherwise.

Somewhere along the Metrorail that shoots you from grammar school through college to a corner office at Goldman Sachs, you'll notice a crumbling stucco alcove festooned with Day-Glo graffiti: "Work Hard, Play by the Rules, Get Screwed." The symbiosis between material success and self-amputation never gets much play in college catalogues and corporate orientation manuals, but it's there, and it always has been.

Unless you have the stamina or perversity for a lifetime of bohemianism, the pressure to conform puts the squeeze on early and never lets go. Middle-class life is more regimented than it looks. It seems to offer an infinity of choices, but the basic menu never changes: career, marriage, family, car. Boat and vacation home, optional good luck. What sustains an illusion of ongoing, limitless choices are consumer products, ranging from the brand of toilet paper you prefer to the type of house you take the mortgage on.

These aren't desolately empty forms, empty marriage, empty houses. They simply can't welcome every need or gratify every desire. They incubate secrets and fantasies. They force us into unpleasant realizations—that we don't really know ourselves while building the hives we plan to spend our lives in, and we don't honestly, profoundly know each other. Often the more we know, the less we like what we've sealed ourselves in with.

This wouldn't change terribly if gay marriage were legalized tomorrow morning, though it should be, anyway. It wouldn't change certain realities. We build compartments to keep difficult feelings from spilling into places in our lives where they can hurt us. We disconnect who we are at work from the role we play at home.

One day, outside our protective, stifling shells, we find, somewhere, a comfort zone where we can gratify a private, embarrassing desire. Over time, with practice, the shame and embarrassment wear off. And the desire assumes a vital, even obsessive importance. The idea of legal contracts that don't require the expensive formalities and idiocies of divorce proceedings, at least from this perspective, are less oppressive than "sacred" matrimony. If people deeply, really want to be together, they don't need the state to ratify their desire—just the same rights that come with the necessary paperwork, if they want them.

McGreevey's compartments were peculiarly rigid and overstuffed. The falsity inside wasn't a gnawing torment, perhaps, but a thing that poked to the surface when conjugal duty called for more than the mere act—uninhibited invention, novelty, rubber toys, poppers, abandon instead of a little tenderness or a plea of exhaustion. Still, you wouldn't need to be gay or straight to feel the same thing in an institutional straightjacket bonding you to your partner "forever." Forever and yesterday have the same quality of fast evaporation.

Legions of men and women find the wine of married life curdling into vinegar, lie awake calculating asset distribution and alimony percentages and child support figures. The "shocker" in McGreevey's case was that he was a public, political figure, closing on 50, homosexual, who never made a life he really wanted in the first place. The only newsworthy part was being a public, political figure. I assure you he was not the first gay state governor in the U.S. He was the first to publicly say so. Thanks to the turds in power currently, he may also have been the last for a long time.

"This, the 47th year of my life, is arguably too late to have this discussion," he told the world when he resigned. He'd gone a little nuts over some jerk he met in Israel, and maybe, whether consciously or not, he'd engineered his escape from a stale travesty he'd been raised to believe was the "right" kind of life. Options had closed, you can't recover time you've wasted.

On the other hand, better 47 than 57 or 74 or never. It's never really "too late to have this discussion" with yourself and decide what's true about you and what isn't. There are many important things you'll never know, but who you feel like having sex with isn't one of them.

Modern unhappiness isn't reliably, or even often, eradicated by love, however predictably "love" presents itself as the happy end of romance novels and Hollywood films, a non sequitor wet kiss that shows how love melts away pesky irrelevant things like mortgages, credit card bills, car payments, medical expenses or sudden unemployment. Most of us realize that love is a nice thing to have, and unless we're exceptionally lucky, it doesn't last forever and it doesn't pay the bills.

Chronic loneliness, unendurable abjection, and lack of authentic adult experiences, the reflexive repression of our need to share sexual pleasure—afflictions unique to no sexuality, nor to the physically unblessed or the less than affluent—conjure unreal fantasies of what "relationships" are, the work they require, whether a sketchy road map exists for one kind and no map at all for another kind.

"Falling in love" in such circumstances, as McGreevey apparently did, is often a form of insanity, demolishing the structures that ensure our status in society. Irrational obsession with an unavailable or slyly exploitative "love object"—as Golan Cipel, McGreevey's presumed boyfriend, evidently was—is a gorgeous subject for fiction. In real life, it's schizoid. But sometimes worth it, in a completely unexpected way. Under a spell of projected wishes and unsatisfied longings, we may lose our jobs, our families, our homes, our friends. Maybe the Governorship of New Jersey. We may even lose our instinct for self-preservation. And, in some curious instances, losing it all is exactly what we want.

III

SURREALISMS AND
THE POWER OF EMOTION

OF CAROLINE BLACKWOOD

ORN IN 1931 into an aristocratic Anglo-Irish family, Lady Caroline Blackwood came late to fiction, in her thirties, after some forays in journalism
that were not uniformly impressive. During a stay in Hollywood she had an
affair with producer Ivan Moffatt; she was introduced to Cary Grant, who was
undergoing LSD psychotherapy and persuaded her to do the same. Psyche-
delics pushed open the stuck door of Blackwood's creativity. She had been married to Lucien Freud, composer Israel Citkowitz, and later to Robert Lowell.
She has been typecast as a "muse to genius" (indeed, her sole biography has the
unfortunate title *Dangerous Muse*). As a Guinness heiress she was expected to
marry well and learn good horsemanship. She was, however, a staunch woman
of considerable mental prowess and a wide reputation as an accomplished
mimic, raconteur and collector of stories, something owed perhaps to her Irish
background. She was an immensely charming yet troubled woman. Until her
death in 1996, she was still renowned for her wit, her sly gamesmanship in her
personal relations, and her stoicism in the face of deadly disease. I would argue
that she was equally the artist to any of her paramours and husbands.

Blackwood's dry humor, the note of bemused astonishment she strikes in
the recounting of human foibles, serves as a kind of party mask for dire and
unbearable truths. She presents us something raw in the guise of something
cooked. She is the master of the dubious qualifier, the droll double take, the
ludicrously shifted point of view from dire to antic. Aunt Lavinia, in the 1977
novel *Great Granny Webster*, after recounting at hilarious length her near rape
in a mental ward by her appointed psychiatrist, puts the finishing touches on
her nails and muses to her niece:

"In one sense he was rather a character, that Dr. Kronin," she said reflec-
tively. "By no means an enjoyable character . . . But in his peculiar way the

amazing thing is that I think he really viewed himself as a romantic. So that with his incomprehensible mentality one has to admit there was something quite individual about the little pig all the same."

A frequent triggering event in Blackwood's prose is the sly disclosure of contractions that emerge in those testing moments thought to define "character." Her people seldom make a positive resolve to act, yet they often experience moments of near revelation, realizations of the truth of the state of things. Blackwood's characters are often people who fall short of themselves, transgress their own convictions, fail to meet life's occasions with a full deck. Inadequacy, haplessness, passivity and self-absorption are typical traits of her creatures, though they may also be monstrously consistent with themselves, aggressively engaged in a futile argument with the world.

On one hand, there are short stories like "Matron," in the collection *Good Night, Sweet Ladies,* published in 1983. Matron is a dutiful workhorse and tyrant of a head nurse, ruling over her hospital wards with an unbendable set of regulations and an almost nuclear response to anyone who disregards them. Yet she has a moment of weakness, a disastrous spark of human feeling, when she sees that a dying patient's wife is virtually starving herself in order to never leave her husband's bedside. Matron orders the woman to eat and breaks one of her strictest rules by giving her hospital food. This almost microscopic violation of Matron's seamless martial armor destroys her very idea of herself and results in her total collapse.

On the other hand, many of Blackwood's characters refuse to crumble or to give an inch. Other people's sensitivities cut no ice with them. Among such stolid gargoyles as the eponymous Great Granny Webster or the Duchess of Windsor's forbidding lawyer Maître Blum in *The Last of the Duchess* (1995), the habit of being always staunchly, inflexibly oneself is shown to wreak as much self-defeating damage as spinelessness and indecisiveness.

[Maître Blum] kept glaring at me with the utmost hostility. She answered my questions with ill-mannered abruptness. Her slanting, unblinking eyes had a snakelike malevolence. She was perverse. If she wanted favorable articles written about the Duchess, she seemed reckless in the way she deliberately tried to antagonize her interviewers.

Blackwood's writing is subtly gothic, and exaggerated in a manner designed to reveal the shocking apathy or terrifying forwardness of her subjects. The accretion of lowering detail in her 1976 novel *The Stepdaughter* is characteristic. The epistolary narrator, J., has been abandoned by her husband, Arnold, and subtly blackmailed by him into caring for her unwanted stepdaughter, Renata, in the luxury apartment Arnold continues to maintain for them.

Renata is a ghastly, lumpish, sullenly withdrawn girl who leaves great quantities of unflushed paper in the toilet and feeds exclusively on rocklike muffins she constantly bakes from a packaged mix. J., a frustrated painter, highly educated, articulate, observant and powerfully bitter about her victimization by Arnold, gradually persuades us to detest and dehumanize the unbearable Renata, whose baleful presence is a constant reminder that J. is trapped and stultified by her feckless, estranged spouse.

We are cleverly led to overlook the obvious fact that J.'s prison is an enviable address where she lives without financial worries and that her own idleness and obsessive feelings of betrayal cause her to magnify Renata's unpleasantness into almost criminal proportions. Indeed, one character who remarks on the beauty and privilege of J.'s surroundings is depicted as an insensitive oaf. And then, with an excruciatingly deft turn of the screw, we realize that we have been drawn into complicity with the destruction of a 13-year-old child, through our identification with J.'s self-conscious and seemingly self-critical lamentations.

This kind of reversal is one of Blackwood's most accomplished effects, typically, though not exclusively, achieved via use of self-deluded or solipsistically limited narrators, such as the hypocritical, misogynistic, emotionally constipated husband whose side we reflexively take, in ever greater exasperation with the people around him, for at least two thirds of *The Fate of Mary Rose* (1974). The agonizing pleasure of this novel lies somewhere in our half-registered sense that the person we're listening to is revealing himself as a loathsome fool; yet the extremity of the situation he describes, with what eventually proves to be wildly biased single-mindedness, deflects close scrutiny of his own outrageous behavior.

Blackwood's earliest stories exhibit a richly nuanced appreciation of the monstrosity of ordinary life. The indifference and callousness of one person toward another tend to level any form of suffering to triviality, and the world goes on in its casually murderous way. The most horrific example, because its reverberations on the victimizer are shown to be so very tiny, occurs in the short story "Who Needs It?" (from the 1973 collection *For All That I Found There*), in which the proprietor of a hair salon finds it necessary to fire her Saturday helper when the woman's concentration camp tattoo sours the giddy atmosphere the customers insist on.

> Angeline waved her plump little dye-stained hands as she pleaded with her husband. "Look—use your nut, Herb. If you had seen that woman's arm— you wouldn't be so mad at me. . . . You should have seen the size of her numbers. They were like something you see on the backsides of a bunch of cattle. . . . I mean Christ, Herb! You could get a customer and she just want to relax and have her hair shampooed—and she might take a look at that arm and it would really turn her stomach. And, well, she might just figure like—who really needs it?"

Blackwood loves monsters. No character in modern literature is more obdurately monstrous than Great Granny Webster. An Edwardian relic, this utterly pleasureless, stingy, censorious, ossified banshee, forever ensconced in her painfully stiff chair before a fireplace laid but never lit, is the stuffed and essentially powerless dragon of a musty castle, the remnant of hidebound and pointless traditional values, someone who has never in her life given anyone a reason to like her. Compared with the child narrator's descriptions of her ebullient, hard-drinking, promiscuously fun-loving Aunt Lavinia, Great Granny Webster is a black hole, swallowing and extinguishing any mote of liveliness that flashes into her ken.

> It seemed to be her heart that Great Granny Webster really lived for. Her own heart was all she cared about. She had produced three generations of descendants and lived to know that none of them could have the slightest importance to her, any more than all the leaves that have flown yearly from its branches can have much importance to an aged oak.

Yet we cannot get enough of this horrible woman. Blackwood's macabre descriptions of Great Granny Webster's fanatical parsimony—"her stingy and minute portions of rubbery, unseasoned canned spaghetti"—inspire a ghoulish appetite to learn what accounts for such an inflexible and pathetic human being. The real magic trick Blackwood pulls off is to keep us wondering what buried primal trauma or tragic life event froze this character into a charmless fortress of withholding even after we realize there isn't one, or just one.

For what transpires throughout *Great Granny Webster* while Blackwood seems to be mainly relating something else is a miraculously terse family history so appallingly mad and dangerous that Great Granny Webster's stiff-mouthed silence and infuriating immobility could almost be considered a dignified withdrawal from decades of psychic mayhem.

One might say Blackwood practices a bullfighter's feint. The author waves a red cape at us, knowing we will charge at the wrong target. The best example of this approach is *Corrigan*. This 1984 novel is Blackwood's loveliest and most craftily assembled work of fiction and, strange to say, her sunniest, though the sunshine arrives late in the day and in an extremely perverse yet logical manner. A lonely widow repining for the past while enduring the boisterous attentions of her clumsy Irish housekeeper encounters a cripple collecting money for an invalid hospital. The eponymous Corrigan is a compellingly handsome and eloquent man, alarmingly uninhibited in his chair-bound lucubrations, whose company has an enervating and eventually transformative effect on the listless and mournful Mrs. Blunt.

The jacket of the new edition of *Corrigan* tactfully describes its charismatic protagonist as an "arch manipulator." There is a surprise lurking in its pages that overturns our understanding of what we've read about for a hundred pages or so, an enriching surprise that has been basking more or less in plain sight, but perhaps even more striking is the uncharacteristically wily optimism of *Corrigan*. For the book insists on the salubriousness of deceptions that cut rather deep into the foundations of mutual understanding. To put it another way, we may need to tell one another and ourselves major whoppers, and not just little white lies, to replenish our interest in life.

This notion, developed so ingeniously in *Corrigan,* is a vital ingredient in Blackwood's work. On the far from simple level of its own abundant jouissance, the story of her prose is its artful and marvelously apposite quality of exaggeration. *Corrigan*'s characters seem credible and alive precisely because the habits that define them are so theatrically overdrawn. The telltale squeak and rumble of Corrigan's wheelchair and Mrs. Murphy's outlandish method of washing a floor become daft and freighted signs of something oversize and ludicrous about to spill into the narrative. In *Corrigan,* Blackwood gives us a sense of ordinary life becoming a breathless adventure, through the catalytic effect of Corrigan, who has the grandiose dimensions of sham and poetry we associate with theatrical illusion.

Blackwood is every bit as antically hyperbolic in ostensible nonfiction as in her novels and stories. What she imagines going on in other people's minds is perhaps more true to their character than what really might be found there. Blackwood rarely wrote journalism, but her forays into nonfiction display an acute sense of the foibles and tics that define the briefly encountered, the verbiage that delineates a mentality and sensibility, the sartorial and other quiddities that give us a character whole. And she is, of course, broadly satirical in doing so. She takes enormous liberties with hunters and their animal-loving opponents in *In the Pink* (1987), her book on fox hunting, and with the boorish ratepayers opposing the Greenham Common antinuclear women in *On the Perimeter* (1984), and in a truly monumentalizing way with Maître Suzanne Blum, the French lawyer who virtually imprisoned the Duchess of Windsor in the latter's Paris mansion during the last years of the duchess's life. Blackwood has a genius for zeroing in on the most resonant and defining absurdities the people she encounters cling to as cherished "ideas" and fervently held "principles." Her tone is both incredulous and searching, in the manner of an especially lingering documentary camera that simply keeps running while its subjects hang themselves.

The flavor of Maître Blum's portrait, in *The Last of the Duchess,* reflects the idea of art as a lie that reveals the truth. Maître Blum must surely have been a detestable woman in every way, yet Blackwood's speculative projections of Blum's inner life are both bizarre and truer-sounding than her account of their actual meetings. "It was impossible to visualize her lying throbbing with unabashed passion and pleasure in the arms of her husband, the General," Blackwood writes. "Her whole personality was too essentially unyielding. It seemed almost obscene to try to picture her in the nude let alone in some subjugated erotic position."

Maître Blum was an actual person, but in Blackwood's treatment she joins a garish array of fictional relatives. Blackwood developed variations on a set of stock characters throughout her career, including the stout or over-weight, pestiferous, and sometimes hoggish female "sidekick" to the central figures. Renata with her cakes, the mother-in-law in the short story "Please Baby Don't Cry" with her sausages and waffle syrup, the obscenely breasty Miss Renny in "The Baby Nurse" are endlessly masticating, insatiably ap-petitive obstacles to someone else's happiness. They are lumps in the land-scape who are half Greek chorus, half Minotaur. More rounded versions of this stolid figure appear in "Matron," in "Taft's Wife" (in the figure of the otiose, obnoxiously flirtatious Mrs. Ripstone), and most sympathetically as the clamorous Mrs. Murphy in *Corrigan*. The most sinister version is no doubt Maître Blum, the servant virtually become the master, no longer content at gobbling up any food in the vicinity or asserting her riotous presence everywhere, but actually gaining vitality and vividness in direct proportion to her employer's corporeal shrinkage.

In contrast to these girthy ladies, other Blackwood women are wraiths and ambulating phantoms, eaten up by anxieties and rage. J., in *The Step-mother*, never touches food; the wretched Cressida in *The Fate of Mary Rose* is so consumed with worry about a child killer on the loose that she shrinks away to a stick figure; Olga, in her eponymously titled story, is one of many faded women of the world, often retired actresses, whom Blackwood de-picts as rudderless, weary, haunted vestiges of dubious former glory.

Her simple, even naive-sounding sentences lure us into assuming these wan, preoccupied, abrasively self-obsessed women will prove bloodlessly one-dimensional, but they quickly acquire bewildering complexity and painfully acute verisimilitude. They are burdened by children who consider them burdensome, used and discarded or kept and untreasured by men whose attentions are elsewhere. At the same time, Blackwood resists strik-ing any plangent notes on their behalf. Life has deformed them into the shape of their own nightmares. One could fall in love with what they were, but it's quite impossible to even like what they've become.

Blackwood's portraits of men are hilarious and frightening. In the highly defective families and affairs in which we find them, they are wretchedly de-pendent on a shifting maternal magma rather than any clearly apprehended partner. The narrator of *The Fate of Mary Rose* is a kind of Blackwood everyman. His girlfriend is a shrew. His estranged wife is a veritable witch. He finds fault with everything and everyone. Frustrated by one woman's oppressive idiosyncrasies, he instantly seeks sympathy and comfort from another, even if it's the blustery lush he despises who lives next door. Any reminder of his responsibilities sends him into a panicked flight. He even manipulates his secretary into staying with his deranged wife, rather than deal with a crisis that endangers his daughter.

> I didn't want to lie to Fay Wisherton but I feared that if I gave her my truthful impression of what Cressida was like at the moment, she would refuse to come down to the cottage. I therefore made a dithering attempt to describe Cressida in phrases which were not strictly dishonest although they gave no accurate picture of her personality. I said she was country-loving. Although this was true, it was not quite as healthy and normal as it sounded. She was country-loving but only in a negative sense because of her phobia that Mary Rose would come to harm in any city.

If the women in Blackwood's books all have a skewed relationship to food, the men have a similarly disturbing relationship to women. If they have sex at all, it tends to be quick and unpleasant. In "Who Needs It?," the hairdresser's loser husband tells her he wants to come in her hair, perhaps the only carnally enthusiastic statement ever uttered by a male Blackwood character. Men are breadwinning absentee sperm donors who beget impossibly awful children. They have jobs that command every drop of what little passion they have.

In the center—one could say the vacant center—of the reverse magnetic field that Blackwood's men and women create between them is an abstraction called "the family." While the tenor of friendships and the flavor of social life are trenchantly telegraphed in Blackwood's fiction, virtually all of it is an appalled meditation on the destructive, warping potential of family intimacy and blood bonds. One of the most curious moments in *The Stepdaughter* comes when Renata reveals to J. that she is not, in fact, Arnold's daughter. J. tells her it was "very cruel of Arnold to tell you all this." Renata replies, "I don't think it was cruel of him. . . . He said that I would have to understand that as he had nothing to do with me he would never be able to love me. I think he wanted to stop me from ever feeling hurt and disappointed about him." And, she adds, she stopped feeling disappointed by him on the spot. The mere verbal removal of the blood tie erases an entire universe of unreal expectation and letdown.

Blackwood's writing contains remarkably little fat. There is, in fact, nothing to spare, which is strange considering how freely she employs her manic imagination. Like certain other writers associated with the famously iconoclastic avant-garde literary journal *Bananas* in the '70s—Emma Tennant, J. G. Ballard, Angela Carter—Blackwood approaches fiction as a site of fantasy and speculation where the norms of realism need be only sketchily deployed. This kind of writing acknowledges the filtered quality of all perception and the status of all narrative as fiction. Its ideal form is the fairy tale, a container of myth related in the simplest language. Blackwood's books have a kinship with fables and conjuring acts and a sly understanding of their compact with the reader. They move along the same spectrum of extremity as modern life itself. Their sensibility is one of stoical fortitude. Their modes are those of the cautionary or improving tale, like the picaresques of the eighteenth century.

At one end of Blackwood's spectrum is *The Stepdaughter.* Here are the harsh rewards of solipsism, self-pity and emotional dependency. At the other is *Corrigan. Corrigan* does not suggest that anything can truly end well; everything ends in death, an ending that is neither happy nor unhappy but merely final. But it does recommend that pretending life is what you make it can be better for your health than knowing all is futile and that everything we do is an inane but solid argument for our own extinction. Blackwood's writing revels in pessimism, but its calm, surefooted sentences, its grace and humor, and its gleeful eye for human absurdity gently nudge us toward the pretense.

WURLTIZER'S WILES

Yesterday afternoon a girl walked by the window and stopped for sea shells. I was wrenched out of two months of calm. Nothing more than that, certainly, nothing ecstatic or even interesting, but very silent and even, as those periods have become for me. I had been breathing in and out, out and in, calmly, grateful for once to do just that, staring at the waves plopping in, successful at thinking almost nothing, handling easily the three memories I have manufactured, when that girl stooped for sea shells.

RUDOLPH WURLITZER'S *Nog* opens on a solemn, unexcited note. Its protagonist has emptied his consciousness of most of its baggage, retaining only a few recurring landmarks: *New York for adventure, beaches for relaxation, the octopus and Nog for speculation. No connections. Narrow all possibilities. Develop and love your limitations.* Wurlitzer's first novel is like an accretion of calcium, a shell deposited by tiny increments of grammar.

Nog became a cult favorite when it was published in 1968 and was, like Wurlitzer's three other novels, out of print until Serpent's Tail reissued them in the early '90s. This is a scandal, but not really a surprise. The world of his fiction is a bleak Beckett desolation, a nihilist's purgatorial slag heap where virtue and survival are mutually exclusive. The disaster of being muted by a feckless market is a minor one. Wurlitzer's resignation encompasses much less capricious and arbitrary catastrophes; from novel to novel, his sensibility evolves from anarchic despair to Buddhist transcendence, retaining throughout a broad American genius for slapstick. An air of fizzled machismo surrounds his protagonists, who tend to be drifters, diminished personalities, and losers given to odd flights of lyricism.

I hesitate to characterize what Wurlitzer's novels are "about." His first three books—*Nog, Flats* and *Quake*—display an anxiety about language so extreme that their accumulations of narrative constantly hover at the edge of collapse. What the books describe are random bindings of human particles, which then break apart, regroup, or slither away from each other. One thing happens, then another, the actors respond to trivial and important changes in their situation with the same clumsy immediacy, an acceptance of fate that becomes monstrous in the absence of any functional value judgments. The figures in the landscape are mainly defined by pathology—bellicosity, murderousness, desultory nymphomania, scab-picking preoccupation with irrelevant problems, tics, injuries, functional aphasias, addiction or old-fashioned death wish. Wurlitzer shares Diane Arbus's instinct for the mesmerizingly repulsive detail.

Nog's subject, if it has one, is solipsism. It attacks the first-person form like a desperate convict busting up a prison cell. Wheeling himself onstage, the narrator immediately calls his own identity into question. He isn't really Nog. He travels under Nog's name, and sometimes, maybe, he is Nog, but Nog—most of the time, anyway—was a Finnish mystic and itinerant carny who once sold him a lifelike rubber octopus in a bathysphere mounted on a truckbed. Like Ur-Nog, Nog II has traveled up and down the Pacific Coast exhibiting the octopus, charging money for it, getting into fights with skeptical audiences. But that was a long time ago. Or recently. Perhaps he only got rid of the octopus last night. He isn't sure. Now the man calling himself Nog is living in a seaside boarding house, "successful at thinking almost nothing."

An elderly, unpleasant Colonel Green is sandbagging the jetty against an oncoming storm. The girl on the beach, Sarah, invites Nog to a Fourth of July party where the guests hear nothing he tells them: that he's making a study of beaches (he lists many), that he's investigating cephalopods. Little happens besides a vicious game of ping-pong with Sarah's husband, but these micro events, flaccid washes of human contact, rendered in a bleary montage of synecdoches, stir Nog from his torpor.

Next he is shoplifting in a San Francisco supermarket, trailing another shoplifter, Meridith, who takes him to a hippie crash pad with a bay view. "The women wore simple print dresses and no make-up, and the men blue jeans and faded work shirts. Everyone wore medallions around their necks. One woman nursed a baby, while the other two slowly shelled peas into a metal bowl. The men sat silently, their eyes blank, reaching out to eat from the bowl. They seem young although it is hard to tell. I seem young although it is hard to tell." There is a man, Lockett, more willful and decisive than Nog; several unexcited orgies in bathtubs, on crumbling mattresses, etc., a long imprisonment in a hall closet; an escape into mountain country; a bewildering finale in the locks of the Panama Canal.

It is often difficult to determine exactly what's going on in *Nog,* since past and present are shuffled into each other and given exactly the same stress. Wurlitzer is indifferent to the conventional methods of "making a picture," in medium shot so to speak, which afford the reader an encompassing vantage point. *Nog's* consciousness and its unfolding private narrative, pared to ontological basics, its fetishistic swervings, its upswelling flashbacks and sudden diminishments or crescendos are all that we are allowed to know. External geography has little significance beyond its impact on Nog's ganglia. Yet the flat, drained tone of the narrator's reporting secretes architectures and landscapes of paradoxical stolidity, perhaps because their details seem so grudgingly surrendered.

Nog has an endgame feeling, beginning at the point of impossibility where narrative typically splutters into silence, and it proceeds in a series of improvised moves, like a story by Robert Walser. Each sentence threatens to pull out the underpinnings of the whole structure, to dissolve whatever sense the accumulation of sentences has managed to contrive. ("I'm cold. Or I was cold. I might be approaching a warmth. I don't remember when I've last fallen asleep in a warm bath. There is a slight rocking. . . . I met Meridith in a warm bath. I followed her down metal steps to a darkly lit room with a round ceiling. One wall was an aquarium. . . . The inside of me is becoming a swelling assemblage of shells.") The book owes something to Blanchot, a lot to Beckett, and probably a good deal to Wittgenstein, too: the syllogistic and self-devouring procession of statements, memories, and observations, the abrupt shifts in tense (sometimes within a sentence), the unexplained and alarmingly natural-looking confusions of Nog's identity with the "real," remembered Nog, with Lockett, with "Lockett's boy."

Nog works as a period piece, though its literary audacity is more apparent now than it was in 1968. The rootless and relatively affectless human debris floating through it mirrors the youth zeitgeist of then-California, when armies of drugged nonverbals ranged all over the place, connecting and disconnecting without exchanging résumés or last names. In fact, all of Wurlitzer's books can be read as sociological artifacts: You can "get" 1968 America in a more visceral way from *Nog* than from reading other prose of the period—Tom Wolfe or Ken Kesey, for example. (The same is true of early '70s malaise in *Quake*.) Aside from the quotidian formal approach of such writers generally, most books dealing with the counterculture seem defensively loyal to 19th-century conventions, probably in reaction to the psychic and social chaos they describe. Wurlitzer, like many other American writers, understands that we are living in Disney World. Unlike most of them, he presents this nightmare amusement park abstemiously, from inside "altered consciousness," in the terse staccato of a Sarraute or a Compton-Burnett.

Wurlitzer is one of the very few American novelists who hasn't rejected or ignored the European evolution of the novel; Dos Passos and Burroughs also come to mind. (Tom Wolfe's manifesto of a few years back, calling for a return to the techniques of Balzac and Thackeray, seemed less absurd for its Tory oafishness than for the fact that most American novels still do read like Balzac and Thackeray, only not as good.) Dos Passos and Burroughs reflect the expansion of the novel form found in Joyce, Céline and Gertrude Stein. Wurlitzer's work takes its cue from the microscopy of Pinget, Beckett and Duras. Wurlitzer and Burroughs are both drawn to mythic American figures (the cowboy, the vagabond, the traveling con artist), recasting them as apocalyptic absurdities.

Flats (1970) surpasses *Nog* in opacity. For many pages it seems to defy anyone to read it, its tangled rhythms suggesting the dense compression of a philosophical tract. There is not simply one unreliable narrator, but many, passing the baton back and forth around the (literal) campfire. These nebulous presences are all named for cities—Flagstaff, Omaha, Memphis—and have (apparently) converged in a post-holocaust wasteland. They have minimal distinguishing characteristics as people, and are sometimes described in terms befitting the urban clusters they're named after.

Flats could be a linguistic implosion of a Louis L'Amour novel, enlarging the Wild West pastiche of *Nog*'s later chapters. The real model, evident in *Flats*'s opening echo of *Light in August*'s first line, is Faulkner, the gnarled, cryptic Faulkner of *As I Lay Dying*, transposed into a high camp funeral ceremony for the myth of the cowboy. (Wurlitzer is the bad conscience of those latter-day "sensitive macho" Cowboy Liberals like Wim Wenders and Sam Shepard. Like them, he wants the pleasures of the myth without its intrinsic psychosexual odium; unlike them, Wurlitzer really understands why it's odious.) Here, the tragic rituals of masculinity are reduced to petty squabbles over cans of soup, a pair of orange socks and other trivia, the grandiose spaces of John Ford shrunk to a territory measuring a few square yards.

While *Nog* is full of cinematic action despite its underlying entropy ("life's principle is to make shells"), *Flats* empties the kill-or-be-killed Western genre of its violent epiphanies; it's a text of pure immanence, something akin to Robbe-Grillet's most inert and topographical inventories, like a camera incessantly ranging over the same puny collection of damaged objects. Here there is no hidden Sphinx, unless it's the novel itself. The characters mark their positions in the landscape, speculate on the inner workings of the others, form momentary allegiances, consider possible modes of action, do nothing, and then retreat to their solitudes—the Wild West according to someone who's read too much Chekhov. *Flats* is remarkable for its refusal to coalesce into the familiar stories its floating paragraphs evoke, bringing the act of reading (and assigning meaning to language) into a rebarbative foreground. Wurlitzer trumps later baroque examples of postmodernist fiction with a kind of scurvy minimalism.

Sex is not a charged event in these books, having devolved to the condition of a monstrously inappropriate reflex. Wurlitzer's characters have burnt out on love, along with most other complex emotions. They cathect on bodies, mostly on parts of bodies. The rampant fetishism in *Nog*, *Flats* and *Quake* can easily be read as necrophilia, since the quality of communication between the characters amounts to near-complete objectification. Each is a radio station broadcasting its inexorable tape recordings, receiving little from other stations. For Wurlitzer, death is truly the only subject, to which all else is grotesque foreplay.

I sat down on the edge of the bathtub. The door banged open in the other room and a lamp crashed to the floor. A small man in black silk jockey shorts crawled towards me. His black hair was parted in the middle and there was an oblong birthmark the size of an ostrich egg on his left shoulder. He managed to crawl to the doorsill of the bathroom before he collapsed. After a long moan, he began to cry.

"The ceiling fell in on me," he whispered. "My hips are crushed. My leg is broken and something bad is happening inside. You got to help me."

He propped himself up by the door, his eyes full of rage and shock . . . .
Blood was forming on one side of his mouth. His head tilted back. Then he
threw up in short violent spasms. When he was finished he wiped his mouth
on the back of his wrist and looked up at me again.

"It's going to be a long day. But if we're not dead now we probably won't
be. I'm hemorrhaging or something. I'll wait here. But don't forget me. You
forget me and I'll come after you. Everything is in my wallet. Room six. I got
credit cards."

Quake is a disturbingly good-humored look at the end of the world.
Compared to Wurlitzer's early books, it is practically outgoing, arranged on
the page in conventionally alternating passages of dialogue and description.
One could even say it has a beginning, middle and end, though I am not
exactly sure where the middle or the end are.

Quake describes the aftereffects of a 7.5 earthquake on Los Angeles, commencing as the nameless narrator is thrown from his bed at the Tropicana Mo-
tel. Numerous residents of the Tropicana make their way to the pool, including
a rock groupie who has sex with the narrator on the diving board. Inside cabin
5, he encounters a large "singing family" plotting to disrupt an upcoming TV
appearance with an incestuous orgy. A dead dog is lying on the floor.

Once he leaves the Tropicana, our hero finds himself in an inferno of disintegrating buildings, collapsed freeways, toppled skyscrapers, burst gas
mains, vigilantes and ordinary, disoriented Americans. These hideously vulnerable figures, full of short-term peasant-cunning and long-term, lethal
neuroticism, make their little moves in an incomprehensible landscape.
Few survive for more than a few paragraphs. They are so inadequate to the
scale of the disaster that virtually any authority figure wins their instant
obedience. After a series of strange interludes with armed psychotics and
injured people trapped in toppled apartment houses—all of whom are obsessed with getting their next meal, sex or pills, or simply with injuring or
killing someone else—the narrator is captured by a paramilitary group,
stripped and herded, along with dozens of other naked survivors, onto a
football field near a freeway off-ramp. Order breaks down among the sol-
diers, and he escapes into further chaos.

The descriptive side of *Quake* is incredibly odd. Wurlitzer puts us inside
a teetering building with a sentence or two, then plays out a long, compli-

cated scene of people communicating in Morse code through perilously angled walls. Everything wobbles, shakes, hostility and fear saturate the atmosphere; through some little miracle of brevity the text creates unbearable frustration and claustrophobia. John Berger once located the essential horror of both Walt Disney's movies and Francis Bacon's paintings in the viewer's act of imagining a world in which there is nothing else. This readily applies to Wurlitzer's technique. We cannot imagine a context beyond the narrator's sensorium. The pitched-over house and its labyrinth of demolished rooms presents a perspective that can never be put right, though it's the natural instinct of the reader to straighten things up, adjust the inner gyroscope, make sense of the world.

In *Quake,* the world has its own crushing logic, but makes no sense at all. It is already the cretinized mass-culture universe where everyone has information and nobody has knowledge. One major rumble of the fault line reduces advanced society to atavism; implicitly, it is fascist from the beginning. As the corpses pile up, it becomes obvious that no one really knows how to do anything except consume: products, relationships and each other.

> "Take my ring," the woman said to the girl. She tried to pull a diamond ring off her finger but she wasn't strong enough. The girl pulled it off for her and slipped it over her own finger.
>
> "Tell Harry Stralinger that I didn't make it," the woman said. "He lives on 302 Cuesta Way. Tell him that he can go to all the Holiday Inns he wants to and that I would have gone to Acapulco with him, only not on that weekend that Robert was around. He wouldn't have survived against Robert."
>
> She died on the grass in front of us. I raised my hand to stop the girl from standing up and a bullet went through my palm. The girl smiled.
>
> "You won't be able to wave to me now," she said. "You'll have to use your other hand. But maybe you're left handed anyway."

Wurlitzer's repudiation of sentiment and rejection of humanist values (which are not at all the same thing) parallel his mistrust of language. His protagonists stifle the code of sentiments embedded in everyday discourse, aware that genuine and inauthentic emotions are hopelessly jumbled together as commodities in a dead world. In this respect his characters are noticeably different from J. G. Ballard's Delvaux-like sleep-walkers or the cartoon incubi of William Burroughs, who've entered a strangely sanguine inner-space age. Wurlitzer's people have simply numbed out because the world is too full of crazy shit to risk caring too much about it.

Slow Fade abandons the signature style of *Nog, Flats* and *Quake.* Written 12 years after *Quake,* it is an elegy for Old Hollywood, and for Wurlitzer's own adventures in New Hollywood, rendered in a limpid, accessible manner. No doubt the externalized prose of *Slow Fade* evolved from years of writing scripts. (Wurlitzer is now better known as a screenwriter—of Alex Cox's *Walker,* Robert Frank's *Candy Mountain* and Volker Schlöndorff's *Voyagers,* among others. He is working with Bertolucci on a life of Buddha. The eccentric nature of his film credits reflects his Hollywood reputation as a "literary" type, slightly too cerebral and arty for mainstream sludge, dreck and splatter. His connection to the jukebox fortune is entirely nostalgic. "It's the classic American story. One generation to get there, another generation to establish it and the third generation to lose it. I'm the fourth.")

Slow Fade has two, at times three, contiguous stories: the escapades of Wesley Hardin, a John Huston-like director of Westerns, as he prepares for and resists his coming death; those of his son, Walker, and A. D. Ballou, a musician-drifter, who're collaborating on a film script for Wesley; and the script, which transposes the spiritual quest and ultimate death in India of Wesley's daughter, Clementine, into a fictional treatment. One of *Slow Fade*'s surprises is the sympathy it mobilizes on behalf of Wesley, a crustily intelligent exemplar of old-style patriarchy. His ability to act decisively, without self-pity, while up to his neck in messes he's created himself (the comeback film he's shooting has degenerated into a drunken carnival) has tragic grandeur beside the spineless studio executives and media drips who dance attendance on him. A. D. and Walker, on the other hand, are grown-up versions of Wurlitzer's earlier heroes, debris from the Age of Aquarius, still drifting from hustle to hustle.

Tricked out as a Didionesque, jaundiced look at the picture trade, *Slow Fade* is really about two generations eyeing each other's metaphysical inadequacies and the inevitable betrayal of the body. It's also about karma. Wesley buys off A. D., who's lost an eye after wandering onto Wesley's set during an Indian attack, by hiring him to write the story of his greatest failure, i.e., parenthood. He hopes thereby to understand his own life, and to recover his spiritual losses by shooting the scripted film. But the world in which this would be possible has vanished; the rugged values of his art are museum pieces, and his own decline is fodder for a tabloid culture that values nothing besides sensation.

For A. D., the lost eye stakes him to a spell of survival. We lose parts of ourselves as we go along. The price of Clementine's enlightenment in India is illness and death. Like Wurlitzer's other books, *Slow Fade* maps a meaningless journey from one place to another. But here things change within people, something develops, the meaninglessness . . . means something. Wurlitzer's flawless prose style takes on a hallucinatory brilliance in this book; the story construction is near perfect. It's rare that a book about the getting of wisdom actually sounds wise, but this one does. Until Wurlitzer writes another one, *Slow Fade* will stand as the exemplary Buddhist novel of American literature.

Wurlitzer's books can easily be seen as premonitions of postmodernism; one can even read *Slow Fade* as a repudiation of techniques Wurlitzer pioneered, and which are now commonplace among more academic writers busy "doing things with language." But Wurlitzer's books are also "original" in an old-fashioned sense, attempts at finding (or at least impersonating) a voice, moved along by a desire to say something, and not simply ruminative exercises in distilling literature from its own oozing corpse. If these books are haunted by the impossibility of writing novels in a time when all experience is spurious, all consciousness blunted and devolutionary, they also refuse, through a kind of mordant silence between horrors, to celebrate the condition of emptiness.

POSTSCRIPT (2007): Since the above essay was written, Rudy Wurlitzer has published two books, as well as the screenplay of *Walker,* the film on which he and Alex Cox collaborated in 1987. *Hard Travel To Sacred Places* (1995) is a work of mourning for the son of Wurlitzer's wife, the photographer Lynn Davis. Ayrev died in a car accident in 1992 on his way from Los Angeles to Arizona.

The devastated couple go first to Thailand, then Burma, finally Cambodia. The bewilderment and exhaustion of extreme grief is a visceral sensation on every page of this book, which records the moment-to-moment effort of going on with life when its most important element has been lost, and the struggle to accept the unassimilable fact of a child's death: The collision of modernity with the archaic in the ancient cultures they trek through, often in abysmally bad health, mirrors the confused distractedness of everyday life and the hole blown through it by the irremediable.

Davis and Wurlitzer struggle to reconcile what has happened to them with an acceptance of the overarching truth that all existence is a mote of dust in eternity, seek out spiritual guides to help them face the void, but mainly undertake the full experience of grief and mourning without the palliatives that Western culture bombards us with to anaesthetize us to the fact of death. Their journey is an end in itself, however, in the sense that they never consider abbreviating it for the sake of their physical survival. Accepting Ayrev's death means accepting their own disappearance, and the ultimate disappearance of everything.

Hard Travel To Sacred Places is almost too painful to read at times: Wurlitzer evokes the ultimate loss as a permanent fissure, a wound that can never close. This book conveys how it feels for everything we carry inside to be at cosmic odds with the transactions we conduct with the outer world. Yet the inability to heal gradually proves to be precisely what we must acknowledge, both to go on living in this world and to leave it without fear, and what Davis and Wurlitzer learn is what they have known from the outset. By the end of the journey they have simply learned it thoroughly and surrendered themselves to the truth. The world's sadness and their own are the same, the condition of things and not an eruption of some anomaly or exceptional trauma.

It's fascinating to consider the relation of this book to Wurlitzer's first novel in over two decades, *The Drop Edge of Yonder* (2007). The author's prodigious tinkerings with the Western genre, from the anti-imperialist screenplay of *Walker* to the metanarrative of the film being shot in *Slow Fade* make *The Drop Edge of Yonder* a logical and inevitable subversion of the cultic violence of a genre as well as a farcical, epically rendered pandemonium. The "instant modernity" that constitutes its own wreckage in *Hard Travel*'s Bangkok, Rangoon and Phnom Penh is the world under bloody construction in *The Drop Edge of Yonder*. The progress of Zebulon from the primitive mountain settlements of Colorado to the urbanizing end of the frontier illustrates the essential sameness of one kind of human wreckage and another:

The survivalist mode of life among trappers and traders simply acquires more complex organization of injustice, exploitation, chicanery, murderousness, betrayal, and greater depths of depravity.

Zebulon epitomizes the pathology of his age, but also embodies the ineradicable wiring that has, throughout all kinds of human history, manifested the desire to do the right thing, and sometimes prodded people into actually doing the right thing—transcending self-interest, protecting a core of decency, dealing with others as we'd wish to be dealt with. Wurlitzer's philosophy of accepting whatever shit happens as neither good nor bad but the fluctuation of the world's fever allows him to load up his characters with every imaginable vice, weakness, duplicity and low cunning, without removing their existential freedom to override their wretchedness and risk themselves for other people. Yes, some people are just shits, as the wise black drag queen once told William Burroughs; but a lot of people only act like shits until they're given an opportunity to become something better. Wurlitzer is a master at showing the human heart and its manifold imperfections as a gift that we trash and honor, both, in the course of a human life.

BULLE OGIER,
PHENOMENON WITHOUT A PAUSE

In the course of a meeting with Bulle Ogier in the former piano bar of the Gramercy Park Hotel—one of many attempts at an interview—I discover, by knocking it over, that the electric lamp on the table is actually a little candle in a frosted glass shade. After contemplating the waxy mess for a while, we notice that the wall sconces are really dim. Huh. It even looks like ... teensy candles flickering behind them. One of my three favorite rooms in New York for 25 years no longer has electricity.

After the interview, we're supposed to join Bulle's husband, Barbet Schroeder, at a restaurant around the corner, but we both feel a lazy aversion to turning on the tape recorder. I hate the artifice of interviewing people and I don't think Bulle is crazy about being interviewed: Everything turns awkward and pressured when you switch on that little machine. I can't bear reading interviews or giving interviews or "conducting" interviews; what turns up in print is never quite what either person wanted to say. Quite often what turns up in print isn't even what anyone did say.

It's that week between Christmas and New Year's when nobody wants to do anything, and this room isn't helping things . . . it's like that stage set in The Discreet Charm of the Bourgeoisie *where a rubber chicken is served for dinner and all the furniture looks like cardboard. . . .*

We shift to another table. It's even darker, and there's a draft. Somehow, dark as it is, we resume as if it . . . no, it's impossible. We move all our stuff to a third table. Which is just as bad. I feel we're ... sinking, somehow, into a prehistoric cave lined with furry upholstery. We can barely see each other. I try to formulate a question. I can't see the tape recorder. Maybe I left it—no, here it is, I can feel it in front of me. Bulle thinks she's lost a glove. They're nice gloves, not the kind you don't care about. Now we're both crawling around on the floor, blindly feeling under chairs. I get up and stumble into the cathedral of light that is the main cocktail lounge. I ask the bartender for a flashlight. He hands me a burning candle.

"Maybe this wasn't such a good idea."

"It's terrible. Let's get out of here."

I think some version of this happened last year, too. . . .

BULLE OGIER first grabbed the attention of American moviegoers in Alain Tanner's second film, *La Salamandre,* in 1972. In the ever-darker aftermath of May 1968, young people everywhere identified with Bulle's character, Rosemonde, a Genevan girl who shoots her guardian-uncle because he bores her. She migrates from one unskilled job to the next, her aimlessness and alley-cat survival instinct exemplifying the intense alienation of the early seventies. Young and adrift in a rich, lifeless city of bankers and bourgeoisie, her only defenses against early brain death are music, sex, indifference.

Rosemonde's first job consists of slipping condom-like casings over an industrial nozzle that shits out macerated sausage meat. The finished product looks like an enormous penis. Rosemonde is a blank slate. Only her eyes indicate that she's fully conscious, deliberately affectless as a form of defiance; the job and everything about it is so bizarre she can't be bothered to show her disgust. Later, working in a shoe store, she fondles the feet and legs of customers in a trance of abstracted lubricity.

Rosemonde navigates on impulse, indifferent to social structures, mores, the opinion of others. She isn't sleepwalking, but she hasn't thought anything through. Two journalists trying to write a screenplay about her become instead her mentors/lovers/guardians: leftist intellectuals adjusting to lowered prospects, they can help Rosemonde understand the system and survive within it while waiting for a better time. *La Salamandre's* great appeal was its essential hopefulness.

Tanner's movie created the perception of its star as an ideal medium through which the rebellious energies surviving 1968 could be transmitted to film. Blonde (but "dirty blonde"), delicate as porcelain, her face as instantly unmistakable as Audrey Hepburn's, Ogier's gestural purity and the telegraphic quality of her smallest expressions suggested the flexing tensions of a high-wire acrobat. Renato Berta, also cinematographer on Ogier's films with Daniel Schmid, lit a seraphic but unobtrusive nimbus around her features.

Soon after *La Salamandre*'s US release, Luis Buñuel's masterpiece *The Discreet Charm of the Bourgeoisie* (1972) opened. In *The Exterminating Angel*, an earlier nightmare party of middle-class frustration, Buñuel had slyly made the trapped houseguests almost interchangeable. Recasting the post-opera feast of the damned as an oneiric sequence of thwarted dining experiences, *Discreet Charm* tacked in the opposite direction. Its dim-witted, criminally prosperous, essentially hideous flock of well-heeled consumers are so simpatico and elegant it's impossible to dislike them: their discreet charm, in a phrase.

Bulle plays Florence, and she gets some of the film's funniest business. As the youngest of the swank band of perpetually frustrated dinner guests, she has the thinnest veneer of manners and the fewest inhibitions. Arriving at the home of the Sénéchals, Florence instantly takes back her floral gift when she realizes Mme. Sénéchal will not be serving dinner. With this hilariously casual gesture of carnivorous reverse etiquette, Florence's personality is established, along with the ceremonial insincerity of middle-class social form.

Buñuel showcased Bulle's meticulous timing and gift for physical comedy. Florence vomits out the window of the town car after too many martinis—this happens in an eyeblink, but the camera catches both that special involuntary spasmic look the second before everything comes up and Florence's abrupt resemblance to a limp rag doll half-draped out the window a second later. During the pile-up of absurdities involving the billeting of an Army division in the Sénéchal's neighborhood, Florence is seen inhaling a whopping hit of Mary Jane as she passes a joint to the commanding officer. The moment is loaded with sight gags: her widened eyes signaling industrial-strength dope, her mouth open as she passes the joint as a visual synonym, and a tertiary, contrapuntally slower style of inexplicably funny gesture in the way her fingers hold it. In another highly risible scene, Florence, demonstrating various salutes—fascist, communist—adds the vulva-shaped symbol of a feminist group, made with the thumbs and forefingers.

"I'm too old to play the heroine," Bulle recently told a journalist. Maybe, but she's blessed with the kind of imperishable attractiveness and sensual dignity Jeanne Moreau has, an autocratic imperviousness to the aging process. Last year, in Luc Bondy's stage production of Yasmina Reza's *Une pièce espagnole*, a highbrow boulevard farce in which large pieces of the set were rolled on castors all over the stage throughout the performance, Bulle's reedy frame, in a flame-red dress, exhibited the prehensile torsion of Gumby while stalking the stage like a cougar. For someone movie-star small, Bulle is a formidably physical actress. Watching her perform live, one automatically thinks of the multidisciplinary training that actors in the "big" Russian theater undertake, where every movement has a specific weight and intention, however natural it looks.

Yet in a manner of speaking, she wandered into acting. She was born in Boulogne-Billancourt, on the outer edge of the 16th district of Paris, in 1939, the year of the "phony war" described in Sartre's novel *The Reprieve*. Her mother, a highly talented painter, took her to exhibitions and concerts; she rarely saw movies. She briefly studied journalism and first saw a stage show on a class outing to see a production by Jean Vilar starring Gérard Philipe.

She came to discover her own private Paris in St-Germain-des-Prés, still the St-Germain of Sartre and Beauvoir, Boris Vian and Juliette Gréco, and, most significantly for her, the St-Germain of Guy Debord, the Situationists, and the radical energies that culminated in the phenomenon of May 1968. Despite the fact that Ogier was out of town that month, she has been associated with it ever since—one of the Revolution's three Mariannes (along with Juliet Berto and Anne Wiazemsky). Vian, by the way, appears in Bulle's very first movie, Jacques Baratier's short *Voilà l'ordre* (1966), albeit via archival footage: The author of *I'll Spit on Your Grave* and *Mood Indigo* had died in 1959, felled by a heart attack at the premiere of the film version of *I'll Spit on Your Grave*—surely the most devastating act of film criticism in history.

Working at Chanel, Bulle met Marc'O, who was conducting theater workshops at the American Center in Paris. By that time, she had been married, had a baby (Pascale, who became a distinguished actress, and starred with Bulle in Rivette's *Le Pont du Nord*) and gotten divorced. She first acted with Marc'O's group in 1960, in Marivaux's *Triumph of Love*.

The most innovative theater in the sixties simulated the "voluntary" madness Rimbaud prescribed for poets. Antonin Artaud likens his ideal art form to contagion in *The Theater and Its Double*. The aesthetic vocabulary of the Living Theater, Peter Brook's London company, and other experimental troupes like Marc'O's, has obvious sources in Breton's *Nadja*, Unica Zürn's novels, George Bataille's *Death and Sensuality*, the theater of Genet, and the writings of R. D. Laing and Norman O. Brown. For actors, the seminal influence was Artaud. Marc'O's players were fluent in the psychodramatic methods of Artaud—the sudden rages, the abrupt vocal switches to near-inaudible whimpering, the subversion of naturalism into a kind of menacing deception between eruptions of violent physical movement. (Pierre Clémenti's performance in Bertolucci's *Partner* is the quintessence of this method.)

One of Bulle Ogier's earliest films is an expanded adaptation of *Les Idoles,* originally performed at La Grande Séverine in 1967. Three pop stars—Gigi la Folle (Ogier), Charlie le Surineur (Pierre Clémenti) and Simon le Magicien (Jean-Pierre Kalfon)—are attractions in a glitzy extravaganza, half-press conference, half-circus. The parody of the yé-yé cliché of a rock & roll band, their sexual charisma sells cultural waste to the consumer. The theater functions as a display window for the commodity fetish—them. The film ends with the dissonantly frothy wedding of Gigi and Charlie, shown earlier in private moments more redolent of psychosis than sex. *Les Idoles* mixes artificial and natural spaces, interrupting filmic and theatrical modes of reception. An action that starts in one place continues in a different one, often in mid-dialogue. The acting is loud, physical, abrasive, somewhat disconnected from any text and shifts tone with menacing abruptness, like large cats turning feral. (Seen today, Marc'O's film forces us to consider how hostile film and theater audiences have become to the idea of difficulty.)

Les Idoles helped inspire Jacques Rivette's *L'amour fou* (1969), a four-hour experiment using two formats: 16mm to document rehearsals for a fictional production of Racine's *Andromache,* directed by Sébastien (Jean-Pierre Kalfon), who also plays Pyrrhus opposite Claire (Ogier) as Hermione; and 35mm for the parallel story of an affair between actress and director with certain echoes of the play's sexual derangements: The lovers are symbiotically "mad" and pass a kind of sacred delirium back and forth, regressing to childhood while holed up in their apartment for two days. The couple's intimacy is a kind of unstable compound, highly flammable, probably toxic. This craziness is the spirit of the age. When Kalfon takes a razor to the clothes he's wearing, the two effectively switch roles—a refashioning of the vampiric epiphany in Bergman's *Persona.*

Never a couple in real life, Ogier and Kalfon were cast several times as one, in a nontraditional sense, typifying their generation's attempt to enlarge its sexual and spiritual possibilities. They appear together in Philippe Garrel's *Un ange passé* (1975) and, unforgettably, in Barbet Schroeder's *La Vallée* (1972)—where they're a couple in the most literal and nonproprietary sense.

Schroeder's film is both fiction and a document of its own production—cast and crew spent half a year in New Guinea, where, 30 years ago, primordial nature and the planet's last Neolithic tribe still existed. Ogier plays Viviane, the wife of a diplomat, who supplies exotic bird feathers to Paris boutiques. She joins a hippie expedition into the rain forest, planning to buy feathers from the natives and return home, while the others proceed to "the valley obscured by clouds," a nebulous white patch on aerial maps.

The landscape, the Mapuga tribe's fantastic otherness, the sexual ease of the explorers, and the local hallucinogens wear away Viviane's attachment to the reality she knows; in the end she becomes more intent on reaching the valley than the others, prodding the expedition forward after the food and water run out. The chance that death instead of paradise waits in the valley no longer bothers her.

Bulle's performance registers this self-abandonment with amazing subtlety. It's as if she were absorbing faint, cumulative vibrations from the landscape; she glides across a spectrum of delicate chords. *La Vallée* is an homage to the counterculture's search for the absolute, and a gorgeous dramatization of its futility. More than the many things said to mark "the end of the sixties," it actually does.

She has had so many distinct, long-running affiliations with important directors that charting them would require a cartographer. One of the most important, in theater and film, is with Marguerite Duras, starting with Jean-Louis Barrault's 1975 production of *Des journées entières dans les arbres,* and Duras's film version that same year. The films with Duras include *Le Navire Night* (1979) and *Agatha* (1981). Several of these feature Bulle's sublime chemistry with the legendary Madeleine Renaud.

In Duras, Ogier's feminism, her melancholy, and her intricately inflected seriousness find an ideal expressive discourse; something deeply lovely in her character corresponds to Duras's simplicity of heart, the emotive clarity of her language.

There's also the Bulle Ogier of ensemble cinema. In André Delvaux's *Rendez-vous à Bray* (1971), a somber chamber work adapted from a Julien Gracq novel of WWI, her character appears only in a succession of flashbacks and supplies the film's single, strategic comic caesura as she struggles to use a knife and fork on a precariously balanced plate of buffet food. In Rivette's *Céline and Julie Go Boating* (1974), the ghosts played by Barbet Schroeder, Ogier, and Marie-France Pisier inhabit another discrete narrative, perpetually re-enacting a Jamesian melodrama in a sort of waxworks-play-inside-the-film accessed by the film's protagonists via hallucinogenic candies. Daniel Schmid's *La Paloma* (1974) is full of Guignol tropes and Gothic howlers: a casino in Shanghai, a creepy Swiss castle, infidelity seen through a keyhole, a family curse, suicide and self-embalming by slow poison. Ogier shows up in an antique limousine as Peter Kern's mother (they're roughly the same age), a grande dame draped with feather boas. Barbet Schroeder is the priest officiating at Kern's wedding to Viola (Ingrid Caven); in this pivotal scene, the actors speak different languages. (Schmid told his producers that no one would notice; in fact, nobody did.) Recent films include *Venus Beauty Institute* (2000), with Ogier as the proprietor of the salon; *Seaside* (2002), as a slot machine addict living year-round in a forlorn summer resort; a gorgeous turn in Werner Schroeter's *Deux* (2002), playing the blowsy, eroto-maniacal mother of twin Isabelle Hupperts and the ecstatic victim of a contemporary Jack the Ripper. Not to mention the exacting drama teacher with a secret life in Rivette's *Gang of Four* (1988) and the brief, smartly crafted roles in *Irma Vep* (1996) and Raul Ruiz's *Shattered Image* (1998).

The Bulle of Schroeder's *Maîtresse* (1973), in a radical revision of her screen image, is the ultimate sin-queen in a Louise Brooks wig, Vampira eyeliner and dominatrix gear so skintight that in one scene it begins to suffocate her. Here, the stylized fragility of her character in *Céline and Julie* reverberates against the hilariously solemn business of abusing a mesmerizing assortment of human ashtrays, pincushions, toilets and footwear polishers feasting on dog food, drinking urine and having their penises nailed to boards. *Maîtresse* is a farewell to ingenue roles, though Ogier still looks suspiciously young in it. The Bulle of Schmid's *Notre Dame de la Croisette* (1981) is more or less imprisoned in a Cannes hotel suite, hanging on to the telephone, trying to rummage up a pass to get into the festival screenings. In Schroeder's *Tricheurs* (1984), forgoing makeup and the jumped-up glamour of the standard casino femme, she reprises the obsessive misalliance of *L'amour fou* as a Dostoevskian folie à deux with Jacques Dutronc, gambling all-or-nothing. Like *Maîtresse*, *Tricheurs* defiantly refuses the unhappy ending the narrative seems to demand and concludes instead in the spirit of a Breton poem: *Plutôt la vie.*

I find it impossible to write about Bulle's film career without calling Pierre Clémenti to mind, and remembering him in an immaculate white suit, holding a cane, in the Berlinale Filmmesse. Beautiful Pierre, le vrai Artaud of the New Wave, Tempter of Buñuel's *The Milky Way*, and the ravishing street punk of *Belle de jour,* who could evoke, like Bulle, the glamour of dereliction and the orgiastic underside of glamour. But this boulevard of reverie begins with Fassbinder's *The Third Generation* (1978) and Bulle's role as Hilde Krieger, theoretical girl of the "salon terrorist" cell that kidnaps Eddie Constantine—quite possibly Fassbinder's most important movie, more relevant today than when it was made.

A postcard Bulle sent to Rivette proposed a sequel for Hilde Krieger, about a female terrorist released from prison. This became *Le Pont du Nord* (1982), set in the dour, hopeless Paris of Giscard d'Estaing's presidency. Marie (Ogier) returns from incarceration on a truck and hooks up with Baptiste (played by Bulle's daughter Pascale) in the occult way Rivette characters often encounter each other—like people drawn together in deciphering a partially ruined map, often a literal one. The pair commence to live entirely out-of-doors, like clochards, while Marie half-revives a former liaison with Julien (Clémenti), once her lover and partner in crime.

Le Pont du Nord is a maze, reminiscent of Rivette's first film, *Paris Belongs to Us*—another Alice in Wonderland spill down the rabbit hole into a mysterious, subterranean world under a gelid, gray urban surface. Baptiste, a Quixote battling windmills with karate, hasn't conceded that there are no maidens left to rescue; Marie and Julien have outlived their illusions. The period of *Le Pont du Nord* gives the reunion of Ogier and Clémenti, ebullient rebels in so many other films, a particularly loaded pathos.

When Baptiste swipes Julien's briefcase, she and Marie discover old newspaper clippings, among them the story of the bank heist that landed Marie in prison. Watching the film after 20 years, I discover that many of the clippings concern the police killing of Jacques Mesrine, "public enemy #1," a much-romanticized master criminal whose 1978 autobiography, *The Death Instinct,* is now a two-film project Barbet Schroeder is developing.

This previously unnoticed detail is the kind of retroactive jolt that opens a window into a shared but differently selective history. There's a character named Mesrin in Marivaux's play *The Dispute*, and Rivette's *Gang of Four*, in which Bulle plays the demanding drama instructor, is organized around rehearsals of Marivaux's *Double Infidelities;* and Bulle's stage debut was, as noted earlier, Marivaux's *The Triumph of Love.* The Mesrine affair belongs to the finale, the unanticipated end of the Giscard era, the moment before Mitterand's election, and, another coincidence, the time in my own life when I first lived in Paris.

In the disenchanted texts of *Maîtresse* or Rivette's *Duelle* and *Le Pont du Nord,* a kind of involuntary reenchantment of Paris conjures what remains unique and magical about Bulle Ogier, along with the suspicion that every real story I know begins and ends, like *La Paloma,* in a glass of champagne.

CUNNING, EXILE, CONTINGENCY

P ERHAPS NO great writer of the 20th century has been so persistently, cele-
bratedly obscure as Witold Gombrowicz. Although much of his work was
made available in English by Grove Press in the 1960s, Gombrowicz never
greatly profited from America's brief enthusiasm for arcane Euroculture. He
was a bit *too* weird, his writings suffused with gnarled, foggy themes. His novels hint at pedophilia and homoeroticism, but contain nothing resembling
pornography. No one chose to play Sartre to Gombrowicz's Genet. Only in
the '60s, the last decade of his life, was he recognized in Europe as a "world-
class" author. His American audience remains negligible.

Never terribly prolific, Gombrowicz wrote five novels, three plays, a volume of short stories, and several volumes of a journal, published serially, between 1953 and 1968, in the Paris-based émigré journal *Kultura*. He came
from a family of Lithuanian aristocrats with estates south of Warsaw, in the
languorous milieu of the idle rich. In his youth, he entertained an absurdist
romantic fetishism of the servant class, and probably indulged it with more
than one stable boy.

Studying law at the University of Warsaw, he sent his valet, "who was more
distinguished," to the lectures. Gombrowicz wrote several failed novels—he
tried, among other things, to write a "bad" novel in which flaws and infelici-
ties would be expanded into a style—while nursing a chronic lung ailment at
the chic resort of Zakopane, in the Tatra Mountains. After receiving his law
degree, he studied in Paris. He later fell in with a gang of white slavers in the
south of France. A Catholic priest, who rescued him from prosecution, sent
him back to Warsaw. The episode remains murky and, of course, rather daring. He became a legal apprentice, writing his first short stories in court-
rooms, where he was ostensibly recording trial testimony.

In 1933, he brought out a story collection, *Memoirs of a Time of Immaturity*. Gombrowicz repeatedly imputed the book's negative reception to its title; reviewers took it literally, and cited the author's lack of development. His first published play, *Ivona, Princess of Burgundia*, received no attention, and went unproduced until 1965.

Gombrowicz's first novel, *Ferdydurke*, created an immense literary scandal, and made him famous—in Poland, where, by mischance, he would soon be utterly forgotten. In 1939, he sailed to Buenos Aires on the maiden voyage of the *Chobry*, Poland's first luxury liner. A few days after the *Chobry* docked in Argentina, Hitler invaded Poland.

He was swallowed up "behind the sea," stranded in a strange country, a strange continent, where he remained stranded for a quarter of a century. As the Argentineans quickly discovered, Gombrowicz was socially impossible. In Warsaw, he had enjoyed shocking café society with displays of atrocious table manners. He drew an entourage from among Warsaw's sleaziest hangers-on and fools. In Buenos Aires, the powerful literary circle around Victoria Ocampo and her magazine, *Sur*, was prepared to welcome the author of *Ferdydurke* with open arms, until they met him. Gombrowicz wasted no time alienating everyone in the Argentine literary world.

He became a fastidious sort of derelict, living for years in fleapit hotels and having love affairs with street toughs. He wrote that in Buenos Aires he became young again, rejuvenated by poverty and faintly criminal adventures. For a while he lived off stiffs, showing up at wakes to eat the sandwiches. After the war, when he might have done well in Poland as a cherished cultural fragment, Gombrowicz stayed in South America. He worked for nine years as a secretary at the Polish Bank and afterwards survived on small grants. He became superstitious, believing that his return to Europe would mean he had accepted death. When he did leave Argentina in 1963, on a Ford Foundation grant, he became seriously asthmatic, and remained so until his death from a heart attack in 1969.

Gombrowicz's life is an intricately scarred mirror of his work. Argentina provided a 23-year reprieve from what he most dreaded: maturity in all its awful prefabricated forms, the respectable life of a man of letters. In novels, Gombrowicz travels under his own name, as an adult narrator who craves the malleable, open-ended, empty-headed existence of Youth. Until 30, we become more and more alive, he believed; after, we become more and more dead. (Thirty does seem about right.)

The young and immature live a different measure of time, and should, by Gombrowicz's reckoning, speak a different language than the old. (And they do, really.) Gombrowicz's writings reveal the terrible secret that "maturity" really amounts to choosing a mask one wears through the rest of one's life, while chaos nibbles at the edge of every gesture, every glance, every word. What people instinctively want is exactly what the social order forbids them: polymorphism, foolishness, what Valery's M. Teste described as "being silly beasts together." Inside everyone lives an embarrassingly awkward, amoral child, picking its nose and plucking wings off flies, while the grown-up exterior politely passes the salt.

These ideas festered within Gombrowicz deeply enough for the books they produced to transcend Freudianism, which, like Sartre, Gombrowicz considered an "essence" that follows after the event of existence. He worked a vast trove of ideas into his journals, articulating a private cult of *life* before *art*. He met Borges in Buenos Aires "once or twice, but we left it at that. Borges already had his rather too obsequious little court. . . . In the Argentine I often heard his 'brilliant' bons mots quoted. Well, each time I was disappointed. It was nothing but literature, and not of the best."

Gombrowicz's disdain for the literary world had little of Lawrence's celebration of Instinct and sweaty loins about it; he was a snob by training, self-indulgent to a fault, and simply difficult to get along with. Argentine aristocrats weren't *real* aristocrats—after all, they were South American.

Severed from his own history, he chose to experience the new life he was forced to invent for himself as a liberation. Homosexual adventures preoccupied him, by inclination but also as a willed perversity. Gombrowicz maintained a furtive literary ambition. He took a clerk's job at the Polish Bank, where he wrote *Trans-Atlantic* "under the desk," sneaking it into existence like a schoolboy sketching obscene pictures in class.

He eventually commenced publishing his diaries in Paris. Through *Kultura* and its lifeline to the greater world, he involved himself in polemical brawls with Camus, Sartre and Cioran, flaunting his acidic views on politics, explaining his own work with the obvious conviction that he was making Literature. Yet there is something deflationary of the literary enterprise, indeed of any enterprise, inherent in Gombrowicz's thought. His practice of stripping the surface off all human activity to uncover grotesque inadequacies reduces any noble posturing to laughable histrionics.

When he savages Neruda in his journals, or Camus's *L'Homme révolté*, the reader gets an acrid mouthful of the inferiority complex Gombrowicz cultivated into a world view. He is at times astonishingly vicious and, more disturbingly, what he writes is true.

> [*L'Homme révolté*] is a work with which I would like to agree with all my heart. But the point is that for me, conscience, the individual conscience, does not have the power which it has for [Camus] as far as saving the world. Don't we see that the conscience has no voice in the matter at any time? Does man kill or torture because he has come to the conclusion that he has the right to do so? He kills because others kill. He tortures because others torture. The most abhorrent deed becomes easy if the road to it has been paved, and, for example, in concentration camps the road to death was so well-trodden that the bourgeois incapable of killing a fly at home exterminated people with great facility. What disturbs us today is not this or that issue, but, how should I say this, the dissolution of the issue in the human masses, its destruction by the actions of people.

Gombrowicz's journal registers every twitter and bleep of his infinitely subtle consciousness. It is not an emotional or autobiographical record, but a philosophical dialogue with persons unseen. His clinical candor about himself has the same flaunting abrasiveness as Genet's sublimely stupid confessions, with the added irritation that Gombrowicz is an intellectual. Like Genet, Gombrowicz led an unusually rangy existence, with the filter of class ripped off the lens, so to speak. He sees through everybody, and carries a large grudge.

Writing of himself, he assumes an inevitable failure or insufficiency. Poland is a secondary, provincial culture; as a Polish writer, he measures himself against the suffocating perfection of "the big cultures." He wants to write like Goethe, Shakespeare and Dostoevsky (and, though he never mentions him, like Chekhov), but "as a Pole and an artist, I was doomed to imperfection . . ." He describes Poland as "a country of weakened forms"; his early works dismantle these wobbling structures with fiercely adolescent glee.

In his major novels, *Ferdydurke*, *Pornografia* and *Cosmos*, Gombrowicz's narrators are creatures of overmastering passivity, living quietly desperate lives, until some external agent, usually a maniac, propels them into a diseased paradigm of social order: A situation forms around the hero, like a calcinating fungus. The question becomes when, and how, a state of benign or virulent inanity will mutate or crack into something more extreme.

Unlike the later novels, *Ferdydurke* belongs to fantastic literature. An absurd premise is elaborated through a sequence of broad exaggerations, none of them especially believable. Gombrowicz's novels seldom connect very closely with the literature of verisimilitude, despite their naturalistic style. In every case, the narrator exhibits a psychotic detachment from the world of others, though he passes as an ordinary, if unusually laconic, presence, a sort of ambulatory stick of furniture.

It's a brilliantly skewed first-person tactic. Imagine one of Joseph Conrad's speakers abruptly intervening in his tale as a full-blown sociopath. Gombrowicz's confidence trick is to place a reasonable-sounding madman among lunatics who *sound* crazy.

> I lay in the dim light, while mortal fear lay heavy on my body and invaded my mind, and my mind in its turn lay heavy on my body; and the smallest particles of myself writhed in the appalling certainty that nothing would ever happen, nothing ever change, and that, whatever one did, nothing would ever come of it.

Ferdydurke begins like a dust-coated Existential saga of uselessness-between-world-wars, with the narrator recounting his terrible dream.

> By a regression of a kind that ought to be forbidden to nature, I had seen myself at the age of fifteen or sixteen, I had reverted to adolescence . . . it had seemed to me that the adult, the thirty-year-old who I am today, was apeing and mocking the adolescent that I was then, while the adolescent was mocking the adult; and that each of my two selves was thus taking the rise out of the other.

The dream comes true, an inversion of the 19th-century coming-of-age novel. A deranged second-form master, Professor Pimko, kidnaps Johnnie from his Warsaw flat and forces him to attend grammar school. Life begins running backwards. Johnnie remains 30, but no one seems to notice. The school is a Wilhelmine hangover where students are drilled in Latin and Polish classics. It teaches infantile submission to authority, received ideas, nationalism, "tradition"; these things are all represented by infantile adults. In *Ferdydurke,* childishness is an inescapable condition, the logical product of a national backwater. Poland, Gombrowicz implies, forever at the mercy of pushy neighbors, is an adult reduced to helplessness, a process replicated in each of its citizens. Since life offers no real choices, people can only repeat inanities.

> ". . . Well, then, why does Slowacki arouse our admiration, love and ecstasy? Why do we weep with the poet when we read that angelic poem In Switzerland? Why does exaltation swell our breasts . . . why is there no escaping the magic and seduction. . . . Why? Because, gentlemen, Slowacki was a great poet. Walkiewicz, tell me why! . . . Why the enchantment, the love, the tears, the exaltation, the magic? Why are our hearts rent? Tell me, Walkiewicz!"
>
> ". . . Because he was a great poet, sir," said Walkiewicz.

For an American reader, one of the unintended ironies in this satire of education is that however idiotically it reads, its 13-year-olds are already better educated than most American college graduates. There's a similar irony about Gombrowicz's complaints against the provincialism of Warsaw in the '30s, which was radiantly cosmopolitan compared with New York or Los Angeles. But this too had its dark side, its desperate wish to be something else—a mania for "advanced" Western cultural products like G. B. Shaw and Greta Garbo. The curse of profound insecurity hangs over everyone in *Ferdydurke*—the progressive-minded Youthful Family, prattling at breakfast about the abolition of the death penalty, the promise of modern science, and birth control; the puberty-haunted boys striking vapid poses of idealism and depravity in the schoolyard; the seedy aristocrats who regularly whip their servants and don't know how to tie their shoelaces. Gombrowicz even throws in a village of human dogs, peasants regressed to all fours.

Ferdydurke's characters are overtly monstrous, like Dostoevsky's creatures who chatter freely about their murkiest urges. Gombrowicz's people, though, are more or less oblivious obsessives, nearly automata. Only Johnnie notices the fixations of others as well as his own; this enables him to manipulate people into catastrophic self-exposure.

The stock epiphany of a Gombrowicz novel comes when an assortment of cohabiting delusions uses up all the available oxygen and starts emitting an explosive gas. People suddenly regress into puddles of infantile craving, baby talk, uncontrollable libido, murderous enthusiasm. This process is set into motion by the narrator's erotic frustrations, which warp off into eccentricities, little tamperings with the gestalt that bring out the adult baby in the others. Gombrowicz uses submerged desires as the basis of plot: His protagonists want certain unimaginable icky things to happen, and the sheer force of this want charges banal reality with a greasy kind of sexual ominousness. There is a constant struggle of surfaces against the powers of subjectivity.

In *Pornografia,* the hero's companion, a one-time theater director named Frederick, possesses a charismatic ability to inflict self-consciousness on other people.

> It seemed to me, and I suspected, that Frederick, on his knees, was "praying" too—I was even sure, yes, knowing his lack of integrity I was certain that he was not pretending but was really "praying" for the benefit of others and for his own benefit, but his prayer was no more than a screen to conceal the enormity of his "non-prayer" . . . it was an act of expulsion, of "eccentricity" which cast us out of this church into the infinite space of absolute disbelief, a negative act, the very act of negation.

The spectacularly charmless, mute heroine of *Princess Ivona* makes others intolerably conscious of their defects—so much so that they band together and murder her. In *Pornografia,* the propeller of odium is a voyeuristic wish, i.e., the desire of Gombrowicz and Frederick to effect an "ideal" sexual act between Karol and Henia, who repeatedly fail to interest each other. The adults then contrive to unite the young in an act of killing. As it happens, a Resistance leader who's lost his nerve is stranded at the house. Orders come through to assassinate him. None of the adults has the nerve to go through with it . . . but getting the kids to do it makes it sexy.

> To have brought Karol in . . . to make it all slant toward him . . . thanks to this the intended death suddenly heated up and glowed not only with Karol but with Henia, with their arms and legs—and the future corpse bloomed with all their adolescent, clumsy, rough sensuality. The heat burst inside me: this death was in love.

By joining a politically "responsible" liquidation to the fulfillment of Byzantine perversity, Gombrowicz dramatizes his notion of politics as a mask for ennobling wormy souls. Or as he puts it in *A Kind of Testament:* "In the end both the ideas of 'higher synthesis' and 'higher analysis' become mere pretexts for the pure pleasure of action. As, I assume, does Fascism or Communism."

In fact, none of Gombrowicz's characters is capable of behaving well, unless out of fear of behaving badly. Absolute rectitude is an absolute masquerade. The saintly Amelia, mother of Henia's plodding fiancé and patroness of war refugees, inexplicably attacks an adolescent intruder by sinking her teeth into his leg and stabbing him with a kitchen knife. On her deathbed, her attention strays from the crucifix to the face of the atheist Frederick, erasing a lifetime of piety at the very moment when it should have come in handy.

The irrepressible cruelty of Gombrowicz's work is one of its chief attractions. His narrators feel boredom and twisted lust, with no intermediate emotions cluttering their sensibilities. Fetishism replaces human involvement. The protagonists fixate on body parts, inanimate objects, insane connections between random phenomena. Gombrowicz's specialty (unique in the modern novel, as far as I know) is to make a universe of paranoid symbols coincide with external reality—not in the manner of Gogol's *Diary of a Madman,* or Nabokov's *Pnin,* where the blurring of inside and outside makes the difference between them obvious, but as if a layer of collective psychic topsoil had suddenly blown off.

Gombrowicz is greatly preoccupied with the friction between Form and Chaos. Humans secrete form, rather like beeswax. I behave like this because you behaved like that; the form of our relationship is collaborative, and unique to ourselves. As an extreme refinement of Sartre's line between existence and essence, Gombrowicz defines the interhuman world of form as a theater of ultimately arbitrary actions, with no intrinsic moral or philosophical underpinnings. We may believe we do things, for example, for high-minded reasons, but "high-mindedness" is simply a habitual response we've learned from other people. If we're Communists we will exploit people with one polemical excuse, if we're Fascists we'll use another, if capitalists still another. The fact of exploitation remains untouched.

In this sense, Gombrowicz's books proceed like mathematical formulae, seemingly open to chance and the unpredictable volition of their characters, but the terms set in motion at the outset can only produce one solution.

These novels are wholly incredible, but written in a light, casual style that makes them seem almost plausible. *Cosmos* is the most extreme exercise in arbitrariness: The plot develops out of certain stray features of the landscape, insignificant visual obstructions, a hanged sparrow, a block of wood, a set of bedsprings, things that knit together for no discernible reason. Witold and Fuchs arrive at a country house, they rent a room, the maid has a hideous scar on the side of her mouth. They've noticed a sparrow hanging from a tree, and now this strange mouth . . . it must mean something, and what about that crack in the ceiling, the one that looks like an arrow, pointing into the yard? What's it pointing at? A rake, resting at an odd angle against a tree. The rake seems to be pointing to the garden wall.

> What did this mean? What lay behind it? And what lay behind that glass I had noticed the evening before on the table near the window in the drawing-room, with two reels of cotton beside it? Why had it caught my eye as I passed? Was there really anything curious about it? Should I go down and have a look and make sure?

The clues present themselves because Witold is bored stiff in the country-side and finds himself attracted to the family's married daughter, Lena— whose mouth somehow recalls the scarred mouth of the servant, and the wire mesh of the ashtray used at the dinner table, and a bit of cork sticking to the lip of a wine bottle, and so on. We see him desperately trying to infuse meaning into the static desuetude of the house, the yard, the surrounding woods. Nothing adds up, nothing materializes. The family's little neurotic mannerisms repeat themselves pointlessly at mealtimes: the retired father's anecdotes and rolling of bread pellets, the mother's buttered radishes, Lena's mouth, the bit of cork, the crack in the ceiling.

None of this means anything. But it must mean something, so Witold strangles the family cat and hangs it from a tree in the yard. Now the clues lead directly to this vicious, mysterious killing.

> I had strangled the cat and hung it from a hook, and all I could do was to have breakfast, go downstairs, and pretend to know nothing about it. But why had I done it? There had been such a strange accumulation of things, so many intertwining threads, Lena, Katasia, the arrows, the hammerings and

all the rest of it, the frog or the ashtray would have been enough by themselves, I had been floundering in the chaos, it even occurred to me that the teapot had made me do it, and that I had acted out of sheer excess and superfluity, in other words, that killing the cat had been an extra, one thing too much, just like the teapot. But no, it wasn't true, it had not been connected with the teapot. Then what had it been connected to?

This is "the pure pleasure of action" gone considerably haywire; what's remarkable in this black stream of a book is its sudden change of course. Once the cat is strangled, Witold's obsessively gathered, private symbols take on palpable significance for the others. His dread and insanity become theirs, their little tics inflate into hysteria, and the sleepy world of another middle-class family bites the apocalyptic dust. The cat hanging will now lead to a human hanging, with a logic everyone can see.

For Gombrowicz, chaos isn't simply the action of desire on reality, but an *a priori* condition of things. Complicity influences the shape of reality with infinitely greater force than the individual. Moreover, individual will is not straightforwardly "desirous," but devious and strange to itself, complexly mediated, displaced. The displacement of desire creates the grotesque form of the world.

Like Céline, Gombrowicz maps the foggy territory of delusion, the chasm between what people think they are and what they really are. His work is cold, sinister and cruel, the song of a chronic malcontent determined to squeeze a good laugh from the horror of existence. Gombrowicz's novels suggest obvious 20th-century affinities—with Malaparte and Junger as well as Genet and Céline. But the writer he most resembles is Tommaso Landolfi, another Russophile fantasist devoted to a life of action rather than literature. Landolfi's obsession with roulette and Gombrowicz's relation to the experience of exile have a similarly romantic, literary tinge. Both writers display an uncontrollable modernity, a revulsion against contemporary life quite typical in modern literature. In Céline, this revulsion reaches down to the level of syntax. In Landolfi and Gombrowicz, it produces that mimicry of classical form that links their works to Goethe, Kleist, Turgenev and Chekhov, like a bridge of ice between the centuries.

GERMANY INSIDE HIM
Rainer Fassbinder and the Spell of Dystopia

W HAT CAN be said about a fat, ugly sadomasochist who terrorized everyone around him, drove his lovers to suicide, drank two daily bottles of Rémy, popped innumerable pills while stuffing himself like a pig, then croaked from an overdose at 37? Marlene Dietrich in *Touch of Evil* said it all: I won't repeat it here.

Anyway, there's nothing you can say about Rainer Werner Fassbinder that he didn't say about himself (in countless interviews, in his films and, in the most literally naked way possible, in the horrific self-portrait in the compilation film *Germany in Autumn*). He was the faithful mirror of an ugly world that has grown uglier since his death, without his brilliance, his starving soul, his exorbitantly calculated persona. The contemporary-model artist, countering a century of both exalting and punitive myths, is a sensibly meretricious decorator, good at business, driven by mortgage payments rather than private demons, preferably married with children, or, if homosexual, devoted to plangent little ironies and charity work. Fassbinder, by contrast, thought it was worth dying young if you managed to live at a certain pitch and get your work done: Most people are dead at 37 anyway, they just don't know it.

Fassbinder directed 43 feature films, including many never shown in America until recently, like the seminal five-part television film *Eight Hours Don't Make a Day* and his sole science-fiction movie, *World on a Wire*. An unparalleled achievement, though any five of these films would be hard to take at one go. "Life is pessimistic in the end because we die and in between because of corruption in our daily lives," the artist said, and there you have the unvarying flavor of everything. There are no lighthearted moments in any Fassbinder film that I can recall. If a character's happy, it's because he hasn't yet heard the bad news. There is, instead, a lot of hilarious brutality, suggesting a festering blend of Molière and Joe Orton.

Fassbinder started in the theater, where his will to power quickly manifested itself, though he claimed that his leader status was forced on him by his retinue of familiars. It was, in reality, a symbiosis, not unlike Andy Warhol's Factory, where people of a certain talent and insecurity orbited around a demiurge who needed them rather less than they needed him. In the atmosphere of the late '60s, the search for communal utopia, the ostensible idealism behind Fassbinder's project, produced among "the Fassbinder people," as in many other contexts, a dystopia ruled by the whims and eccentricities of its prime mover.

Both Warhol and Fassbinder, homosexuals with conspicuous, complex attachments to their mothers, used a repertory situation to reenact their childhood humiliations on reversed terms, instilling infantile helplessness in those around them and assuming the dominant role of the withholding/ bountiful parent.

They both thought of themselves as unattractive, unlovable and only able to secure "love" from people by conferring favor on them, i.e., by putting them in movies. The enormity of these unfillable needs may be gauged by the staggering number of films both Warhol and Fassbinder made in a small span of years. That the process was more important than the finished product is obvious in Warhol's case; Ronald Hayman's excellent book, *Fassbinder Filmmaker,* reveals how surprisingly much this was also true of the latter. Paradoxically, in both directors this film-mediated bonding created heightened mistrust of their love objects: greater distance instead of intimacy.

In the parlance of sex, Warhol was a bossy bottom. The obdurate passivity of his films achieves all the hostile effects of silence and noncommitment. Fassbinder's temperament was far more confrontational, and in compromised ways more generous (to better control people, he actually paid them, unlike Warhol, and used them as actors rather than as personalities), but his first nine or ten films share something of Warhol's quietly sadistic *durée,* laconic limpness, and chaos in search of a methodology. But Warhol "professionalized" his film production by turning it over to Paul Morrissey, his imprimatur on Morrissey's films projecting the ultimate passive control. He manifested himself through his absence. Fassbinder, on the other hand, asserted the centrality of his person from the beginning, appearing in almost all of his own films, writing his own scripts, often doing his own camerawork.

Fassbinder's sensibility fully emerged after his encounter with the films of Douglas Sirk. Under Sirk's influence, Fassbinder discovered in the conventions of melodrama the ideal means of showing why utopian wishes are doomed to crash in our system of life, how happy endings are smiles pasted over horror. Perhaps he had this idea long before seeing *All That Heaven Allows* and *Written on the Wind,* but after Sirk, Fassbinder sealed off the utopian exits—with *Beware of a Holy Whore* (1970), his tenth film, Fassbinder dramatized the nightmarish party of collective art-making, the manipulative brutality and deceptive approval essential to his method, and the deformities idealism wreaks on the personalities of idealists. After *Whore—The Rocky Horror Picture Show* for anyone who's worked in movies—Fassbinder no longer heroicized petty criminals, gays, immigrants and other marginals, but instead showed how the system warped them and stunted their possibilities. This might not have activated much hysteria if he hadn't also shown the perverse complicity between the social order and its reformers—if you're part of the solution, you're part of the problem.

Fassbinder was typically attacked by people who needed heroes (in today's cant, "role models") and heroic causes. His enemies included both reactionaries and progressive types who couldn't bear the reflection of their own neuroses. *Mother Küsters Goes to Heaven* and *The Third Generation* alienated the whole spectrum of the conventional left, while films like *Katzelmacher* and *Veronika Voss* exposed the spirit of fascism thriving in postwar Germany. The play *Garbage, the City and Death* (filmed in 1976 by Daniel Schmid as *Schatten der Engel*) brought cries of anti-Semitism from people determined not to understand it. *Fox and His Friends* and *The Bitter Tears of Petra von Kant* outraged gay groups by displaying homosexual relations that were every bit as exploitative as heterosexual ones. (The message: Capitalism turns everyone into a whore; anyone who resists this fate comes to a bad end.)

The bigger scandal was Fassbinder's anarchism, his proclaimed self-exemption from any program or belief system. Our beliefs are animated by feelings, and, as he relentlessly showed, our feelings are manufactured for us, not least by the movies.

A famed quote: "Love is the best, most insidious, most effective instrument of social repression." The tight bonds of Fassbinder's own pathology account for the claustrophobia of the world he pictured. Compare a film like *Lola* or *Beware of a Holy Whore* with, say, Altman's *Three Women* or *The Long Goodbye.* Altman too is a spinner of destructive microcosms, an anthropologist tracking systemic damage in human personalities. But in the margins of his films, Altman always presents evidence of other life, hints of alternative destinies. Altman's late films feel incomplete, complacent, sometimes arbitrary; his endless indulgence of actors "doing their own thing" eventually overwhelmed his ability to shape a film into something more than a string of vivid anecdotes. In Fassbinder the parts are the sum of the whole. He presents a hermetic world, from which there is no escape: The characters, rather than the actors, have collaborated on making the world the unlivable place it is.

The infantile need for love, warped through a lifetime of twisted social forms, produces both the voluntary prison of family life and explosive methods of escape from it. These latter are uniformly self-defeating. One thinks of Hans Epp in *The Merchant of Four Seasons,* quietly and deliberately drinking himself to death. Or of Peter in *I Only Want You to Love Me* braining a tavern-keeper with a telephone. Of Herr R. in *Why Does Herr R. Run Amok?,* killing his neighbor, then his wife and child, finally hanging himself in the office toilet. Or of the final hours of *Veronika Voss,* the last dance in the desert in *Whity,* the hissing gas stove signaling the inevitable ending of *The Marriage of Maria Braun,* Elvira's overdose in *In a Year of 13 Moons.*

These characters have reached their logical dead end, which happened also to be Fassbinder's: The implacable logic that leads them there is Fassbinder's signature mise-en-scène. For an artist who claimed an urgent interest in utopia and liberation, Fassbinder bears a curious resemblance to the Mauriac whom Sartre reproached for robbing his protagonists of free will and setting them down in an airless universe. They are almost always more intelligent than their situation, but between their insight and their emotions lies an area of blindness.

"Human beings have no interest in reality," Alexander Kluge has said, "They prefer to lie than to become divorced from their wishes." The most painful moments in Fassbinder's films come when his characters see their lives clearly for the first time—painful because they immediately flee into delusion. "Each and every one of you makes me want to puke," Petra von

Kant tells her family, honestly enough. A moment later she's running on about Karin, the lesbian girlfriend who's just ditched her: "That little girl's finger is worth more than the rest of you put together." The worst of it is that this is probably true within Petra's libidinal economy, but Karin herself is pretty worthless. Fox knows Eugen is bleeding him white and will dump him when his bank account is empty; he even knows this before Eugen does. But "love" has become everything. Fox would rather die than face the ruin of his "love."

Fassbinder dramatized aspects of his own social relations that reflected truths about society at large. Their overwhelming negativity makes them useful. A film like *Martha,* which pictures bourgeois marriage as a torture chamber built on the complicity of its inhabitants, is worth any hundred or so meet-cute Hollywood comedies, bittersweet romances and earnest social dramas. Fassbinder didn't make "art films" in opposition to Hollywood; he put as much Hollywood and as little artiness into things as he could.

At the same time, no one as truly, brilliantly obdurate and unyielding as Fassbinder would survive for a second in the American film industry. It's a pleasant exercise to imagine him alive, in Los Angeles, making incredibly sinister movies about AIDS, immigration, race relations, the treatment of old people, the health-care system, prisons, corporations and other things that are rarely the subjects of first-rate films. But who in the American system would let him? There are sites of cultural dissonance and critique in which Fassbinder's view of things isn't entirely unwelcome (mainly on cable TV), but his impermeable fidelity to that view, and his explosive personality, would be. We prefer our geniuses to be passionately stupid and entirely complicit with the whims of the marketplace, and Fassbinder plainly wasn't. Like so many seminal artists of our time, he destroyed himself before others could do it for him.

VIENNA III, KUNDMANNGASSE 19

T HE HOUSE Ludwig Wittgenstein built between 1926 and 1928 is, in the words of Valie Export's film *Invisible Adversaries*, "an unexampled piece of architecture in the 20th century." It is an enigma, a myth, a Rosetta Stone of lucid, yet impenetrable ciphers. A system of spatial circuit breakers, noetic riffs in glass and steel, a palimpsest, a joke, it is like the iceberg in H. M. Enzensberger's epic poem "The Sinking of the Titanic":

> *It is none of our business,*
> *it will drift on in silence,*
> *it needs nothing,*
> *it has no offspring,*
> *it melts away.*
> *It leaves nothing behind.*
> *It disappears to perfection.*
> *Yes, that's the word for it:*
> *perfection.*

My interest in Haus Wittgenstein began in 1977 when I first saw *Invisible Adversaries,* in which the house's strange career is touched on in the course of an architectural survey of Vienna. I was haunted by the idea of a one-of-a-kind artifact by Wittgenstein, whose writings had influenced me, in many different ways, since my initial encounter with *The Blue and Brown Books*. But I was even more haunted by the fact that the house had narrowly escaped demolition in 1971, saved at the last minute by protests and petitions. But a rather lowering victory, indicating as it did that culture has at all times to be rescued from the society it supposedly serves. When I visited the house for the first time, in 1981, I realized how Pyrrhic the victory of that preservation battle had actually been.

I

Es ist passiert, "it just sort of happened," people said there when other people in other places thought heaven knows what had occurred. It was a peculiar phrase, not known in this sense to the Germans and with no equivalent in other languages, the very breath of it transforming facts and the bludgeonings of fate into something light as eiderdown, as thought itself. Yes, in spite of much that seems to point the other way, Kakania was perhaps a home for genius after all; and that, probably, was the ruin of it.
—ROBERT MUSIL, THE MAN WITHOUT QUALITIES

By 1889, the year of Wittgenstein's birth, the architecture of mid-century, epitomized in the pseudohistorical structures of the Vienna Ringstrasse, had become a focus of cultural anxieties that eventually spread to every corner of the Robert Musil's *Empire of Kakania* (*Shitland*). In that year, Camillo Sitte published *Der Städtebau* (City Building), a Volkish polemic advocating the organic growth of the city over the planning schemes of an industrializing state. Architecture, along with painting, sculpture, music, decor and crafts, would function within a total orchestration of the environment. Sitte's book provided momentum to a burgeoning arts-and-crafts movement, whose artisans were being displaced by new manufacturing methods. His thinking appealed precisely to those yearnings for permanence embodied in the borrowed classicism of the Ringstrasse. It was not the Greek and Roman mannerism of Ferstel's Votivkirche and Siccardsberg and van der Null's Staatsoper that Sitte execrated, but the vast open spaces between the Ringstrasse structures. The monumental blanknesses around buildings of heroic scale dwarfed the populace, instilling collective agoraphobia.

Four years after *Der Städtebau* appeared, Otto Wagner won a municipal competition for a city plan. Wagner's scheme centered on practicalities of industrial development, encompassing modern sanitation methods and inner-city transport needs in a utilitarian esthetic. The next several years brought a flowering of architecture geared to industrial expansion, typified not only by Wagner's block-long Postal Savings Bank (1905), the Josef Olbrich's cabbage-domed Secession building (1898), Joseph Hoffmann's Stoclet Palace in Brussels (1905–14) and the later, drastically purist works of Adolf Loos—but also by a proliferation of low-cost housing projects, the first amelioration of a 50-year-long housing shortage. In this period, use value gradually nudged folkloric and nostalgic design tendencies into less obtrusive fields like painting and decoration. And, as the specter of the 1848 Revolution receded, so did the military notion of city planning that had created the open spaces Sitte dreaded. (The same notion had inspired Haussmann's Paris boulevards.)

Agoraphobia, however, persisted. It wasn't a perception of spatial disorientation that plagued the Dual Monarchy's cosmopolitans, but a sense of immanent temporal disjunction. Throughout the '90s of Wittgenstein's childhood, and until the shots at Sarajevo, Hapsburg culture jerked forward in steadily more ominous convulsions. The culture's desperate will to dance to history's accelerating tune, while maintaining an appearance of immutable order, produced a hyperproduction of art objects and literary works that filled—or at least cluttered—the dizzying temporal voids created by a disappearing past and an imponderable future.

The period's best minds, coming of age in a society that embraced irrationalism in art while maintaining a mindless faith in scientific rationalism, experienced the opposite of the general agoraphobia. Thus Paul Engelmann answers Stefan Zweig's remark in *The World of Yesterday* (1942) that "it was the golden age of security":

I believe that Hitler's blind ravings about his thousand years to come have nearly found a match in the purblindness about a thousand bygone years which is reflected in this statement by a well-known writer, who here identifies himself with the deceptive sense of security of a generation that had from childhood lived on the fat of the land. Otherwise he could not have failed to feel the atmosphere of this security like a stifling noose round his neck, like the writing on the wall, a warning that such a life simply could not end well either for himself or for the world at large.

That culture might be powerless to affect the movement of history was a perception Viennese society held in abeyance for half a century, by endorsing every avant-garde that appeared in its arts and literature. These were received as the challenging aesthetic byproducts of industrial and commercial progress. The scandals caused by the Secession could only have occurred in a society anxious to assimilate them for tonic purposes. It's true that a large reactionary element resisted cultural innovation, and often went on the attack. When the certainties of the codified professions were questioned—in medicine, physics and jurisprudence, for example—this resistance turned violent and ugly. But among the enlightened newly rich and established upper classes, art enjoyed such esteem that even its most radical practitioners (along with its most patent mediocrities) were given the honor of excited debate and the security of responsible patronage.

It was a period of liberal complacency, an era of ornament. Man would be perfected by technical progress, and the civilizing presence of Art. Art wouldn't simply hang on walls; the practical, material stuff of daily life would become art, as artists in increasing numbers applied their talents to silverware and glass design, tea-services and carpets, furniture and interiors.

Ornament had its double in the information field. The *feuilleton,* an impressionistic mélange of literary fantasy and journalism, provided a veil of illusion between reader and raw event. Facts, in the land of Kakania, became matters of opinion. The imprecision of public discourse injected the moral flab of the status quo into reportage, government decree and legal statute alike. While the Baroque had fallen away a century before, during the Napoleonic Wars, the spirit of the Baroque returned in Austria-Hungary with a vengeance, tarted up as stylistic innovation. It disguised the nature of the age for an aspiring middle class. For those who knew better, it kept the inevitable at arm's length, like heroin.

The Empire of Kakania, which had covered nearly every inch of territory between Italy and Russia until 1914, vanished so swiftly and completely that for 60 years, fin-de-siècle Vienna was vaguely pictured as a ballroom of waltzing Wiener schnitzels draped in diamonds and cavalry sabers, an image eventually modified to include Dr. Freud peering down from the balcony. In more recent years, through reawakened interest in Musil, Broch, Schnitzler and Canetti, figures such as Karl Kraus and Adolf Loos have been better understood, as radical thinkers reacting to a profound cultural crisis.

Kraus's importance, for English readers, can still mostly be inferred from writings about him, since a fraction of his work has been translated into English. Much of his writing poses thorny translation problems. It could hardly be otherwise, since for decades Kraus exposed linguistic nonsense and idiomatic coercion in the Viennese press.

Kraus began his career as a book and theater reviewer for various German and Austrian publications, including the influential *Neue Freie Presse.* His reputation widened with the publication of two satirical pamphlets, one a pastiche of current literary styles, the other attacking Theodor Herzl's Zionist movement.

In 1899, after a year as editor of *Die Waage (The Scales),* a political magazine, Kraus commenced publishing his own paper, *Die Fackel (The Torch),* to the displeasure of Vienna's press lord, publisher of the *Neue Freie Presse,* Moritz Benedikt. Benedikt's paper was Vienna's journal of record: by reputation, at least, an unbiased, highly respectable source of news.

Kraus considered Benedikt's paper the wellspring of public stupidity and civic corruption, worse than the yellow press because its guise of reasonableness made it harder to see through. It was *Die Fackel*'s chief target. Reading Kraus's attacks on it today reflects extraordinary prescience about what the newly invented trade of journalism was destined to become. The *Neue Freie Presse* dealt with persons and ideas it didn't approve of simply by never mentioning them.

While Kraus's public stature grew enormously, his name never appeared in Benedikt's paper. Kraus, more generously, awarded Benedikt a place in his epic play, *The Last Days of Mankind* (1922), as Lord of the Hyenas.

Until 1911, *Die Fackel* carried contributions from Strindberg, Heinrich Mann, Georg Trakl and Oscar Wilde. subsequently, until his death in 1936, Kraus wrote the whole paper himself. His savage exposure of Austrian hypocrisy, hatred of war and manipulative patriotism, the moral attractiveness of his beliefs and the limpid clarity of his writing attracted a huge following, especially among young people. Canetti describes him as "the real, the rousing, the tormenting, the shattering Karl Kraus," and every chronicler of the period describes the electric excitement of Kraus's public readings, and the eagerness with which every issue of *Die Fackel* was snapped up as it appeared.

Kraus's dismantling of the obfuscative language of press was a form of ethical battle. Reproducing verbatim samples for public ridicule, Kraus revealed thick deposits of nonmeaning that *feuilletonistes* and reporters created from incessant repetition of cliches and received ideas. Karel Capek (whose own parodies of journalese in *War With the Newts* [1936] mimicked the Newspeak of fascism) wrote of Kraus: "He taught us how to read, how to appraise accurately sense and nonsense in printed words, their contradictions, their frightening recurrence. Whoever has gone through the school of the red paperbound issues of *Die Fackel* has completed, as it were, a course in moral philology." When Wittgenstein moved to Norway in 1913, he had his *Die Fackel* subscription forwarded.

Certainly Kraus, who "had a gift for condemning people out of their own mouths" (Canetti), inspired Wittgenstein's methodological approach to purifying philosophical discourse. Moreover, what Kraus attempted in the area of public utterance—i.e., dissolving ethically indefensible statements—had the same purpose as the exclusion of metaphysical speculation from philosophy demanded by Wittgenstein's *Tractatus:* to demonstrate that spiritual values could not be legislated in discourse, but could only be conveyed in language that did not concern them, or expressed through an individual's actions. Both Kraus and Wittgenstein sought to make certain kinds of statements impossible.

II

The search for an authentic ethics of language was an experiment in conceptual mapmaking. To define what each field should concern itself with placed intangibles beyond the reach of any system's claims and distortions. Private life and extrasocial values could then exist behind a civic facade of utilitarian relations.

Adolf Loos saw an urgent need for the corollary purification of practical design. Loos proposed separating art, which dealt with inner life, from architecture and crafts. Utilitarian objects should reflect their nature in their design. Buildings should serve practical needs of their users. Loos despised the habitual practice of sticking an "edifying" Greek facade on a Baroque parliament building, attaching imperial-looking entrances to Vienna's rent-palaces, and similar anachronistic decoration. He also loathed the unwarranted novelty and utopian agendas of modernism. Loos maintained that when historical forms remained the most practical ones, they should be adopted. When new materials and objects required invention of new forms, the craftsman or builder—not the artist—should decide a thing's logical design.

"The evolution of culture," Loos wrote in *Ornament and Crime* (1908), "is synonymous with the removal of ornament from utilitarian objects." By making things uselessly precious, art expended in ornament degraded art to mere decoration and alienated people—whose "private mess" necessarily generated the decay and damage of used objects—from the world of things. Loos's famous essay was directed specifically against the *Heimatkunst* produced by Joseph Hoffmann's Wiener Werkstätte and the foray into crafts manufacturing that marked the Secession movement's degeneration from cultural revolution to cottage industry. Loos's essay also signaled an exemplary shift in architectural thinking, away from both purposeless historicizing and purely formal displays of modernism.

Loos was hardly alone in rejecting ornament: Precautions concerning ornament can be found in all architectural writing of the prewar period, from van de Velde's have-it-both-ways *Vom Neuen Stil* (On the New Style, 1907) to Sant'Elia and Marinetti's martial *Manifesto of Futurist Architecture* (1914). But Loos was singular in proposing ornament's rejection as an *ethical* imperative, an idea he elaborated with meticulous thoroughness. The extraordinary essays Loos published between 1897 and 1900 rail against "retro" styling in underclothes, furniture, glassware and hats, celebrate the plumbing and silversmith trades, survey the history of building materials and explain the evolution of footwear. Loos took a thoughtful interest in everything from counterfeit pleats in the Norfolk jacket to the suspension springs of English mail coaches. He decries the unnecessary, the superannuated, the dysfunctionally "beautiful," pinning the false in cultural artifacts to a deep falsity in the culture's premises. Loos's style is relaxed and good-natured, not curmudgeonly. His way of deflating arty pretension is to show how function rather than fashion determined the design of historical artifacts, how technical advances made some styles obsolete, others not. "If progress in technique makes possible an improvement of form," Loos wrote, "it is always necessary to adopt that improvement." Loos was no conservative.

He was an anomaly. In 1893 he traveled to New York; he spent three years in America, taking in Philadelphia, Chicago and St. Louis. He discovered the buildings of Louis Sullivan and Frank Lloyd Wright, the cast-iron structures of Griffith, Hatch and Kellum (most of them later destroyed to accommodate the World Trade Center), Burnham and Root's Monadnock block, the residential structures of H. H. Richardson. Aside from the impact this unprecedented architecture must have had on him, Loos's three-year absence from the European scene coincided with the Austrian effulgence of Art Nouveau, which may have looked a rather unsatisfying revolution when Loos returned. He never built skyscrapers, but Loos applied these American visions by using new materials more audaciously than any European contemporary besides Peter Behrens.

He devised his buildings according to his published credo. "The building should be dumb on the outside and reveal its wealth only on the inside," Loos wrote. His buildings shocked the Viennese, who expected public surfaces to come embellished with Ionic columns, caryatids, acanthus leaves, egg and dart molding, Corinthian entablatures and gargoyles. The City Council forced him to add flowerboxes to the mute, square windows of Looshaus in the Michaelerplatz; his Café Museum in Elisabethstrasse was instantly dubbed the Café Nihilismus by architects who later imitated it. It wasn't the absence of the past that gave Loos's buildings their startling appearance, but the absence of pointless decoration. Loos adapted features of Schinkel's illuminist versions of late Roman, Ledoux's Romantic Classicism and the pared-down Baroque of Fischer von Erlach, as well Louis Sullivan's stark modernity. Extracted from historical moss and disencumbered of inert embellishment, classical borrowings looked as disturbing as Americanisms: dumb, solid and threatening.

Loos reserved interiors for the "private mess"—the inner, inexpressible values whose bogus articulation he condemned. The bald exteriors provided no indication of the spatial organization within. The ideal of transparency that Gropius and Bruno Taut extrapolated from Paul Scheerbart's *Glass Architecture* (1914) was anathema to Loos: It violated private space. Loos thwarted intrusion with windows set deep into thick walls and radical dissonances between core spaces and shells. His buildings taunted the outside world with casually wrought secrecy. Inside, elaborate geometries of ovoids, squared arches, trapezoidal perspectives articulated in parquet patterns, marble and mahogany facings, depths protracted by mirrored walls, space construed to anticipate the imprint of organic patterns, rationalized to absorb the overrun of daily jumble and successive generations of furniture. The Loos house made space receptive to the accretions of aura that transfer the structure from architect to inhabitant. Its exterior was a veil of silence: stingy or inoffensive, depending on your point of view.

Loos gave some of his works rather conventional outer structures, harmonizing them with the surrounding architecture, subverting it on the inside. A curious echo of the many years when his only commissions were remodeling assignments. In his final works, Loos devised interior space with essentially the same negative or neutral muteness as the outer walls, as if clearing off even minimal traces of anticipated function. While the separation of public and private is maintained in a formal sense, the value of the "private" assumes a sudden zero aspect. The space becomes inhabited but its articulation is left blank. It appears as a minus sign set against a future plenum in which every detail is alien.

III

The insidious thing about the causal point of view is that it leads us to say: "Of course, it had to happen like that." Whereas we ought to think: it may have happened like that—and also in many other ways.

—LUDWIG WITTGENSTEIN, NOTEBOOK ENTRY, 1940
(PUBLISHED IN *CULTURE AND VALUE*)

If there were many Wittgenstein buildings with which to contrast his philosophical writings, the exaggeration of the latter influence might be less conspicuous. We could study the abstract for concrete residua, reducing the philosopher's life to a set of pronouncements and some statistics, perhaps augmented by a few snapshots.

In the histories we find a retroactive application of a mythos to events it couldn't have played any part in. Ludwig grows up in a prosperous, refined Vienna family. Educated first by private tutors and later at a Linz secondary school, he enrolls in 1906 in the Technische Hochschule in Berlin-Charlottenburg to study engineering. In 1908, he proceeds to Manchester University, where his work in aeronautics (specifically, a mathematical model of a propeller design) inspires his investigations into the foundations of mathematics and logic.

In 1911, at the prompting of Gottlob Frege, he becomes a protgé of Bertrand Russell at Cambridge. There he commences formulating the propositions of the *Tractatus Logico-Philosophicus*. After two years at Cambridge he spends a year in a small Norwegian village. At the outbreak of World War I, he volunteers for the Austrian Army, eventually serves in the front lines, is captured by the Italians in 1918, completes the *Tractatus* in a prisoner-of-war camp at Monte Cassino. After considerable wrangling with publishers, the book appears in 1922.

Instead of returning to Cambridge, Wittgenstein enrolled in the Teacher's Training College in Vienna, where he obtained qualifications to teach in elementary schools. During vacations he worked as a gardener's assistant in a monastery. Between 1920 and 1926, he taught in three provincial grade schools: Trattenbach, Puchberg and Otterthal, all in lower Austria. Then, after another spell of Norwegian solitude, he took over the design and construction of a house at Kundmangasse 19, Vienna, originally commissioned by his sister Gretl from the architect Paul Engelmann. After completing the house, he returned to philosophy, and in 1929 returned to Cambridge.

The Wittgensteins were one of the richest families in Austria. Karl, Ludwig's father, had performed Krupp-like miracles in developing Austria's iron and steel industries. Like other industrialists of the period, he lavishly supported culture, acting at various times as patron to Brahms, Mahler, Bruno Walter and many others; he also financed Olbrich's Secession building. He wasn't a parvenu, and declined the Emperor's offer of a title. While instilling the era's liberal values in his nine children by maintaining a perpetual salon at Palais Wittgenstein, he refrained from the arriviste practice of pushing the children into the arts. (They were, without exception, gifted.) In line with more conservative custom, he expected his sons to follow him into business.

The fate of these sons played some role in the mysticism beyond the border of the expressible drawn by the *Tractatus*. Hans, a musical prodigy, killed himself in Havana in 1902. Rudolph committed suicide in 1904. A third brother, Kurt, shot himself in 1918. Hans and Rudolph were known homosexuals, a devastating fate at that time; perhaps relatedly, neither wanted to pursue the manner of life laid down for an important fortune's senior heirs. (Kurt, on the other hand, killed himself to elude capture at the Italian front.)

Ludwig Wittgenstein's life was extraordinarily marked by harsh exposure to death. He prepared to study statistical mechanics with Boltzmann, the disciple of Hertz; before he could do so, Boltzmann killed himself, driven to despair by the violent criticisms of Mach and Ostwald. Summoned to the poet Trakl's bedside in the Krakow Military Hospital, Wittgenstein arrived to discover that Trakl had been dead for three days, suicided on an overdose of cocaine. According to recent biographical accounts, Ludwig was a homosexual with mortifyingly eager sexual appetites who suffered almost crippling guilt whenever he satisfied them. In 1913, in a conversation with Bertrand Russell, he mentioned the possibility of suicide.

The picture of Wittgenstein, tortured genius, familiar from Cambridge lore, is strikingly redolent of Hapsburg-era values and an unusually exacerbated moral sense, revealed in the specific actions of his lifetime. Besides Karl Kraus's epistemological relentlessness, Wittgenstein was strongly influenced by Tolstoy: *What Is Art?*, *Selections from the Gospels* and the twilight stories in which Tolstoy—privately, by then, deranged by celebrity, persecuting his wife, converting his literary estate to the custody of spiritual frauds—publicly exalts the dignity of manual labor and idealizes the "noble peasant." If, in matters of logic, Wittgenstein had Kraus's surgeon's touch, his moral perceptions, as well as a frequently disastrous optimism about other people, came straight from Tolstoy's fantasy of "innate" Christian virtue.

The 1919–28 period has been referred to as Wittgenstein's "worldly period," his "mystery years," his "years of renunciation." These years are indeed mysterious, though not inexplicable, given Wittgenstein's quite sincere belief that doing philosophy was effectively useless. If we assume that his method, like Kraus's, consisted in taking propositions at face value, this period becomes less mysterious. Wittgenstein distinguished metaphysics from philosophy, not to deny the existence of a metaphysical realm, but to exclude this realm from the depredations of discourse. The religiosity of Wittgenstein's actions, unusual in its intensity, doesn't entirely contradict the agnostic character of his philosophical teachings. Real life, active life, was another way of teaching; in this Wittgenstein followed the Gospels and the progressive social ideas of his family and class.

Five years before divesting himself of his fortune in 1919, Wittgenstein anonymously donated part of it to Trakl, Rilke and Loos, via Ludwig Ficker in Innsbruck. He chose Ficker to determine the beneficiaries, because Kraus had praised Ficker's periodical *Der Brenner.* (Without regretting the bequest, Wittgenstein later deemed *Der Brenner* twaddle; as for Loos, Wittgenstein describes himself in 1919 as "horrified and nauseated" by a visit to the architect, whom he judges "infected with the most virulent bogus intellectualism.") While the largesse of 1914 made no appreciable difference to his income and continued the family tradition of art patronage, his more radical decision of 1919 had the upsetting character of a religious event. Wittgenstein was exasperatingly thorough about getting rid of his money, which had multiplied into several millions thanks to wartime investments in US Steel. His anxiety to rid himself of every penny is duly registered in his sister Hermine's memoirs. Hermine also observes where his inspiration came from:

> Anyone who knows the *Brothers Karamasov* by Dostoevski will remember the place where it is said that while the frugal and careful Ivan could no doubt get into a precarious situation some day, his brother Alyusha, who knows nothing about money and has none, would not starve because everyone would gladly share with him and he would accept from them without hesitation. I, who knew all this for a fact, did everything to fulfill Ludwig's wishes down to the smallest detail.

He rid himself of the power of money, and the myriad, irrelevant options it made possible. Without money, he could deal on equal terms with other people, and engage in useful work, or so he thought. With it, he could only play at making a living, or assume the unappealing role of philanthropist. *Vide* Loos, the money was, for him, a surplus of obstructive ornament.

Wittgenstein wrote to Engelmann in September 1919:

> I have taken up a career (I was not pulling your leg). I won't keep you guessing any more, as the matter is now finally settled. I am attending a teacher's training college in order to become a schoolmaster.

Wittgenstein apparently didn't consider himself in temporary exile from his true calling. Even though Russell had told Hermine in 1912, "We expect the next big step in philosophy to be taken by your brother," an entire world war in which Wittgenstein had served very actively, and in which the world of his youth and childhood had been completely vaporized, separated him from Cambridge. Moreover, Russell had completely misunderstood the finished *Tractatus Logico-Philosophicus;* Wittgenstein's disinclination to use Russell's introduction was the main obstacle to getting it published. For another thing, Wittgenstein had written in his own preface: "I am, therefore, of the opinion that the problems (of philosophy) have in essentials been finally solved."

Wittgenstein may have become a schoolmaster for civic reasons. Austria had been devastated by the war, to put it mildly. A progressive plan for economic recovery through educating the peasantry was being implemented by the ascendant Social Democrats. It was hoped that new teaching methods, based on Socratic techniques of reciprocal learning, would replace the Wilhelmine drilling methods that had been the pedagogical norm since 1848. Wittgenstein came from an enlightened class, possessed appropriate talents, wanted to be useful. It would not have been out of character.

W. W. Bartley's remarkable book *Wittgenstein* gives the only detailed account of the period to 1926. Bartley examines significant connections between Wittgenstein's later philosophy and his firsthand discoveries about the learning process. He cites affinities between language-acquisition concepts in *The Blue and Brown Books* and precepts of Gestalt psychology employed by Piaget. Bartley also relates a depressing tale of "noble peasants" obstructing their children's education and ultimately running the schoolmaster out of town. The end of Wittgenstein's career in lower Austria coincided with the provincial resurgence of the Christian Socialist party, which overthrew the school reform movement in stages, as part of the general rehearsal for fascism. Lowering though the story is, Wittgenstein "achieved stunning results in mathematics, teaching 10- and 11-year-old boys advanced algebra and geometry. . . . He also took his students far beyond ordinary elementary-school standards in the study of history, and in literature he and his students read together not only folk and fairy tales, but also the type of poem that they would usually not encounter before the equivalent of the American junior high school."

He built remarkable models of machines, motors and practical equipment. The cat skeleton he used to teach anatomy was still being used, into the 1970s, in the Puchberg village school.

A fascinating work of that time exists in facsimile: *Dictionary for Elementary Schools.* Compiled from word lists his students copied down in uniform notebooks that were then bound and used for reference, Wittgenstein's dictionary eventually was printed and distributed throughout the Austrian school system. Given the avalanche of printed works written by, recorded by students of, and concerning Wittgenstein in the last 20 years, it seems historically impossible that besides the *Tractatus,* the *Dictionary for Elementary Schools* was the only book he published in his lifetime, but it was.

It's hard to decide which of the following two statements, one from an Italian architect, Francesco Amendolagine, the other from an English philosophy instructor, W. W. Bartley III, is the more ridiculous:

A letter written by Wittgenstein in 1925 to the architect Paul Engelmann, before his involvement with the project, stating his interest in the scheme on which Engelmann and his sister Gretl were already working, reveals the importance Wittgenstein himself ascribed to the design in terms of his own "development" and shows how determined he was to undertake the task. In the light of this fundamental historical document, Gretl's statements—regarding her own attempts to get Ludwig involved in the project by arranging that he work as an assistant to Engelmann, as therapy for some imaginary disturbances caused by the war—prove totally meaningless.

If one accepts that the ways in which one styles oneself—the games one plays with one's own name—say a lot about who one is or would like to be, then how revealing it is to find out that Ludwig Wittgenstein characterized himself in the . . . Viennese City Directory, in each edition from 1933 to 1938, as "Dr. Ludwig Wittgenstein, occupation: *architect*. . . ."

Taken together, these two passages indicate a range of incomprehension manifested in specialized professions when a practitioner demonstrates the desire to do more than one thing in life; in their respective contexts, each proceeds from a puerile notion of consistency. Amendolagine is keen to prove that Wittgenstein's architecture provides the missing link between the *Tractatus* and the *Philosophical Investigations.* When he isn't just gassing, he proposes some interesting ideas; by reading Wittgenstein's life as a demonstration of philosophical, rather than psychological, consistency; however, Amendolagine paints the philosopher as a servomechanism without interiority, adaptable to any task.

Here is Wittgenstein's (undated) letter to Engelmann in its entirety:

Dr. Mr. E.,
I shall be very glad to see you at Christmastime in Vienna. I should also be very interested in the building of a house. I shall be in Vienna from 24.12 to 2.1.
Yours, L. Wittgenstein

I also have various personal matters to discuss with you. Whether we shall be able to understand each other this time will become clear soon enough.

Master of aphoristic compression though he was, even prolonged scrutiny of the above fails to reveal "the importance Wittgenstein himself ascribed to the design," or to indicate characteristics of a "fundamental historical document." (It does contain an interesting ambiguity in the indefinite article, but that does nothing for Amendolagine's argument.) What's revealing is Amendolagine's attempt to remove any therapeutic taint from the design process; the idea that Wittgenstein's involvement might have been initiated by other people, rather than impelled by implacable inner processes, strikes him as beneath consideration.

Bartley, on the other hand, shrinks Wittgenstein's architectural career to that of a neurasthenic site-supervisor, seizing fatuously here upon the irony of the designation "architect" as a Freudian wish-fulfillment. According to Bartley, Wittgenstein's spells of asceticism—the retreats to Norway, the flights to the Austrian hills—were the anguished antidote to furtive sexual binges in public parks and the shabbier type of homosexual bars. In this particular projection, which conjures images of Spencer Tracy subsiding back into Dr. Jekyll after an especially ghoulish bacchanal, there is every reason to telescope two years of architectural work into a fast paragraph.

Bartley represents each of Wittgenstein's absences from academic philosophy as a geographic escape from urban academia's sexual temptations. The two years at the Teacher's Training College are depicted as an aching stretch of intense sublimation punctured by several spectacular falls from grace. As it happens, the Teacher's Training College had been located in the same Vienna street as the building site, minutes away from Wittgenstein's old cruising grounds, but since Bartley has nothing fresh in the fellatio department to report (and perhaps no interest in architecture), his history simply flutters a few calendar pages into the Kundmangasse and wings swiftly onward to Cambridge.

The "imaginary disturbances" Amendolagine mentions are a solecism, if he means to say that Wittgenstein imagined them, since Wittgenstein would have had to have been disturbed if he thought he was; if Gretl, on the other hand, is being blamed for imagining disturbances in her brother that did not exist, Amendolagine's phrasing fails to make the accusation clear. It's my own guess that Wittgenstein was extremely disturbed, not only because of the war, but as a result of his disillusioning encounter with the Austrian peasant Volk, the deaths of his favorite uncle Paul, his closest friend David Pinsent in 1918, and the suicide of his brother Kurt in the same year—to say nothing of the total transfiguration of Austrian society after the collapse of the Empire, the steady rise of right-wing fanaticism, and the virulent resurgence of anti-Semitism. (Wittgenstein was three-quarters Jewish.) For concrete evidence, besides Gretl's statements, which Amendolagine disputes, a considerable correspondence with Paul Engelmann survives, of which the 1925 letter above is probably the least revelatory item. There is, too, Hermine's pleasantly written memoir, which touches on Wittgenstein's condition after the war:

> I told him . . . that imagining him as an elementary school teacher it was to me as if someone were to use a precision instrument to open crates. Thereupon Ludwig answered with a comparison which silenced me for he said, "You remind me of someone who is looking through a closed window and cannot explain to himself the strange movements of a passer-by. He doesn't know what kind of storm is raging outside and that this person is perhaps only with great effort keeping himself on his feet." It was then that I understood his state of mind.

Making a building is one of the few efforts that, if completed, results in a self-sufficient act of creation. Buildings are not ephemeral, like ideas, yet they can incarnate ideas—ideas, that's to say, about buildings. The satisfaction of building is, as far as I know, singular, personal and objectively substantive, in the sense that a structure occupying real space exists for others as much as for oneself. It becomes a palpable feature of the world. It can't be stored in a closet, or rolled up and removed to a warehouse, or, except in rare instances—Wittgenstein's house being among these—revised after completion.

It is, moreover, an elitist activity that doesn't require an elite sensibility, simply the will and means to do it. It's not impossible to think of architecture as something carried out in a state of agitation, but unimaginable that a solid building would exhibit qualities of "nervousness," "insecurity," or the ambivalence and ambiguity involved in purely mental operations, or in more malleable forms of art-making.

I imagine an inner tranquility, almost bovine, possessing the Facteur Ferdinand Cheval, completing his daily postal route, then calmly setting to work on the fantastic, vegetal spires of his Palais Idéal, a veritable Pantheon of the irrational. Or the numberless instances of chthonic *Gesamtkunstwerk* issuing from some bromidic mental peace.

In a reverse image, Haus Wittgenstein is a concretization of logical space, the stasis of true materiality imposed on a kind of demonic abandon. For Wittgenstein was obsessed with the house, hypervigilant regarding every detail. One can look everywhere for the slip, the flaw, the sentimental archaism. Nothing of the kind existed in the house Wittgenstein completed, though later, ill-guided efforts to restore some of its ruined features resulted in gross imperfections that are all the more striking in contrast with the intact original parts of the building.

Its modernity is strictly that of its materials. Wittgenstein's house opens no dialogue with other architecture. Wittgenstein lavished an obsessive mathematical precision on the interactive volumes and circulation scheme of the house, attempting nothing less than perfection—and, one should add, nothing more. The building had only to "make sense." If it needed also to be beautiful, the beauty Wittgenstein achieved was entirely resident in its proportions, its logical flows, the appropriateness of every design item—door handles, chandeliers, the access scheme from one area to another. By rigorously avoiding conspicuous idiosyncrasy, Wittgenstein managed to suffuse the entire house with it.

Semper's three requisites of formal beauty—symmetry, proportion and direction—comprise the total contents of the building. Wittgenstein invented his architecture from point zero, limiting its spatial possibilities to the minimal criteria for urban, residential, upper-class housing. The building imposes an austere harmony of materials at every point.

Entering Haus Wittgenstein is like walking into a blueprint. On the ground level, the grid-lines of a stone floor visually intersect the slender glazing and mullions of several glass doors opening on a terrace. Inside, the square pillars of the main entrance hall expose the support structure and form a directional grid. Naked light bulbs set in the ceiling provide even, unemphatic illumination. The effect is one of ample horizontality and tranquilizing balance. But the visual emphasis is on the vertical. The parallel glazing of two-winged double doors and windows—the door type used throughout with few exceptions—produces multiple optic interruptions as doors and windows open and close, kinetically section space as one moves past them, and outline volumes that would otherwise dissolve in flooding natural light.

The elevator shaft is clear glass, providing more linear configurations calculated to the merest shadow. The staircase winds around the elevator shaft;

its outer wall is sliced by a recessed slant-topped window, sectioned vertically to echo the horizontal lines of the stairs. The window dividers cast
thin shadows, forming triangles with the stair edges; the triangles are bisected by the metal frames of the elevator glass. More pedestrian design
problems posed by shelving, closets and other storage space have been
solved with the same didactic linearity, and with such avoidance of miscal-
culation, such fanatical meshing of proportions, that the house gradually
resembles an extravagance beyond Gaudí's wildest hallucinations. An extravagance of negation; an epic of correction.

The design sets its limit at the requisites of form: The house means to accommodate an identifiable manner of life, and, in a fundamental sense, imposes it. As an ensemble of logical relations, a machine of interdigitating
vital parts, it nullifies the possibility of remodeling. Hence what restoration
has been undertaken has served to destroy rather than preserve the thing
Wittgenstein made.

It has no appendix, no vestigial tail. Its tone, its resonance, are pitched to
reciprocal vibrations of its materials: the gray stone floor, the unpainted
stucco walls, the blunt, ingeniously seamless door handles, the compactly
volumed corner radiators. The place obviously wasn't intended for the opu-
lent, prewar belle époque domesticity of rooms stuffed with objets d'art and
hierarchical divisions of intimate from public space, but for a less showy,
less ostentatious affluence. Hermetic in one sense, in another it presumes
easy communication between its inhabitants.

Just as the house exposes its structural mechanics and moving parts as vis-
ible design components, it opens large passages of traditionally sequestered
space to visibility. In addition to fairly aesthetic, or at least unembarrassing,
living habits, the house takes for granted a prodigious capacity for silence,
for thinking. It promotes this in a number of ways—for example, by making
hallways and routes through connecting rooms into nonlinking circuits.

The height of the door handles and slightly resistive weight of the tall
metal doors that divide the salon from the entrance hall produce a just-
perceptible fortress feeling that Wittgenstein repeats elsewhere, notably in
the clifflike height of the basement pantry windows and the mechanical
opening-rods he devised for them. (The pantry contains a dumbwaiter,
contrived somewhat like a miniature of the elevator.) In a more conventional way, three unconnected terraces accessible through window-level

glass doors on the third floor act as inducements to solitude. The prescriptive aspect of Haus Wittgenstein, its gentle, firm little shoves toward meditation, is an emanation of its total ordering of space.

The house is basically a cube with projecting volumes that it exceeds in height. Within the cube, each floor radiates from a set point of symmetry (the elevator shaft and staircase) into horizontally arranged blocks (rooms) of varying size grouped in different configurations on either side of a divider-space (the hall), whose size and placement is different on each floor. As one ascends from floor to floor (there are three stories, not including the basement), the preceding pattern of intercommunicating blocks almost immediately disintegrates. Places accessible from the hall on one floor may now be reached only through an entirely different network of rooms.

Distances between rooms and patterns of movement on the ground floor reinforce the house-as-game idea. To reach the breakfast room, isolated like a sentry box above and adjacent to the vestibule, one must do an about-face, reversing the path from entrance and vestibule. Functional distances are impracticably vast, the kind of passages usually routed through walled corridors and back staircases. Spaces here, for all their circuitous baffling, are transparent, passageways simply defined by glass doors.

Privacy is sometimes emphasized with translucent glass on inner doors: Wittgenstein's concept of privacy, however, transcended the visual. The house contracts and compresses distance through its ever-present dichotomy of transparency and solidity. Everything you can see through is also weighty. The clarity of space invites rapid passage through it, but its organization requires a measured, methodical pace. The doors and windows are Viennese double doors and windows—the wings must be closed synchronously in order to join. All that's offered by that inviting openness is a different species of difficulty.

The site itself guarantees privacy, since it is raised considerably above street level on the grounds of a large, walled garden. Just inside the grounds at street level, contiguous with the street wall, we find a guard house at the public entrance and, near the service entrance, a gardener's quarters. The total surrounding structure serves all the barrier requirements that Loos typically incorporated in his shell designs since so many Loos buildings are flush with the street. While there were several tall apartment buildings near the site, the house was surrounded by trees at the time of construction. All the trees were cut down in 1971 and the relative privacy of the site has been further diminished by closer construction.

One doesn't feel here the tacky awe of Versailles or the bloblike excess of Le Corbusier's Notre-Dame-du-Haut. Nor does the building's unadorned frankness inspire, as Gropius buildings often do, the vain wish that one *could* like it. As with Loos, Wittgenstein's architecture is not just rigorously logical—a raison d'être operating by itself that produces repulsively inhuman environments—but logically transparent. As Loos untiringly demonstrated, a thing that makes sense to the person who uses it will be enjoyably used, however new the form. For Wittgenstein's clients—Margarethe Stonborough-Wittgenstein and her family—the house as executed made perfect sense. From sketches Hermine drew in the '30s, we see how sparingly furniture and paintings were disposed in the uncarpeted rooms. The arrangement, as well as the style of objets d'art, reflect a classical, ascetic sensibility: the ideal tenant.

Haus Wittgenstein is not modest; it is discreet. Its extravagance is conceptual, subtle and elitist in the canniest possible sense. To insensitive eyes, it is an unassertive, anonymously "modern building" on the outside, while on the inside its radical difference from vernacular architecture of its period is only evident in details that elude categorization. That each lock, door handle and window frame was specially fabricated according to Wittgenstein's specifications, and is totally unique, takes a long, considered look. Perfection in architecture is always invisible. We certainly can't see that Wittgenstein raised the salon ceiling an inch and a half after finishing the interior, just when his sister was preparing to move in. We might have sensed something off if he hadn't.

Francesco Amendolagine observes that to credit Wittgenstein's design method to the influence of Loos is to misconstrue it completely. Loos's architecture posits a polemical reproach to other architecture. Loos attacked problems dialectically, in relation to an existing canon of solutions. For Wittgenstein, these problems simply didn't arise. Yet it isn't surprising that the two men's diametrically opposed notions often lead to the same place. In overall form, for instance, Haus Wittgenstein strikingly recalls Loos's Scheu House of 1912, while Wittgenstein's famous door handles resemble those of Loos's 1906 Villa Karma near Vevey, Switzerland—a building Wittgenstein most likely never saw. (It seems to me quite possible that Wittgenstein's writings influenced Loos, rather than vice versa.)

Wittgenstein treated architecture as a tabula rasa—just as he treated philosophy. The intersection of Wittgenstein's basically ahistorical style of epistemological inquiry with the penultimate questions Russell and G. E. Moore distilled from the entire congested maze of Western thought since Aristotle is one of the leveling ironies the Age of Einstein has perpetrated in virtually every discipline.

The fact that Wittgenstein designed and built a house has always registered with his Cambridge followers as deeply peculiar, as if defections from academia and secularized production were not strategies shared by important thinkers of the last 200 years. Well before Hegel, philosophers foresaw the shrinkage of formal philosophy from cultural envelope to university cubbyhole. The Encyclopdistes carried out philosophy by other means—e.g., the novel—while post-Hegelians alternated the production of thick *Bildungsphilosophie* with more accessible short books. Lichtenberg anticipated the aphoristic tendency continued by Nietzsche and Kierkegaard. In our era, prescriptive philosophy has mainly taken aphoristic or essay form, traveling as cultural criticism and aesthetic research: Benjamin, Adorno, Habermas, the Enzensbergers, Barthes, Kluge, Canetti, Horkheimer, Arendt and Bachelard all can be considered philosophers, though Arendt, particularly, resisted the title.

Architecture, of course, remains an anomalous item among the "worldly" productions attached to the names cited above. But the *un*worldly character often ascribed to Wittgenstein by his followers (in light of which the house becomes an extraneous sacred relic, a stucco grail) mystifies his actual connectedness to the secularizing trend of recent philosophy, and obscures his real usefulness as an exemplary figure.

Vitruvius, the earliest authority on architecture whose writings have survived, gives us the definitive job description and qualifications:

As for philosophy, it makes an architect high-minded . . . furthermore philosophy treats of physics where a most careful knowledge is required. . . . Music, also, the architect should understand so that he may have knowledge of the canonical and mathematical theory. . . . Let him be educated, skilful with the pencil, instructed in geometry, know much history . . . and be acquainted with astronomy and the theory of the heavens.

Besides the above, Wittgenstein had practical training. He built not one house, but two. In 1921, he designed a two-story chalet, which he constructed with his friend Arvid Sjogren. It overlooks a fiord near the village of Sjkolden in Norway, monastically isolated at a cliff summit. It consists of a trapezoidal base structure topped by a triangular balconied cap. Obviously less ambitious than Haus Wittgenstein, this is, however, a house, not a "hut," as it's often been described. It belongs to a family of objects that includes Haus Wittgenstein, conceptually integral in its strict matching of form to function. Within this family, there is a curious theme of doubling: under "house," the Vienna mansion and the Norway cabin; under "book" the *Tractatus* and the *Dictionary for Elementary Schools.* The large elevator, the little dumbwaiter. Then we have "atomic propositions": the cat skeleton, the lost maquettes of machinery, the classical bust Wittgenstein sculpted in the '20s. Then there is Wittgenstein's own judgment on Haus Wittgenstein: ". . . the house I built for Gretl is the product of a decidedly sensitive ear and *good* manners, an expression of great *understanding* (of a culture, etc.). But *primordial* life, wild life striving to erupt into the open—that is lacking. And so you could say it isn't *healthy.*" And then there is silence.

IV

There are ideas and events which win instantaneous and universal recognition for their social value and broad international dimensions. They embody definite spiritual needs, fascinate and sweep over more and more people, become a powerful impetus to progress and creative work. Such events have marked the present of socialist Bulgaria since April, 1956.

—FROM *BANNER OF PEACE*, No. 13, 15–23 AUGUST 1983.
DISTRIBUTED AT THE BULGARIAN EMBASSY IN VIENNA,
FORMERLY THE HOME OF MARGARETHE STONBOROUGH-WITTGENSTEIN

As the above extract of committee-speak has it, there are indeed ideas and events that sweep over more and more people—rolling over the ones who resist sweeping—claiming hearts and minds so decisively that often nothing except smoking debris is left in their wake. Such ideas and events went vacuuming through Austria after the Dollfus assassination in 1936, embodying spiritual needs that were all too definite and, sure enough, rapidly acquired broad international dimensions. But the ubiquity of such winning ideas and events in today's world should not blind us to the significance of much smaller ideas that churn through little individual brains and expel themselves as little actions: These too can betray the character of a whole era. I have described the house as it was, not as we find it.

The house became a Red Cross hospital during the Second World War. It was used to quarter Russian troops and their horses in 1945, and, later, a demobilization center. Mrs. Stonborough reoccupied the house in 1947, and lived there until her death in 1958. In 1971, Dr. Thomas Stonborough, the heir, arranged to sell the property to a developer; demolition was already scheduled when the architect Bernhard Leitner, arriving in Vienna at the eleventh hour, marshaled opposition in the press and mobilized an international effort by artists, philosophers and architects to save the building. Stonborough, embarrassed by the publicity, embarrassed himself further by claiming that Engelmann had been the sole architect; the city government supported this view until the air of scandal became uncomfortably thick. Finally, the Vienna Landmark Commission declared the house a national monument—without, however, purchasing the property. When the hue and cry subsided, the commission allowed the sale of the place to Bulgaria.

It is important to counteract the spontaneous generation of clichés concerning the former world menace whose outposts, ranging in size from a substantial former colonial holding to a tiny Caribbean terror island, were held equally culpable in exporting "terror" into the nervous systems of declining megastates and their senile rulers. Austria is not a wealthy nation, but Bulgaria is a much poorer one. Wittgenstein was not Bulgaria's son, but Austria's. Thomas Bernhard, who is widely considered the greatest Austrian writer of our age, has used Haus Wittgenstein as the inspiration for his novel *Correction,* and provides a context for Austria's sale of national landmarks to its ideological adversaries:

> Because he realized that while on the one hand he loved Austria as the land of his origin, he also hated it because it had rudely affronted him all his life long, it had always repulsed him when he needed it, it had never let a man like Roithamer come close, basically men, people, characters like Roithamer have no business in a country like his homeland and mine, where they have

no chance of developing and are continually aware of their inability to develop, such a country needs people who are not angered to the point of rebellion against the insolence of such a country, against the irresponsibility of such a country and such a state, such a totally decrepit, public menace of a state, as Roithamer said again and again . . . this state has countless men like Roithamer on its conscience, it has a most sordid and shabby history on its conscience . . .

To invert one of Ingmar Bergman's profundities, one can deduce the imperial shell from the nascent reptile client state.

The house *as it is,* or rather, as it was when this essay was first written: In the vestibule one comes across an ugly metal rack offering assorted booklets and magazines of an inspirational nature, among them such treasures as the "Constitution of the Socialist Republic of Bulgaria" and the uplifting weekly, *Banner of Peace.* The breakfast room serves as a dismal reception area.

Throughout the house, proportions have been wrecked by the removal of room dividers, creating L-shaped spaces where none had existed. The division between salon and dining room has been removed. The area has been converted into an exhibition gallery for joyful Bulgarian folk art revealing the infinite versatility of batik. The walls, which Wittgenstein had left their natural color or else painted a pale yellowish beige, have been uniformly assaulted in strident appliance-white. They are, without exception, filthy. Where chipping hasn't left blotched indentations on the surface, streaks of dirt smudge the walls all over the house, at a bewildering variety of angles and elevations. Wittgenstein's chastely naked light bulbs have gone the way of the Bulgarian Royal Family, replaced by fat pendant globes of white plastic that shoot their 40 watts wherever with Halloween abandon.

The first floor bathroom greets the visitor with a Gothic display of light blue stalactites of peeling paint, dangling from ceiling, pipes and wall corners. Wadded rags litter the window ledge and sprout from out-of-the-way places. The windows themselves sport sinuous cracks. The second-floor bathroom offers the same spectacle, but there whole window fragments have been smashed out. The damage is hardly recent, judging from the grimy layers of paint dust and caked soil. Every underutilized area looks totally shabby, but even what *is* used is either smeared with effluvia, "improved" in some obnoxious manner, or damaged.

The residential suites are inaccessible—during our visit a cleaning woman, exactly resembling the garrulous domestic gargoyle in *The Bride of Frankenstein* who grumbles about "that strange Dr. Pretorius" and later incites the villagers to kill the monster, observed our every move through those handy arrangements of glass, breaking into a vowelless Bukovinian shriek whenever we approached forbidden turf. However, one unauthorized peek into the third-floor domicile disclosed a sort of Balkanized Playboy-mansion motif, replete with gaudy shag carpets, satin eiderdown on the orgy-sized bed, and an imitation zebra rug on the wall above. The connecting bathroom contains new, mass-produced fittings.

Examples of a touted "restoration" occurring twenty-some years ago offend at every turn. Much of the internal logic of the house has simply been destroyed. Built-in closets have been ripped out, walls removed, a fireplace has simply disappeared. The beauty of the door handles doesn't simply inhere in their form, but in the ingenious design that allows one bar to slip into the hollow sheathing of another bar on the other side, so that both are fastened by a single mechanism inside the door. This gives a striking elegance to the juncture of door and handle. Where restoration has occurred, one now finds washerlike metal plates screwed into the door frame, effectively ruining the design. Furthermore, the wrong door handles have been fitted to the wrong doors: The shorter ones that go with the smaller second-floor doors were cast from the original mold and bolted into the large doors on the first floor. Similar destruction of the house's subtlety proceeds wherever individually fabricated elements need replacement (if they're replaced at all).

The glass door of the dumbwaiter and part of its shaft are broken, but the real atrocities on the basement level lie beyond the pantry. On this, the floor least visited by architectural tours and Wittgenstein historians, the Ministry of Decor has fully unleashed its imagination, creating a wholesale destruction of original design—most of this basement never existed until the mid-'70s, when an Austrian architect, Karl Auboeck, working with a Bulgarian designer, took it upon himself to enlarge the basement. (To the credit of the embassy staff members, they all seemed embarrassed about it.) A cocktail area boasting that type of squat wooden-frame chair that once graced the domestic flights lounge of Chicago's O'Hare Airport, ranged about a Scandinavian hibachi affair (the grill stuffed with cigarette butts), is a premonition of things to come. Frescoed into the glazed wall opposite this boar-roasting facility, a helmeted Bulgar charioteer drives a team of heroic steeds, presumably away from another cocktail lounge, this one fabricated from smoky wood and stained glass designs inspired by the glorious history of Bulgarian tablecloth patterns. The chariot ensemble has the high color of DC Comics, whereas the Spanish hacienda scheme of the barroom beyond it conveys that tastefully muted brown-and-burnished-gold feeling endemic to East Side singles bars between 60th Street and Yorkville. Arches and elliptical openings heighten the peek-a-boo atmosphere of this naughty Marxist-Leninist Hernando's Hideaway—functionally a pit-stop en route to the very Temple of Culture.

Yes, the concert hall. What embassy can do without one? This one jazzes up your basic slope design with sound-absorbent carpeting and a veritable forest of blond wood paneling, Style 1955 Parochial School System of Industrial Suburb. Czarist-cum-Minsky's red theater curtains and the introduction of a numbing, chalky gray wherever possible, more as a suffusion or a way of life than as a color, further enhances the noneffect. Bathing it all, or rather draining all of it, is the Soviet International Style rectangle of tubular fluorescent lights embedded across the ceiling and diapered (no other word comes to mind) with flimsy-looking grids of pale plastic, rather like ice-cube tray dividers that have mutated to giant size, perhaps after passing through some lethal phlogiston escaping from the furniture.

The first-floor living room functions today as a conference room. A long black oblong extracted from precious Formica waits silently within a girdle of matching office chairs for an inevitable round ashtray of ruby glass. Spiderishly facing the table from far across the room, flanked by shelves of hallucinatory legal codes and hideous abstract paintings, the desk of highest authority stands, its chair poised at an easy viewing angle to an enormous color television set. On the desktop, gazing imperturbably at the gradual, certain death overtaking "an unexampled piece of architecture in the twentieth century," is a bronze cast of the terra-cotta head Wittgenstein made in Michael Drobil's studio, his only work of sculpture. Its calm form rests like a bowling trophy, next to the ambassador's DVD player.

In fairness to Bulgaria, had the country not stepped in and attempted, however ineptly, to salvage at least the house itself and some of its unique internal structures, Austria, which had no use for Freud, Bernhard, Kraus or any of its men and women of genius, would have blithely razed the place to the ground. As has often been remarked, Austria—never de-Nazified, a country still scandalized by public mention of its own sordid history, where Kurt Waldheim got elected president and the squalid little corporal from Linz was rapturously welcomed on the Heldenplatz on the night of the Anschluss—was never a home for genius, but remains the same Kakania, minus the empire, that it always was, a nation of pastry chefs and peasant cunning, so intrinsically awful that the Russians actually returned it, still in its wrapping paper, after it was handed to them at Yalta.

MAJOR MOTIFS

madness

    suicide
    attempted suicide
    cripples
    wheelchairs
    crutches
    malicious gossip of cunning peasants
    National Socialist mentality of ruling classes
    mental and moral ruin produced by Catholic Church
    National Socialist mentality of lower classes
    greed and philistinism of bourgeoisie
    stepsibling incest
    Ludwig Wittgenstein
    hypocrisy of Catholic Church
    Glenn Gould
    hateful pathology of families
    Arthur Schopenhauer
    malevolent soul-destroying State
    the Impossible

ALONG WITH all that: internal contradictions, meaningless or arbitrary; in-consistently stated opinions (a character *highly esteems* Robert Musil at one moment and in another dismisses Musil as "a bureaucratic writer"; the characteristic Thomas Bernhard narrator *reveres* Bach, a few pages later *despises* Bach, finds *even Bach* lacking in the highest sort of artistic qualities).

The distancing strategies of a Bernhard novel, which place the narrator at several more or less honorary removes from the "character" at its center, like Joseph Conrad at his most structurally convoluted (the Conrad of *Chance,* say), leave an open question as to whether this or that protagonist (and what a ridiculous term, *protagonist,* for a Bernhard character) in a work by Thomas Bernhard accurately speaks for Thomas Bernhard, in the matter of his enthusiasms, his phobias, his imperious aesthetic hierarchies; it would not be unnatural, after reading five or six Bernhard novels or plays, to say, or to think, anyway, *What do I care what this beetling twit thinks about anything, this absurdly superior nit-picking nattering shit—*

It wouldn't occur to me, unless he'd quoted someone saying it about him, to throw in the term *nest-fouler,* but that too: this *infuriating nest-fouler,* as Bernhard considered it his business to irritate people, to stir up trouble, to foul the Austrian nest. And besides an obvious talent for doing this, he exhibited a self-congratulatory confidence that he really did foul the nest, that the people he wanted to offend were truly offended.

This procedure, like any tic evidenced through several dozen artistic works, over a long career, can be wearying and irritating in ways that the author didn't quite intend; it's hard to read the description (in *Wittgenstein's Nephew*) of a state minister's outrage at Bernhard's acceptance speech for the Austrian State Prize for Literature except as an almost fatuous demonstration that the author is *truly, significantly irritating.* ("After I had delivered my speech . . . the minister, who had understood nothing of what I had said, indignantly jumped up from his seat and shook his fist in my face. Snorting with rage, he called me a *cur* in front of the whole assembly and then left the chamber, slamming the glass door behind him with such force that it shattered into a thousand fragments.") In this regard, if getting a prize is the same thing as getting pissed on, as Bernhard says in almost the same breath, why list these prizes on all his book jackets?

This belongs among the contradictions Bernhard reveals as hapless inevitabilities, as aspects of the poisonous, irremediable human condition, the perpetual *love-hate* collaboration with the very things that stifle and frustrate creative effort, that ruin our development, that destroy the possibilities of human existence, that bedevil and devour us over time—the corrosive and inextricable bonds between ourselves and our families, for example, but also between ourselves and those we've fallen in with over the course of a lifetime, wittingly and unwittingly: This is the awful glue between Bernhard and the dreadful Auersberger couple in *Woodcutters,* between Rudolf and his sister in *Concrete,* and most morbidly and funnily between Konrad and his wife (who are, typically, said to be half-brother and -sister) in *The Lime Works.* We desperately need the people we love and hate, and who love and hate and need us, because our lives, which are nothing in the end, are inscribed in their lives, which are also nothing.

Bernhard insisted in his writing (and, as far as it goes, in his acceptance speech for the Austrian State Prize for Literature) that our existence is meaningless, that there is no God, no afterlife, and that *when we think about death everything becomes ridiculous*—but this wasn't the reason his books and plays were continually attacked in Austria. The truth that we spend all our lives denying the certain knowledge of our own extinction is a commonplace of postwar theater and literature, an uncomfortable but by no means unassimilable "theme" for consumers of Beckett or Ionesco. Like any other metaphysical truth, this one can be swallowed whole by the culture industry without leaving the slightest impression on the consumer. The bourgeois learns that he is alone in the universe with the same bovine complacency that he learns that he is speaking prose.

Bernhard, however, added to the immutable existential truth found in Beckett the specific ugly truth about Austria—its Catholic–National Socialist condition, its unregenerate, corrupt continuity with its National Socialist past—and because of this, campaigns were whipped up against him in the Austrian press. His final play, *Heldenplatz,* which conjures ghosts of Austrians hysterically welcoming Hitler into Heroes' Square on the night of the *Anschluss,* was denounced by the Austrian president, the former Nazi Kurt Waldheim, even before it opened in 1988, mere months before Bernhard's death. Waldheim denouncing *Heldenplatz* is almost too good to be true, one of many bizarre episodes in Bernhard's career that convince us that his work is inevitable and necessary. It is not only an effort of execration and exposure of contemporary hypocrisy and madness but an obstinate reminder of Austria's disgraceful role in Hitler's Reich and the country's unregenerate anti-Semitism.

The memorial aspect of Bernhard's work organizes his language around a never-closing wound. His world is a dead world, a world in the process of total demolition, where the past can never be overcome or recovered from.

Bernhard's Austria is an older and even more crumbling version of Musil's Kakania, or Shitland: Shitland plus Auschwitz and defeat.

Bernhard's parti pris is for warmer climes in every sense, for Portugal and Mallorca, Rome, even London, even *emotionally* warmer countries like Poland, anywhere but this cold, heart-dead Austria. Yet Bernhard never went into exile, never left for good like Ingeborg Bachmann; instead he shuttled back and forth between Vienna and the farming regions around Salzburg, "where Catholicism waves its brainless sceptre." Since Austria is dead, Bernhard perhaps reasoned, it's also powerless, defunct, and metaphorical, a country of dead souls that encompasses the whole world.

The spiritual, emotional, and intellectual blockage experienced by Bernhard's characters is a universal condition, regardless of Bernhard's Austrocentricity, the heavy local flavoring of moribund Austria and the many bleak Austrian histories that feed into his novels and plays—the history of Ludwig Wittgenstein, for example, of Wittgenstein's vast fortune and renunciation of that vast fortune, and of the house the philosopher built for his sister, an obsessively redesigned house that the state never bothered to preserve but instead sold to Bulgaria; or the history of Karl Kraus and his news magazine *Die Fackel,* that is to say, Karl Kraus the *gadfly,* also denounced in his time as a *nest-fouler;* one could also cite Odon von Horvath, Robert Musil, Stefan Zweig, and Arthur Schnitzler as precursors in a long tradition of denouncing Austrian hypocrisy and Austrian state-worship and Austrian brainlessness.

Bernhard goes much farther than earlier writers in his *manner* of excoriating what he perceives as false and hypocritical. Despite the fastidious tenor of his language and its lack of obscenity or even ordinary vulgarities, its galloping syntax and obsessive *fixes* place it with that of modernist fulminators such as Céline, who breach any sort of narrative convention to directly address the reader and to attack, with hysterical energy, a vast jumble of unrelated irritants. Bernhard's favorite effect is one of sublime overkill, as in his comparison of Jesus Christ with Adolf Hitler in the second volume of his autobiography, *Gathering Evidence,* and his exhaustive, exhausting demolition of "that philosophical ruminant" Martin Heidegger in *Old Masters:* These ludic passages are not asides, but the virtual content of Bernhard's books, which don't really tell stories that are possible to digress from. Someone starts telling someone about someone else, recounting the minutiae of the third party's daily habits and thought processes, and by the end of the book that someone else is dead, usually by suicide—there you have virtually all Bernhard's "plots"; he takes absolutely no trouble to invest these saturnine histories with anything like suspense or narrative tension, relying entirely on a protracted and intricately tangential verbal process to hold the reader's interest.

The central tragedy in Bernhard's work is the way the time of our lives gets wasted—by ourselves, through relentless, compulsive ambivalence and, in the Sartrean sense, sheer *force of habit;* by other people we really shouldn't know; by a pathological inability to start or complete the only actions that could "save" us; in a larger, more annihilating sense, by a civilization rotten beyond redemption that dooms any effort to escape our impasse—and the intolerable reality that everything comes to nothing in the end, that time erases us and everything we do. The fact of time passing is itself a source of horror, or blackest comedy, in Bernhard's works: When Bernhard encounters the Auersbergers in *Woodcutters,* it's the 20 years that have passed since he last saw them that suffuse the novel with anguishing heaviness and grotesque absurdity; the information that Konrad in *The Lime Works* and Rudolf in *Concrete* have had writer's block *for decades,* or that Reger in *Old Masters* has sat for hours before a museum's Tintoretto, every other day, *for over 30 years,* works on us in true Gothic fashion. Our idiotic loyalty to the very things that have driven us crazy, that have poisoned our lives and made them impossible, lays all our possibilities to ruin. Decades pass, and life's pleasures are instantly forgotten, while its every insult clings to us forever. The darkest secret Bernhard spills is how indifferent we become to our own lives over time and how carelessly we chew up the hours between birth and death.

CURZIO MALAPARTE

IN OCTOBER 1980, the Czech astronomer Z. Vávrová of the Klet' Observatory at Ceske Budejovice discovered planet number 03479, a celestial body the size of a large asteroid, in the nether reaches of the cosmos. The astronomer named it after his favorite writer, Curzio Malaparte. A literary homage drifting in outer space would have appealed to a writer who inhabited an unclassifiable planet of his own, a writer known for ingenious deceptions, morbid hilarity and what one might call heartfelt insincerity.

However engaged he became in the splendors and miseries of the sad century he lived in, Malaparte carried himself with an air of antic dignity, a saturnine detachment redolent of a cosmic private joke. He embraced ideas with the grip of an octopus and abandoned them as casually as Kleenex.

In the many photographs we have of him—reviewing troops in Ethiopia, strutting in jodhpurs at the Russian front, fencing with the Futurist Mario Carli—Malaparte's expressions suggest perplexity and seriousness. His face resents the camera, as if it were interrupting matters of vast importance. He bears a marked resemblance to the German actor Kurt Raab. These fierce looks belie a personality reputed to be oversize, gregarious, playfully argumentative, a bit catlike. His books reflect an addiction to name-dropping. He had the habit, common among the well-to-do, of relating intricately detailed, nauseating anecdotes while others were eating dinner.

Screen-star handsome, sardonic, disarmingly droll enough to charm the feathers off a peacock—Malaparte had the lethal fascination of a cobra. His impeccable manners and easy grace marked him as a born aristocrat, which he wasn't.

Curzio Malaparte was born Kurt Erich Suckert in Prato in 1898. His German Protestant father manufactured textiles. His Catholic mother was a great Milanese beauty. His mixed parentage, he claimed, made him feel less than completely Italian; in compensation, a proprietary chauvinism rarely found in the writing of his contemporaries runs through Malaparte's books.

His most relaxed and amiable book, *Those Cursed Tuscans* (1956), is a mischievously needling celebration of the Etruscans and their descendants. Those who have spent time in Prato will recognize the veracity of some of Malaparte's most hyperbolic arias:

> And there is nothing—absolutely nothing—which the people of Prato cannot turn into a profit, beginning with the rags that arrive at Prato from every part of the world. They come from Asia, Africa, both the Americas, Australia: and the filthier, viler, sleazier and more flea-ridden these rags are, the more precious they seem in the eyes of a people that has learned how to enrich itself out of the refuse of the whole earth.

At fourteen, he began writing poetry. His early verse celebrated, among other things, the Italian annexation of Libya.

Two years later, he joined the Italian Alpine regiment, fighting the Germans in France, an experience recounted decades later in *Il sole è cieco* (1947), a deflationary corrective to Ernst Jünger's *Storm of Steel* (1920) and Henri Barbusse's *Under Fire* (1917). Missing from Jünger's and Barbusse's novels (ideologically opposite, equally "committed" in obtrusive ways) is what Malaparte finds obvious: the fantastic unnaturalness of war, its existential incredibility.

He served the full four years, a cadre of the Fasci d'Azione. His lungs were damaged in a chemical-weapon attack in the battle of Bligny.

Malaparte acted as press coordinator at the Versailles Conference, which had to have sharpened his sense of absurdity (cf. John Maynard Keynes, *The Economic Consequences of the Peace* [1920]). He then served as attaché to the Italian ambassador to Poland. He filed daily reportage to *L'Idea Nazionale* and *Il Giornale*. In 1922, he began contributing to Fascist publications. Patriots of a certain vintage welcomed his first book, *La rivolta dei santi maledetti,* by smashing hundreds of bookshop windows, because Malaparte defended the 350,000 Italian troops who deserted from the battle of Caporetto after a mustard gas bombing.

In 1924, he launched a Fascist weekly, *La conquista dello Stato*. The Fascist cause had begun to splinter, partly in reaction to the murder of Socialist deputy Giacomo Matteotti, presumably the work of Mussolini's *squadristi*.

In January 1925, Mussolini preempted investigation of the Matteotti affair by assembling the Chamber of Deputies and declaring a dictatorship. Just after that, Kurt Erich Suckert adopted the name Curzio Malaparte—bad part," as if proclaiming his role as an irritant to the state.

Malaparte's reputation has been colored by a false impression of his involvement with the Fascist power. In fact, his relations with it were largely adversarial. For a time, Malaparte played at being a theorist of Fascism; he participated, somewhat comically, in the polemical warfare between *strapaese* (Fascists advocating a return to bucolic life and traditional values) and *stracittà* (those favoring Mussolini's state-shaping schemes by means of technology and urbanization). Consistently inconsistent, Malaparte wrote articles for the *strapaese* journal *Il Selvaggio* arguing one side of the question, while simultaneously launching *900,* a journal supporting the *stracittà.*

He had access to the powerful, including Mussolini, but that wasn't unusual in a society where artists and writers enjoyed at least as much status as politicians, if not actual power. Mussolini distrusted him. Malaparte reciprocated. He thought Fascism could get along without a dictator. Later, he concluded that Italy could get along without Fascism.

Despite many editorships and publishing boards he circulated through in the '20s and '30s, Malaparte played no significant part in Mussolini's regime, and had negligible influence on Fascism's theoretical permutations.

Malaparte retained a pragmatic, honorary allegiance to Fascism, as many Italian writers did. Some simply avoided overt political statements in their work. Malaparte's case is more complicated. His egotism repeatedly drew him back into one kind of complicity or another. Yet his compulsive candor invariably landed him in trouble. He repeatedly failed to compromise himself, especially when he tried to.

He withdrew from politics for several years. He managed a publishing house and edited a daily Neapolitan newspaper. He published books of poetry. He assumed directorship of *La Stampa* in Turin, owned by the proto-Taylorist

Fiat manufacturer Giovanni Agnelli. He traveled in the USSR and Eastern Europe, and wrote two books about Lenin.

In 1932, Malaparte published *Coup d'État: The Technique of Revolution.* In *Coup d'État,* he views the state as an industrial machine that any determined individual or faction could operate, a gear works lubricated by human labor. Malaparte speculates that a figure like Max Bauer, a key strategist behind the Kapp Putsch in Germany in 1920, might have derailed Louis Bonaparte's coup d'état on 18 Brumaire; he dissects Trotsky's mistakes in his struggles with Stalin.

Coup d'État's neutral exegesis is a model of clarity, but its chapter on Mussolini, withering and flattering by turns, enraged Il Duce. Malaparte sensed the wisdom of an extended trip to Paris. His Parisian journals record his estrangement from a country where, as an Italian, he was often suspected of being a spy. (*Diario di uno straniero a Parigi* remained unpublished until 1966.)

A still-obscure contretemps between Malaparte and Italo Balbo resulted in the former being convicted on charges of slander and defamation and exiled to the island of Lipari, off the coast of Sicily. Balbo, Italy's hero of long-distance aviation, moonlighted as a *squadristi* assassin. He had the dash of Lindbergh, and, also like Lindbergh, the morals of a flea. Mussolini appointed Balbo air minister but later hustled him out of the country by making him governor of Libya, after discovering the vast extent of his financial chicanery.

A popular story claims that the real reason Malaparte was banished to Lipari was for criticizing Mussolini's neckties; if such stories concerned irrefutably stable personalities, they would sound insane. But dictators generally follow the advice William S. Burroughs has one judge offer another: "If you can't be just, be arbitrary."

Malaparte spent a year on Lipari. In *The Skin* (1949), he fumes about his sufferings in exile, defending himself against the ridicule of some young Communists. Alberto Moravia's autobiography, however, discloses that "the arrest was a joke. . . . Malaparte saw his friends, his women, strolled along the beach in a bathing suit, holding his Lipari greyhound on a leash."

Galeazzo Ciano, Mussolini's son-in-law, facilitated his friend Malaparte's transfer to Ischia; Malaparte considered buying a house there before his sentence was commuted to house arrest at Forte dei Marmi in Tuscany—a location too enviably splendid to be considered exile.

Released from custody in 1935, Malaparte founded *Prospettive,* a monthly journal, two years later. The first phase of its publication championed Mussolini's regime; Malaparte needed to get back into the public eye. In this instance, playing the strumpet had salubrious results.

Prospettive restored Malaparte's visibility and useful contacts within the regime. Rehabilitation enabled him to transform *Prospettive* into an important outlet for the most progressive and experimental modernist literature.

The revamped *Prospettive* ranged across international boundaries. It published works by Claudel, Apollinaire, Picasso, Beckett, Giraudoux, Breton, Éluard, Montale, Lorca, Rilke, Sartre, Heidegger, Morante, Landolfi, Joyce, Hesse, Eliot, Pavese, and Moravia. It featured essays on Lawrence, Gide, Freud, Kafka, Cézanne, Lautréamont, Rimbaud, and other, emphatically "European" voices.

In the late '30s, Malaparte acquired property on Capri, intending to build a house. The writer redesigned every detail of his planned villa after disputes with the architect, Adalberto Libera, ended in an impasse. With the contractor Adolfo Amitrano and Amitrano's two sons, Malaparte built the place himself.

In *The Skin,* Malaparte relates that when German Field Marshal Erwin Rommel visited him on Capri, the Desert Fox asked if the writer had designed the house. "No," Malaparte replied. "I created the scenery." Malaparte had likely rehearsed this response to a yearned-for query for years in his bathroom mirror; it was too good a line to throw away, so he simply invented a visit from Rommel that never occurred.

Casa Malaparte bears a glancing resemblance to certain naval vessels used in the American Civil War: a long, slightly out-sloping rectangle, slanted on the landward end, where a trapezoidal stairway widens as it rises from the ground, ending level with a flat roof, where a C-shaped *brise-soleil* is the only interruption of the sea view.

The building sits on a plateau, flanked by wind-rustled boas of pine boughs and branches of holm oak overhanging the cliffsides of Capo Massullo. The site is the least hospitable outcrop of tufa on Capri, in spitting distance of Tiberius's grotto where, centuries ago, prepubescent "little fishes" nibbled at the emperor's genitals.

Malaparte referred to this domicile as *casa come me,* "come me" being a favored appellation for things he greatly liked. Another example doubles as a caution against unskeptical readings of Malaparte's fiction: Febo, a dog he rescued on Lipari, inspired a tender prose poem, "cane come me." In *The Skin,* Malaparte tells how, after years of tender devotion, Febo disappeared. The writer, frantic, searched everywhere on the island for the dog. He finally learned that Febo had been snatched by thieves who sold animals to a local vivisectionist. Malaparte raced to the laboratory, only to find his half-eviscerated pet in the wrenching throes of its last minutes.

The scene breaks any reader's heart. It broke mine, until I chanced upon a letter Malaparte's brother wrote, noting Febo's old age.

You know the house, from Godard's adaptation of Moravia's novel *Contempt.* In the film, its owner is the producer Jeremy Prokosch, played to Visigoth perfection by Jack Palance, who tyrannizes director Fritz Lang (playing himself) and cuckolds screenwriter Paul (Michel Piccoli) by seducing Camille (Brigitte Bardot) with Paul's spineless acquiescence. They've come to Capri to finish Lang's version of the *Odyssey.*

Godard implied no parallels between Malaparte and Prokosch. Prokosch is, as Malaparte wasn't, a dictator in his island hideaway, a barbarian who echoes Goebbels with a contemporary twist: "When I hear the word *culture,* I take out my checkbook."

Malaparte's *casa come me* owes nothing to Fascist monumentalism and little to architectural modernism. It is, like the Viennese house Wittgenstein built for his sister, a unique, incomparable architectural anomaly. It was far from perfectly engineered, however. The drainage system wasn't adequate to leach the Mediterranean salinity out of the roof and stucco walls, which were drenched constantly by the Caprian rainfall and occasionally by massive waves. Before its restoration, Casa Malaparte's walls had a consistency of 42 percent corrosive salt.

On the third day a huge fire flared in the Raikkola forest. Men, horses and trees clutched within the circle of fire sent out awful cries. . . . Mad with terror, the horses of the Soviet artillery—there were almost a thousand of them—hurled themselves into the furnace and broke through the besieging flames and machine guns. Many perished within the flames, but most of them succeeded in reaching the shores of the lake and threw themselves into the water. . . .

The north wind swooped down during the night. . . . The cold became frightful. Suddenly, with the peculiar vibrating noise of breaking glass, the water froze. . . .

On the following day, when the first ranger patrols, their hair singed . . . reached the lakeshore, a horrible and amazing sight met their eyes. The lake looked like a vast sheet of white marble on which rested hundreds upon hundreds of horses' heads. (*Kaputt*)

Malaparte wanted, fervently, to be Marcel Proust. History robbed him of the opportunity. He became instead the Proust of Hieronymus Bosch's paintings. His circumfluent sentences conjure flaming cities, war machines laying waste to centuries of civilization, repulsively decayed and mutilated corpses.

Perhaps because of his longing for Proust's rarefied milieu, the associations triggered in Malaparte by apocalypse are escapist memories. *Kaputt* (1944), his ersatz journal of his wartime peregrinations as an Italian officer/observer and newspaper reporter, is a picaresque of violence, but it is also an album of sedative recollection. The desert of the present dissolves into oases of golden afternoons, quiet moments in salons, flirtations, friendships, the pentimento of *la dolce vita*.

Abruptly, the cacophony of war obliterates the sweetness of a dead world. In the fearsome present, the slightest flicker of human decency produces an unnerving shock, akin to finding the Duchesse de Guermantes working in a whorehouse.

Europe is a brothel attached to an abattoir. The Nazis ape the politesse of the vanquished, impersonating the dignified lives they've destroyed, clumsy as children wearing their parents' clothes.

Everything, in short, is *kaputt*.

Kaputt's travelogue of carnage, its scathing set pieces in drawing rooms whose furnishings fell off a truck, its portraiture of the Master Race's demented slobs, surpasses in sheer rage and bilious perspicacity anything written in the era aside from Céline's later trilogy (*Castle to Castle, North, Rigadoon*).

Malaparte describes rooms, landscapes, objects and personalities with prose so replete with uncanny detail one would call it lyrical if *lyrical* didn't suggest vapidity. What becomes lyrical, in that sense, is Malaparte's habit of tossing moralistic asides to the reader, casting himself in the most flattering light possible, and trumping everyone else in conversation. He never gives anyone else the last word.

A writer who compulsively imparts his dissembled noble sentiments while consorting with moral imbeciles has got to be the unreliable narrator par excellence.

Malaparte narrates fiction using his real name, a practice familiar enough from Céline, Gombrowicz and, on occasion, earlier writers like Zola. Today it has become a more commonplace technique, especially since publishers have taken to deciding whether something written as fiction would score better sales as a memoir.

Even among serious writers who use this device, Malaparte's presence in *Kaputt* and *The Skin* complicates the fictional construction of the self, because Malaparte is not reinventing himself. He doesn't function as a doppelgänger with a different life; his character traits aren't molded into an assumed personality whose "I" can be distinguished from the "I" of the writer.

Malaparte is Malaparte. He lives among real persons, witnesses real events. More complicating still, Malaparte sometimes was where he says he was, though quite often he wasn't, and his version of what happened makes florid use of his imagination.

If all his work's ambiguities are part of an aesthetic strategy, it follows that Malaparte enlarged the art of fiction in more perverse, inventive and darkly liberating ways than one would imagine possible, long before novelists like Philip Roth, Robert Coover, and E. L. Doctorow began using their own and other people's histories as Play-Doh.

Surprisingly, many readers have imputed a claim of factuality to Malaparte's fictions. Things that couldn't possibly have happened are cited as facts, or disputable facts, wherever this writer is referenced—and we now have the Internet to thank for blanketing the universe with any mythic whopper the literal-minded choose to swallow. (When I Googled "Malaparte," I found little reliable research in several thousand web pages; what I did find were over ninety citations of a passing reference I made to him in a review I once wrote of Bill Clinton's autobiography.)

Most assuredly, hundreds of horses fleeing a forest fire were not trapped up to their necks in Finland's Lake Lagoda and flash-frozen by an amazing cold snap; Ante Pavelić, the *Ustashi* capo in Croatia, never unveiled for Malaparte's delectation what appeared to be a basket of Dalmatian oysters but proved to be forty pounds of human eyes; Heinrich Himmler and Malaparte never vigorously flogged each other with birch branches upon emerging from a Finnish sauna, before plunging into an icy river. These are, to paraphrase Picasso, lies that show us the truth.

Malaparte's introduction of the imaginary into the ostensibly real has a legible purpose. It reveals a psychological reality—in *Kaputt,* a pathology woven into all social relations by the war. If Malaparte insists that he's witnessed atrocities, he does so in order to undermine the powers of denial shared by the considerable elite who never had to come in contact with the battlefield. (He did, of course, witness many; his dispatches for *Corriere della Sera* from the eastern front are collected in *The Volga Rises in Europe* [1943]. But here there are no surrealist embellishments, only lapidary, unjournalistic but fastidiously accurate observations—too accurate, in many instances, to allow their publication in *Corriere della Sera.*)

Céline and Malaparte were the only writers who directly addressed, with appropriate rage and devastating candor, the dirty secret of World War II: While bombs dropped on Prague and Hamburg and Budapest, the aristocrats of Europe, the owners of the continent, fretted exclusively about whether troop movements were likely to prevent their restorative weekends in Baden-Baden, delay their taking the waters at Carlsbad, ruin their customary month of Mozart and mud baths in Marienbad.

Death and suffering, at least until the final movements of Europe's Götterdämmerung, were for working-class suckers. While employees bled out in the snow around Leningrad and had their heads blown off in obscure parts of Romania and Poland, the old money and the new Fascist oligarchy had their champagne and caviar flown in from Paris and Kiev and Stockholm right on schedule, just like in the old days.

The Skin, a kaleidoscope of the American occupation of Naples, has the densely packed, peripatetic, demonic abandon of a vaudeville revue in hell.

Its premise—that once all ideals have been shattered, a person's only flag is his own skin—is exampled throughout the novel by an array of degradations, including the beneficence of the "liberators":

> If ever it was an honor to lose a war, it was certainly a great honor for the people of Naples, and for all the other conquered peoples of Europe, to have lost this one to soldiers who were so courteous, elegant, and neatly dressed, so goodhearted and generous.
>
> And yet everything that these magnificent soldiers touched was at once corrupted. No sooner did the luckless inhabitants of the liberated countries grasp the hands of their liberators than they began to fester and to stink. It was enough that an Allied soldier should lean out of his jeep to smile at a woman, to give her face a fleeting caress, and the same woman, who until that moment had preserved her dignity and purity, would change into a prostitute.

The Skin makes liberation as gross a nightmare as the Europe of *Kaputt*. Malaparte guides us into a cult of "inverts," a network of intelligence agents extracting secrets from Axis generals fond of sodomy; in this "religion," the central ritual features a godlike androgyne giving birth to a large wooden effigy. (Homophobic as this sounds, Malaparte's treatment is jesuitical in the extreme and can't be dismissed as a simple effusion of prejudice.) The ghastly child entrée served at General Cork's banquet is actually a manatee, the last occupant of the Naples Aquarium—because of a fishing ban, now all the aquarium's exotic specimens have been served up at the liberators' official dinners.

Malaparte's theme takes literal form when the author guides the troops of one Colonel Granger from Naples into Rome: As the Romans ecstatically greet the American military, one of its tanks runs over an evacuee from the Abruzzi. His body, flattened like a pancake, is hoisted on a staff and borne like a flag at the head of the advancing army.

Before the war ended, Malaparte acted as a liaison officer for the Allies. He later joined the Communist Party. He moved to Paris in 1947, where his biographical play about Proust, *Du Côté de chez Proust,* premiered in 1948, somewhat untriumphantly. A play about Karl Marx, *Das Kapital,* fared no better in 1949. In 1950, he directed the film *Il Cristo proibito,* a well-acted, intelligently photographed melodrama that can be read as a plea for reconciliation, a denunciation of war, or one of Malaparte's most extravagant efforts to display his Italianness—the film includes nearly every trope of Neorealism, with a closing scene that virtually copies the ending of Rossellini's *Stromboli,* released in the same year. While *Il Cristo proibito* sometimes appears to have been cut with a pair of dull pruning shears, its pacing is much less soporific than many "classics" of Neorealist cinema. (I know I'm in a minority, but *The Bicycle Thief* is the most boring film I've ever seen.)

None of Malaparte's books of the 1950s have the amplitude or amazing audacity of *Kaputt* or *The Skin,* but neither do they evidence any waning of skill or flagging of prescience; they have a much less ornamental style, an assured concision that gives Malaparte's wit an aphoristic brevity his more celebrated works never really attempt—*Kaputt* and *The Skin,* indelibly horrific and beautifully written though they are, have a deliberate, arguably sadistic long-windedness that Malaparte dispenses with in *Those Cursed Tuscans* and *Il Ballo al Cremlino* (1971), the latter a deliciously deadpan satire of Soviet high society, Communist officialdom rendered in the delicately subtle shadings with which Proust painted the vedettes of St. Germain.

Near the end of his life, Malaparte began traveling in China, and, inevitably, shifted his utopian longings once again, in favor of Maoism. He made a preliminary attempt to elucidate the next-to-last volte-face of a lifetime marked by fervid allegiances and sudden repudiations, in *Io, in Russia e in Cina* (1958), but plans for a more epic work on the new workers' paradise were cut short by lung cancer, diagnosed by Chinese doctors as "a little bug."

As Malaparte endured a horribly prolonged end at the Sanatrix Clinic in Rome, his condition was reported in the Italian press like a national emergency. The lifelong irritant had become a cultural treasure. Malaparte had always been an enigmatic, contradictory, fantastically opaque entity: He has so often been branded an opportunist that it seems important to point out that every time he seized an "opportunity," he did so precisely when it was already, obviously, a liability. It would be more just to say that Malaparte enjoyed the contradictions he epitomized and preferred being contrary to being on the winning side of anything.

CONJUROR OF ST. GERMAIN

JEAN ECHENOZ is one of contemporary literature's rare graceful magicians. While every good novelist ventures a modicum of risk, Echenoz risks everything in his fiction, gambling on the prodigious blandishments of his voice to lure his readers into a maze of improbabilities and preposterous happenings. He might easily be located in the posthuman environs of Michel Houellebecq, Ryu Murakami, and the late Jean-Patrick Manchette, though his imaginative range suggests that, in a different period, he might display the ungovernable exuberance of a Rabelais.

Ours is not an age of exuberance, except for those who have not yet heard the bad news. Echenoz is more likely to bring to mind Goya's black paintings or Jan Potocki's *The Manuscript Found in Saragossa*. His prose carries a busy pentimento of recent voices: Carson McCullers, Alain Robbe-Grillet, Virginia Woolf, Severo Sarduy, Emmanuel Carrère, Boris Vian. His characters are often marginal to the point of near nonexistence, Beckett's clochards with backstories, Conrad's adventurers in a shabbier key. They are blessed with luck, cursed with memory.

Thanks to dazzling translations by Mark Polizzotti (of the fiercely attacked and ferociously honest André Breton biography *Revolution of the Mind*), we now have much of Echenoz's work available in English. His fidelity to this work could not be bettered. Easy to read, this former child psychologist and winner of the Prix Goncourt in 1999 is not at all easy to understand, and retaining both ease and difficulty—as Polizzotti has done—is surely the elusive marrow of translation.

If it's true that photography released painting from naturalism, Echenoz prompts the hardly new thought that film has, or ought to have, liberated the novel from its more plodding expository chores. While his technique mimics film's sleight-of-hand by cutting across time lines, points of view and locations, he also features ample doses of allegory, a strong resemblance to fables and fairy tales, and anthropomorphisms that could resonate only in a linguistic venue. He indicates, at every point, something beyond documentary reality and paints a world where coincidence and the dream state regularly trump logic and verisimilitude.

Like Manchette, Echenoz cannibalizes the *roman policier* and refashions its bones into elaborately unnatural skeletons. *Big Blondes* turns the detective story on its ear; rather than a sequence of clues that leads to a guilty person, the guilty person dispatches a series of detectives. Moreover, she gets away with it and, in the process, reforms herself. *I'm Gone* twists the key conceit of Greene's *The Third Man* into a narrative pretzel, simultaneously revealing and concealing its implausible secret.

Like Houellebecq, Echenoz endows a parade of abject figures with metaphysical and moral resonance; he makes unlikely people vessels of nuanced introspection, quixotic willfulness and weirdly fastidious sensibility. He is neither as overtly bleak nor as complacently provocative as the writers he most resembles—Manchette, certainly, Houellebecq, and in a different sense Marguerite Duras and Robbe-Grillet—whose approach is an ostensibly enlightened sadism toward the reader: that is, a glacial view of human activity as if observed through night-vision goggles or powerful binoculars. At the same time, his novels traverse the same atomized and fate-shrunk territory in which Manchette's and Houellebecq's characters so often encounter the inevitable as the secret side of chance.

A favorite technique in Echenoz's work is what might be called perpendicular, rather than parallel, narratives. *Cherokee, Double Jeopardy, I'm Gone, Big Blondes,* and *Chopin's Move* all commence by splitting into separate, closely parallel stories, then split further, like blobs of mercury, into subnarratives that intersect them. *Double Jeopardy* announces its method in its opening paragraph:

> Thirty years earlier, two men had been in love with Nicole Fischer. The stranger she'd preferred to both of them, a fighter pilot by trade, had had time neither to marry her nor to bail out of his spinning prototype, which slammed into the Haute-Saône under the noonday sun of May. Blonde and baptized Justine three months later, the fruit of his labors would thus bear her mother's name. The latter, her mourning over, her daughter born, conceived the idea of seeing her former suitors, Jean-François Pons and Charles Pontiac; she would

have liked to know how they were getting on without her. But . . . they had loved her so much that their lives had been shattered. . . . Pons and Pontiac had distanced themselves, first from each other, then from the outside world.

A paradox runs through *Double Jeopardy:* Thirty years is a long time; for the emotions, it's no time at all. As that gulf of time gets filled in—Pons has ended up managing a South Asian plantation, where an evidently characteristic *folie de grandeur* persuades him to foment a worker's revolt; Pontiac has become a grubby vagrant among the derelicts and dregs of the Paris subway system and the city's blighted postindustrial moonscapes—a gun-running venture draws the two men, and Nicole Fischer, back into proximity. The plot is thickened, so to speak, by a mutiny aboard a freighter, the intervention of rival weapons buyers, a kidnapping, a massacre, and a continual shifting of geographies and points of view. Everything the novel opens with becomes relevant to the unfolding plot, including Justine. Even the dead pilot's body turns up in a Burmese marsh.

Picaresque echoes of Richardson and Fielding, the ridiculously crammed eventfulness of *Pamela* and the hilarious misanthropy of *Jonathan Wild* exquisitely circumscribed within a couple hundred pages and spliced to the rhythms of a technologically saturated world, direct us back to the first true effulgence of the novel form, when it was a brazenly artificial construction. We don't have to suspend disbelief, since Echenoz doesn't ask us to believe anything. Hallucination is his métier. *Big Blondes* combines the real absurdities of contemporary mass media—a TV producer obsessed by typologies of "blondness" and forgotten blondes who were "famous for fifteen minutes"—with utterly bogus, Shakespearean tropes of disguise, the interventions of a foot-tall incubus lodged on its heroine's shoulder, an evil Indian doctor, a Bombay smuggling operation involving radioactive materials sewn into horses' stomachs. We may not be able to believe these things, but Echenoz compels us to picture them in microscopic detail. In *I'm Gone,* a signature narrative swerve whisks the story from Paris to an icebreaker, then a dogsled expedition in the Arctic; dense clouds of mosquitoes above the timberline, which tilt against any guess of ours about what that frozen region is like, cement the feeling that it's true to life. Maybe not real life, but something like it.

Cartesianism, according to Leibniz, reflects that "man is perpetually created corrupt and erring." Echenoz is an equivocal Cartesian on both points; the implied absence of free will is at least a motif and probably a conviction. Actions

produce paradoxically unwilled outcomes, owing to fateful lacunae in his characters' knowledge, the presence of superior force and overriding systems, and
the failure of emotions to apprehend the reality that produces them. At the
same time, his protagonists experience catharsis, change, modification of
habits; whether they are existentially "free" or not is a matter of some doubt.

Piano, Echenoz's most recently translated work, raises this question in a
perplexing context, since two thirds of the novel takes place in the afterlife.
The afterlife has rigid, if arbitrary, rules, miraculous procedures, and the
lowering prospect of eternity. Max Delmarc, a renowned concert pianist,
has stage fright verging on hysteria and an alcohol problem kept in check
by an assistant named Bernie, who often has to shove him through the con-
cert-hall curtains to propel him toward the piano.

Max complicates and contradicts the normative Echenoz hero in several
unexpected ways. Famous in a limited realm, he has an identity considerably
more distinct than the novelist's usual evanescent, middle-aged scam artists
and subterraneans; unlike the serial monogamists encountered in Echenoz's
other books, Max has remained pathetically faithful to the memory of Rose,
a woman he failed to approach years earlier, who then disappeared, and who,
he learned, was as interested in him as he was in her. The woman we assume
is his wife turns out to be his sister. Another woman who reminds him of
Rose, despite a marked absence of any resemblance, proves unavailable. And
before he can find the long-missing Rose or attract his new infatuation, Max
is murdered by a street tough in the course of a meaningless robbery.

The end of Max's life is only the beginning of his story. But fans of Alice
Sebold will find nothing for them in Echenoz's version of the afterlife, which
is far from heaven and more like a tuberculosis sanitarium, where the violently killed are patched up by plastic surgeons and looked after by dead celebrities like Peggy Lee and Dean Martin—who, like the rest of the dead,
are obliged to take new identities and abandon their previous line of work:

> "What I mean is," Béliard specified, "you're going to have to change profes-
> sions. That's how it is when you come here. It's not my decision, you under-
> stand, the same rules apply to everyone."
>
>   "But what do you expect me to do?" worried Max. "I don't know how to
> do anything else."
>
>   "We'll find you something," said Béliard. "We find solutions for everyone.
> Take Peggy, for instance. She had to change jobs, too. She needed to find

another trade. So fine, she chose health care, and she's not doing too poorly. Besides, she has the right physique—though no matter what we do, she can't quite rid herself of her little movie-star habits. She gets like that now and again, and sometimes we have to take her down a peg."

Posthumous existence conspicuously lacks a deity. After a brief recovery period in the clinic, the dead get sent for eternity to one of two places (except for a few resident celebrities who "have connections"): an Edenic but potentially tedious pastoral landscape, or else the "urban zone," indistinguishable from contemporary Paris. A person's destination has nothing to do with the weighing of vices against virtues, is in fact arbitrary, determined by quotas; either option, however, seems more than slightly punitive. Max, consigned to the urban zone, stripped of his former face and identity, has to work as a bartender in a sleazy hotel lounge.

Besides having Rose as his own spectral Beatrice, the Dantean Max has two Virgils: in life, the affable Bernie; in death, the ascerbic, disagreeable Béliard. Living forever with no discernible purpose is its own form of hell (*vide* Karel Capek's *The Makropoulos Secret*), monotonous in its bland torments. It appears an uncanny dispensation that after much heated argument, Béliard allows Max to break both cardinal rules of post-living: to make no contact with people who knew him pre-mortem and to avoid any trace of his former profession. In fact, the strictures governing things turn out strangely permeable, as Béliard himself, dispatched from the clinic to locate an escapee from the alternative afterlife of the Edenic, endless park, starts drinking heavily and becoming unhinged in Paris, apparently forgetting his mission and letting himself go to seed.

But there is a much more indelible form of hell revealed to Max after his successful rebellion against what turn out to be only superficial constraints. It is deeply horrible because it seems precisely calibrated, not to any evil Max did in life, but to a failure of nerve, a failure to seize a chance at happiness. This implies something far worse than God inherent in the human, even posthuman, condition. Echenoz's endings usually reflect a sense of futility. Even when everything else works out, the most important thing remains out of reach. A person's life returns him to his originary flaw, possibly wiser and more resigned but intractably fucked up.

Dalkey Archive is publishing Polizzotti's translation of Echenoz's early novel *Lac,* retitled *Chopin's Move,* which is rather like a black-and-white silent movie to *Piano*'s Technicolor talkie: *Chopin's Move* is a persiflage of the cold war's gritty friction between two Europes, while *Piano* evokes the ebulliently empty hell of universal capitalism. The English title refers to a life-size chess set on the grounds of the Parc Palace du Lac, a resort hotel outside Paris—figuratively the deer park of royal times, or the somnambulist palace of *Last Year at Marienbad,* and a prototype for *Piano*'s tediously well-manicured version of "heaven."

The title further indicates protagonist Franck Chopin's role as a pawn in a complicated game. And, as Echenoz's novels not only reference music extensively but give particular composers and pieces of music considerable symbolic importance (*Cherokee* is structured in one large whorl around the loan and return of a recording of Lester Young's "Cherokee"), the name makes a playful nod to the Polish composer (a statue of whom causes phobic reactions in *Piano*'s Max).

Chopin, first in a long line of Echenoz heroes conceived in the bowels of a T. S. Eliot poem, is fiftyish, attractive, hapless, desperate. Highly skilled as an espionage technician, libidinally restless, Sartre's Roquentin recast as a reluctant "man of action," in spite of an essential inertia and passivity: Things happen to him, he's compelled to react, and love (if that's what it is) impels him to put himself in harm's way. Trappings of a spy novel flitter in and out of visibility. There are ridiculous, steroidal bodyguards, defectors, double agents. Sinister figures high in the food chain, seemingly opposed, actually work for the same people. A landscape watercolorist whose paintings are clues. None of this resembles a John le Carré novel. Echenoz's language deflates the idioms of genre: "He had immediately been trained in the use of microdots and blank carbon, dead drops, the art of losing tails, and all the rest of that crap."

Through a telescoping effect, as well as various surreal devices, Echenoz situates his preoccupations somewhere beyond plot, which in any event operates like George Bernard Shaw's famous sugarcoating to make the medicine go down. Quotidian realism is jettisoned within a chapter or two, when a Queneau-like playfulness takes over. Chopin, an eminent dipterologist, is shown attaching tiny microphones to the thoraxes of flies, which he then releases in the suite of a certain Vital Veber, "general secretary" of some murky Eastern-bloc bureau: a nebulosity within a nebulosity, gray on gray, whose solitary noises Chopin monitors by means of his flies. The flies have their own affectionately rendered personalities. For that matter, so do inert objects, cars, weather systems, clocks—most things Echenoz describes have nearly as much personality as his human characters.

The animation of insentient or nonhuman entities produces an effect of cacophony and distraction. Objects wheeze, growl, sputter, weep, and complicate space. They exude sadness, joy, disappointment. Objects have needs, hopes, and die a thousand deaths. Observed by human subjects, they acquire a kind of anthropomorphic autonomy that defies the whole idea of actual subjectivity. Chopin has no psychology; the insensible objects around him fairly gurgle with a purposive inner life.

> Outside the light precipitation continued. Droplets of rain hunched on the glass, sparse and immobile. They had to band together, get unionized in one fat drop before they could hurtle gaily down the windshield, on whose verso, inside the car, droplets of fog clustered toward the same end . . . having known only the acid universe of sawdust, cold, and cutting slabs, with no prospects other than to contain blood-stained rags and knives its whole object-life long, this trunk was suddenly facing a warm and miraculous retirement, stuffed with comfortable winter clothing, furs and cashmere, angora, and now it was being carried on men's backs toward the heights of Rue de Rome.

The material world holds its own "against" the personalities passing through it. Events that would occasion great dramatic fanfare in a conventional story occur matter-of-factly, often stimulating zero effect in the people they happen to. Echenoz's people greet catastrophe as if they'd been expecting it and feel a little peeved that it's taken so long to get there. The world, he implies, is too full, too crowded with assertive objects, animals, sidewalks, cars, buildings—it's hard for any person to truly matter, even to himself.

Embedded in the dire business of *Chopin's Move* is a contrary narrative—this is also true of *Cherokee, Double Jeopardy, I'm Gone,* and *Piano,* in different degrees of explicitness. The convolutions of these novels elasticate the temporal distance between a wish and its ruin (or, more rarely, gratification) in the manner of an LSD trip. The sediment of past time, thick and opaque, fills cracks in the present as water colonizes a slow-sinking liner. Echenoz tends to return to the place where he started. But it's never quite the same place. The borrowed vinyl in *Cherokee* returns at last in the form of a tape recording. The narrative, spun from an ancient, murderous antagonism between the detective hero, George Chave, and his insane cousin Fred, ultimately delivers the two men to a state of mutual accommodation, after an incredible series of betrayals, abductions and homicides. This new equilibrium, however, has a kind of winking insincerity, as if the whole comedy could start over on the absent next page.

For Echenoz, space is as malleable as time. *Cherokee* ranges all over Paris and its suburbs, yet Chave's focus is monocular and infallible, to the extent that the city, for all Echenoz's fabulous descriptions, begins to resemble a map strewn with arrows. Spaces between him and the objects of his quest become compressed, as if the sprawling city consisted of four or five buildings and a dozen people. Similarly, the characters in *Big Blondes* streak back and forth between France and Australia, Australia and India, in minuscule narrative space; *Double Jeopardy* flashes between Burma and Paris and points between as if space were made of the latex harvested on Pons's plantation. In *Piano,* Max's expulsion from the clinic causes him to awaken, inexplicably, on a hydrofoil in the Amazon.

The author is concerned less with logic than with the evocation of a restive, unassuageable longing. His protagonists carry an impossible burden of emotion through minefields of intrigue and spurts of violence. This yearning immunizes them against more urgent misfortunes. In effect, it's their only real misfortune.

Each novel casts desire for someone lost and unregained, someone unattainable, in different ways. As in more classical genre works by Raymond Chandler or Cornell Woolrich, desire occupies space between actions that "advance the story," and the desired object is usually entwined in the mystery the hero tries to solve. But in Echenoz the mystery bears all the markings of the dream, a cloaca of violent fantasies produced by desire itself. The frantic succession of events is a garnish metastasized into fantastically twisted, varicolored forms, a prose coral reef, a labyrinth with nothing at its center but a thwarted wish. Echenoz is that inimitable stripe of literary juggler who shows us a wholly different way of thinking about ourselves and our predicament, a juggler of verbal knives who, if not for his preternatural grace, could easily slice his arm off while displaying a hypnotic and arguably pointless skill. I say "arguably" because the vastly entertaining is often mistaken for pointlessness.

EMMANUEL CARRÈRE'S COUNTERFEITERS

"ON THE Saturday morning of January 9, 1993, while Jean-Claude Romand was killing his wife and children, I was with mine in a parent-teacher meeting at the school attended by Gabriel, our eldest son. He was five years old, the same age as Antoine Romand. Then we went to have lunch with my parents, as Jean-Claude Romand did with his, whom he killed after their meal."

So begins *The Adversary: A True Story of Monstrous Deception,* one of the most silkily rancid novels of the past two decades. Its affectless, musing cadence recalls Camus's *"Aujourd'hui, maman est morte . . . ,"* or the early-19th-century confession made famous by Foucault: "I, Pierre Rivière, having slaughtered my mother, my sister, and my brother . . . ."

Emmanuel Carrère's novel is a fantastic tale that happens to be true, a picture of everyday life with its flesh peeled off. The forensic particulars of Romand's existence were themselves clustered around a fiction, like iron filings on a magnet. He dropped out of medical school at the outset of his "career," simply pretending to advance from strength to strength, grade to grade, while in reality he spent most of his time cowering in the apartment his parents had bought him, paralyzed by a failure of will. He even convinced other students at the school that his classes were scheduled at different hours than theirs (which did involve a degree of risky prevarication), and that he passed the same exams as they. It should be noted that Romand kept regular study dates with his ostensible peers, who were impressed by his quick grasp of difficult material.

The lives of impostors and con artists often reveal that to actually become what they pretend to be would take less effort than that required to sustain the deception. This is usually attributed to the thrill of the con. Yet Romand seems not to have experienced any unusual visceral pleasure from fooling other people, merely the banality of a life resembling everyone else's, without the responsibility of "officially" earning it—or, indeed, of even really having it.

After years of parental support, Romand announced his graduation from medical school. He awarded himself an exalted job at the World Health Organization (WHO), headquartered just over the Swiss border from his home in Ferney-Voltaire, in the French Jura. Meanwhile he married a pharmacist, Florence; fathered two children, Caroline and Antoine; and passed as a conventionally responsible, bourgeois civic presence (school boards, community meetings, etc.). To support his immediate family in the stylish manner of Ferney-Voltaire's professional middle class, Romand defrauded his parents, his in-laws, several other relations, and later his mistress Corinne as well, by offering to invest their savings, through WHO's Swiss bank, at a guaranteed 18 percent annual return. Astonishingly, these people surrendered every franc they had put away, without hesitation.

Romand juggled these ever-diminishing funds for *18 years*. Each morning, he drove off to work, often actually crossing into Geneva, where he sat for hours in the WHO parking lot. He selected a window where he fancied "his" office was, pointing it out to his wife and children every now and then, without ever taking them inside the building. He occasionally departed for a week or two "on business." In reality, he spent days wandering forests, or passed his traveling time in Paris hotels and rustic inns a safe distance from home. He established an inflexible rule forbidding anyone, including his wife, to contact him at work. He firmly, weirdly barricaded his imaginary professional life against everyone who knew him.

The charade had to end one day; the fact that it didn't end sooner reflects a ghastly truth about contemporary bourgeois life. Romand never spoke about his work, except occasionally to mention—lightly, with an air of slight embarrassment—his friendships with world-famous cardiologists, cancer surgeons, the director of Doctors Without Borders; his reticence was taken for the extreme discretion characteristic of the professional elite he supposedly belonged to. He pinched brochures and other printed matter from the WHO lobby, leaving these materials casually strewn around the house. Romand's charade, for years at a stretch, required only a modicum of embellishment.

Contrastingly, his more banal secrets required byzantine damage control upon exposure: When Luc Ladmiral, Romand's best friend since medical school, demanded that Romand reveal to Florence his affair with Corinne,

Romand tragically declared that he had lymphoma. He confided this fictitious cancer (in fragile remission, he said) to several intimates at various times, distracting them from gaping improbabilities in his accounts of driving mishaps, deaths of coworkers and mentors, and similar ponderous happenings for which there was no tangible evidence. Certain calamities were fabricated to elicit sympathy and impart the idea of Romand as an especially burdened soul—which he was, albeit for spectacularly different reasons.

Other lies were strictly meretricious. In at least one instance, he sold a bogus experimental cancer drug to a relative for an enormous sum; nobody blamed him when it didn't work. He invented bizarre excuses to explain why his wife and children didn't enjoy perks available to other WHO employees and their families. Somehow, these improvisations were accepted as signs of an admirable, if overactive, moral fastidiousness.

When, very belatedly, people gleaned that Romand's Formica-like normality had unaccountable inconsistencies, he proved incapable of facing public bewilderment and ostracism. Instead of killing himself, however, he murdered his family, including his parents; tried to strangle his mistress; and set his house ablaze, swallowing a Nembutal overdose and inhaling smoke only after he heard the fire engines.

The Adversary demonstrates that the novel form can frame real events more potently than quotidian reportage or generic crime "nonfiction." Carrère doesn't call his book a novel, nor does *The Adversary* disinvite the consumer of true-crime books; still, there are books that ploddingly belong to genre writing, and other, nominally generic works that don't. The appetite for exhaustively detailed, voyeuristic reconstructions of mayhem is unlikely to find much ruminative succor in *The Adversary*'s compression, its poetic angularity, its absence of facile moralizing. Yet it has been hugely popular in France, where it was published in 2000, as has Nicole Garcia's screen adaptation, one of two films based on Romand's story.

Carrère the writer appealingly figures in the narrative. Eventually, he contacts Romand; a correspondence, eventually prison visits, and courthouse encounters ensue. These are revelatory, depressing, essential. People whose entire lives are a performance pull out all the stops in the acts they cook up under indictment.

In the French manner, some would say, Carrère indicates his status in the literary world with scattered allusions to his earlier books. This is not immodesty, but usefully stresses that a singular, fallible observer is interpreting events by his own lights as he reports them; as it happens, Carrère's previous writing directly facilitates an important insight into Romand's mentality. The Romand family had secrets, though none as nasty as the ones in *Class Trip,* and some perturbing events stippled Romand's early years. But I suspect that the darkest parts of Romand's smudgy childhood came directly from reading Carrère's novel, and that he hoped to elicit Carrère's approval by praising its insight, and win his pity by comparing himself with *Class Trip*'s haunted child.

Throughout *The Adversary,* Carrère inserts flashes of his own life, in calculatedly flat counterpoint to the drama of Romand's narrative. He mentions thorny problems with his long-incubating Philip K. Dick biography. A friend with AIDS, suffering third-degree burns from an accident, is dying in hospital. Carrère sees a newspaper account of the slaughter in Ferney-Voltaire. He seems drawn to this story because it is so unlike his own. Yet his children are roughly the age of Romand's; he wonders how a man could kill his own children. He wonders about Romand, who's still comatose from smoke inhalation, having set the fire to disguise the murders, or to feign attempted suicide, or both in succession (he had to have known he'd be found out, and tried to delay the moment of full revelation). At last Carrère decides to write about it:

> I considered rushing to the scene, setting up shop at a hotel in Ferney-Voltaire, playing the nosy, tenacious reporter. But . . . I realized that this wasn't what interested me. . . . The details of Romand's embezzlements, the way his double life had taken shape over the years . . . all that, which I would learn in good time, wouldn't tell me what I really wanted to know: what went on in his head during those days he supposedly spent in the office, days he didn't spend, as was first believed, trafficking in arms or industrial secrets, days he spent, it was now thought, walking in the woods?

Deciphering a sociopath like Romand is not, strictly speaking, a process of identification. Romand is *impossible to identify with. The Adversary*'s title itself places him slightly outside humanity, "the adversary" being a traditional euphemism for the devil. Romand's monstrosity, an eruption of unassuageable evil, is beyond human understanding. A slight contradiction arises. A monster, by definition, isn't subject to human laws or morality, any more than a cow or a cobra is. What Carrère wants to know, perhaps only vaguely suspecting as much, isn't what occurred in Romand's mind when he was, every day, absent from his own life, but when, and why, he ceased to be human.

The fabulous quality of Romand's deception makes it nearly unbelievable, though it may be more accurate to say that we'd like it to seem more incredible than it is. Ultimately, Romand himself is no help in discovering why he started lying—no conscious help, at least, since introspection and narcissism are hopelessly entwined in his personality. (He made up a carjacking incident and other bizarre whoppers even before he made his permanent detour into fantasyland, but has no idea why.) He does, though, by chance, suggest a partial answer. The embellishment of the original lie, over decades, is both logical and insane. He had to say *this* because he'd already said *that*. He had to perpetrate *this* fraud since he'd already committed *that* one. But the solution to the puzzle is so infantile, so stunningly selfish, that it makes Romand more horrible still. It can't fully account for his rampage—yet what if it does? What if modern life is constructed to support the flimsiest impersonation of the real, in order to further undermine and devalue the authentic?

Carrère forgoes the redemptive uplift that high-minded crime literature routinely shoplifts from Dostoevsky and Tolstoy, who invented Ivan Karamazov and Prince Dmitrii Nekhliudov, respectively, in a less morally narcoleptic time than the present. Russian society, in the twilight of czarism, viewed its aberrant personalities as reflections of its own imperfections. Even there, of course, humanity produced unassimilable anomalies that could only be regarded with wonder and attributed to the mysterious workings of a satanic entity. *The Adversary* confronts the more ineluctable problem posed by Iago, or Balzac's Vautrin, or Peter Verkhovensky in *Demons*. As in Bresson's film *L'Argent* and "The Forged Coupon," the Tolstoy story from which it derives, in Carrère's narrative a great crime is only one, conspicuous disorder among many produced, like a poison seeping through society, by "a false coin in circulation," to borrow Heidegger's phrase.

The proliferation of the inauthentic, or false consciousness, is a subject much contemporary literature skirts by fetishizing psychotherapy, itself a ritual of redemption. This is where *The Adversary* most forcefully distinguishes itself from "crime writing" and the sentimental narratives associated with it. In prison, Romand expeditiously finds God. With equal efficiency, he finds others who have found God, in the form of two prison visitors, his "angels," Marie-France and Bernard. (The prison visitor—volunteer friend, self-trained social worker—is a more familiar figure in France than America. He or she is often an exemplar of saintly patience and Candide-like gullibility.) Carrère writes:

> I wound up imagining Marie-France and Bernard leaning over my work to one side of me, rejoicing even more—and all heaven with them—for a repentant sinner than for the ninety-nine just souls who have no need to repent; on my other side, I heard [a reporter covering Romand's trial] saying that the worst thing that could happen to Romand would be to fall into the hands of those people, let himself be lulled by angelic speeches on the infinite mercy of the Lord and the wonders He would work in his soul, and thus lose all chance of someday getting back in touch with reality.

Romand's feral reaction to imminent exposure is hardly more shocking than the dewy-eyed forgiveness of others on ethereal grounds. "He is not putting on an act, of that I'm sure," Carrère concludes after recounting various Christ-inspired encomiums to Romand's essential goodness, "but isn't the liar inside him putting one over on him? When Christ enters his heart . . . isn't it the adversary deceiving him yet again?"

In a document solicited for a Catholic newsletter by one of his "angels," Romand's language echoes *Tartuffe,* euphemizing his butchery as "a terrible family tragedy" and rejoicing that "the presence of God burst upon" him in his blackest hour. In effect, he repudiates guilt while feigning its embrace. Anchored in a humanist ethos, 19th- and early-20th-century literature depicted redemption through piety as authentic: Transgression was a fall from grace; the criminal was an object of pity, regarded as something more, and at least potentially nobler, than his deed, a soul in need of healing.

The recrudescent *Elmer Gantry*-ism of recent decades has given "finding God" a deservedly unsavory reputation. Our age does not believe in God, despite a fervid, universal pretense that its occupants do. For scoundrels high and low, from mass murderers to corporate thugs, historical personalities like Jesus Christ are Band-Aids to plaster over a festering gash in the social contract. Romand's expedient religiosity converts his victims into sacrifices necessary to his own salvation. This self-absorption recalls the group-therapy sessions for war criminals in Liliana Cavani's *Night Porter.*

Romand's "possession" is his own creation, a product of infantile passivity. Carrère's account ratifies Hannah Arendt's speculation that "the activity of thinking as such" could be "among the conditions that make men abstain from evil-doing," a "hypothesis enforced by everything we know about conscience, namely, that a 'good conscience' is enjoyed as a rule only by really bad people . . . while only 'good people' are capable of having a bad conscience." Romand *stopped thinking* the week of his second-year med school finals. Considering the eons of malingering self-pity and inanition that followed, Carrère refers to Romand, in passing, as a "big baby"—the blunt, miserable truth. What passed through his mind all those hours, days and years of killing time was *nothing at all*.

During a recess in the killer's trial, Carrère meets a newspaper sketch artist, a 40-year veteran of courts and trials, who makes a bleak observation reached by many who've probed the mental gearworks of sociopaths: "They think it's a man we've got in front of us, but in fact it's not a man anymore, hasn't been a man for a long, long time. It's like a black hole, you'll see, it's going to spring at our faces. People don't know what true madness is. It's dreadful. It's the most dreadful thing in the world."

Although Carrère could hardly pose it as the central enigma of his narrative, this story is haunted by the inference that "the activity of thinking as such" had atrophied almost as thoroughly in the people taken in by Romand's deception as it had in Romand himself. Exactly how lazily does someone need to dissemble to be seen as honorable, decent, trustworthy? Intimate friend, loving husband, adoring father? In Romand's case, it took only a few phone calls to his imaginary employers and professional organizations for his house of cards to collapse; how could it have held up for 18 years?

The subtitle of Carrère's *I Am Alive and You Are Dead: A Journey into the Mind of Philip K. Dick* is no empty promise. Like Jean-Claude Romand, but in a considerably more baroque sense, American science-fiction writer Philip K. Dick had the reality-testing prowess of a paramecium. Carrère installs himself in Dick's weird cranium with the mimetic dexterity of a pod "taking over" Dana Wynter in *Invasion of the Body Snatchers*. Happily for us, though generally less so for him, Dick translated his pathology into a large body of writing, inventing alternative universes where otherwise debilitating fears and phobias assumed beguiling shapes, becoming containers of widely shared metaphysical anxieties.

Dick was born prematurely in Chicago in 1928. His twin sister died of malnutrition after their mother inadvertently underfed them. Dick's parents divorced when he was five. His father, absent much of the time anyway, then disappeared for good. His mother passed along a rampant hypochondria and festive dependence on pharmaceuticals. Dick also developed a lifelong addiction to psychiatry as a teenager. Mother and son migrated to Berkeley. The community there, with its resemblance to a wildlife refuge for perpetual students, rebels, dead-eyed burnouts and Age of Aquarius would-be's, provided a kind of safety that Dick attempted to replicate, with mixed results, for the rest of his life.

After abandoning school at fifteen, Dick worked at a classical-music store, where he met sci-fi impresario and author Anthony Boucher, who first published Dick's writing in the *Magazine of Fantasy and Science Fiction* in the fall of 1951. On the strength of this sale—not exactly a sultan's ransom—Dick quit the music store, and he never held another steady job after that, eking out a meager livelihood from his stories and novels. Many years, books and marriages later, his royalties brought a modicum of security, but even when he died, famous, in 1982, he was far from affluent, nor had his work been acknowledged by the mainstream American literary world.

Carrère's own works qualify as fantastic literature, or speculative fiction: *Gothic Romance* (*Bravoure*), an early novel, is woven from the Frankenstein story and the circumstances under which Mary Shelley wrote it; another novel, *Hors d'atteinte,* is about gambling, and virtually every fiction centered in a casino belongs to the realm of unreal, alternative worlds, from Dostoevsky's *Gambler* to Tommaso Landolfi's feverish stories of compulsive betting. Carrère has written a book-length essay on Werner Herzog, impresario of the bizarre and uncanny, and another, *Le détroit de Behring,* about *uchronia,* the science-fiction term for an alternate or alternative history.

But as much as *I Am Alive and You Are Dead* lavishes an almost unwarranted degree of attention on Dick's novels and stories, the book is about something else entirely. Philip K. Dick—the person, as opposed to his inscription on the page—is the kind of dysfunctional personality Carrère creates in fiction, and it's arguable, at least, that if this were a book about a psychotic plumber instead of a notable science-fiction writer, it would still exert the same morbid fascination.

Carrere usefully links much of Dick's writing to the somewhat pathetic theater of Dick's life, but *I Am Alive and You Are Dead* isn't very much about writing at all, except as the peculiar secretion of Dick's madness that survives in printed form. Dick's carnivalesque, markedly adolescent mind exhibits a certain rote pattern when Carrère describes him in the act of writing; Dick was always, it seems, on the brink of yet another deluded illumination, and after a while, these eureka moments all sound much the same.

In life, Dick's career was dreary at best. As I find his better works diverting in concept and almost as execrably written as most science fiction, Carrère's biography kept inspiring the question, Why is a writer as brilliant as Carrère so insistent that a nerdy, narcissistic slob deserves all this attention? But the question becomes moot when one considers *I Am Alive and You Are Dead* as the same kind of fictional nonfiction as *The Adversary*—a true story, but only because in rare cases real people resemble the most extravagantly invented fictional characters. In this context, it would be pointless to cavil about Dick's exact literary stature. His life, as Carrère tells it, is one of the most comprehensive illustrations, ever, of the shitty fate awaiting almost anyone—genius, middlebrow or mediocrity—for whom the act of writing is a necessary means of achieving mental and moral equilibrium rather than a career choice.

When opportunities to promote himself in interviews and speaking gigs cropped up, Dick had no idea how to use them to advantage, becoming lost beforehand in whatever byzantine train of thought had lately colonized his brain. He usually came across as a meandering crackpot. Spokesperson for the storming of consciousness's frontiers, Dick dropped LSD exactly once and became so paranoid that it permanently terrified him. His ceaseless industry was a peculiarly ungenerative effort to make sense of reality— ungenerative because his contrarian nature wouldn't abide any truth acknowledged by anyone else: As soon as he had convinced someone that his perceptions were accurate, he immediately became convinced that he was wrong. In everyday life, his personality habitually regressed to an unappetizing stage of adolescence. He was grandiose, abject, cowardly, envy-ridden, emotionally shallow and, quite often, repulsively obese—in short, a can of nightcrawlers, with a brace of diamonds (or, depending on your opinion of his oeuvre, zircons) hidden at the bottom.

Carrère has been a passionate fan of Dick's over-generous literary output since adolescence. (Like most genre writers, Dick wrote too much—almost fifty novels, over a hundred short stories; he needed the money.) Carrère's portrait has no taint of malice, but it's doubtful that any honest biography

of Dick could conceal his repellent qualities, since they manifested themselves in most of the noteworthy moments of his life. The mitigating cir-
cumstance that Dick was clinically insane, enough so to require periodic
confinement, is registered throughout *I Am Alive and You Are Dead,* but it's
hard to finish the book without feeling fortunate never to have known him.

Amphetamines enabled Dick to write novels with the same rapidity
Balzac attained by drinking coffee. Some were written in a week, and many
of them read that way. Usually set in a world of effortless space travel (as fictional today as ever), Dick's novels manifest enough of the familiar to establish a believable reality, then introduce a runaway element that throws that
reality into question.

Dick's best work is speculative fiction of a memorable kind, smartly
crafted, interestingly paced, full of fresh, disturbing images and provocative
ideas—*Ubik, The Man in the High Castle* and *The Three Stigmata of Palmer
Eldritch* are probably his most successful novels. Carrère acknowledges that
Dick's writing often falls short of his intermittent brilliance; what he doesn't
say, and ought to have, is that the bulk of Dick's oeuvre recycles the same projections of financial anxiety and sexual paranoia to ever-diminishing effect,
except on those rare occasions when a new idea actually occurs to him. And
he cannot, as far as I can tell, create a character that isn't cardboard-thin.

There are legible reasons for Dick's prolific redundancy. Balzac wrote
bales of shit to keep creditors off his back, long before producing any of the
novels he later included in his complete works. And, if modern pharmaceuticals had been available instead of espresso, he might well have written
thirty times more dreck, and even made a botch of novels like *Ursule
Mirouet* and *Père Goriot.*

Much of Dick's adulthood passed in a state of subacute amphetamine
psychosis, which accounts for his construction of intricate cosmologies that
resemble each other in many details, and their sudden metamorphoses into
opposite cosmologies, the trick endings that reverse the state of things established by his plots. Carrère treats the fractional differences between one
Dick novel and another with the scrutiny of a psychiatrist listening to a patient's slightly varying recurring dreams. In a sense, this is a more elevated
approach to literary biography than the usual hagiographic sludge. Carrère,
thankfully, mostly references the same five or six important works instead of
running through the whole bibliography.

Ideas of earthquake magnitude struck Dick at regular intervals, scrambling his perception of what reality "meant." While it sometimes crossed his mind that it didn't mean anything, Dick found meaninglessness intolerable and incessantly embraced meaningless explanations as to why there is something rather than nothing. Dick believed a secret lurked behind everything, and that he would just naturally be its intended recipient. He attached occult significance to trivia that caught his attention (numbers, advertisements), certain that they were messages from the unknown, addressed exclusively to him.

Carrère supposes that Dick felt haunted by his dead twin. The idea that he, instead of she, had died in infancy, and that he was being imagined, or contacted from the other world, by her, might account for the fascinating variations on this conundrum found in Dick's novels. A mild brush with the FBI during the McCarthy era seems to have set off inextinguishable brush fires in Dick's brain for decades, culminating, bizarrely, in a strong identification with Richard Nixon. An unexplained robbery at his house generated decades of dithering speculation, including Dick's recurring suspicion that he "might have" burglarized himself.

A latter-day, slobbery romanticism of the "Love me or I'll die" variety lured a succession of insecure women into Dick's surpassingly uneventful orbit. (He hated leaving the house, never exercised, and was only slightly less sedentary than a potted plant. From early middle age, he preferred "cuddling" to sex.) Dick usually ended these liaisons in an access of paranoia, sometimes convincing his cashiered paramours that they actually had been plotting his destruction.

In the circles that formed around his oracular obesity, others existed to nurture him and wax awestruck at his Dexedrine-motored theories. Like most addicts, he grew worse as he got older. In later years, new lovers were quick to notice, and back away from, the heightening symptoms of his impressive inner wreckage. As he deteriorated, Dick developed an avidity for physically unappealing women with fatal illnesses and serious mental disorders; he even cruised psychiatric clinics for potential dates. The objects of this patronizing, late-blooming adoration usually turned out to be saner and less needy than he was, and dumped him.

Summoning Dick's inner states, extracted from Dick's fiction as well as myriad interviews and copious research, Carrère arrives at the kind of slippery truth that empathy sometimes levers out of the unconscious. This intuitive approach, nearer to method acting than ventriloquism, may be the most prescient way to represent someone as trapped in his own neural synapses as Dick, someone so far from endorsement by the people who would later lay claims to his work that he could stand as a monument to the culture's obtusity.

Like *Beautiful Shadow,* Andrew Wilson's biography of Patricia Highsmith, *I Am Alive and You Are Dead* is a surpassingly well-accomplished, unflattering act of love. It depicts an obsessive, self-destructive, frequently insufferable artist, who seems to have had a biologically calibrated sense of how to pace his suicide in order to finish his work first. The very fact of the work—improbable, even miraculous, given the author's bad living and defective inner wiring—is revealed as the reason for the life, exactly as it was lived.

Carrère is immersed enough in science fiction that when French reviewers of his novel *The Mustache* compared him to Kafka, Carrère thought it odd that nobody cited science-fiction writer Richard Matheson. *The Mustache* is a fantastically creepy story about a man going mad, with echoes of stories by Gerard de Nerval, Edgar Allan Poe's "Toby Dammit," Villiers de l'Isle-Adam's "The Desire to Be a Man," Daphne du Maurier's "Don't Look Now," and the cruel tales of Landolfi—works about arbitrary, ludicrous obsessions and recurring hallucinations, pursued to absurd, devastating ends.

In *The Mustache,* a man's capricious impulse to shave off his mustache provokes the unraveling of his existence. Imagining that the failure of his wife and friends to notice the mustache's absence is a deliberate canard, he makes vain efforts to "trap" them into admitting the prank; when people continue treating his mustache as a bewildering fixation of his own, and, finally, as symptomatic of a nervous breakdown, he becomes estranged from his wife, who insists he never had a mustache; he decides that he's the victim of a conspiracy. The man is soon reduced to feigning blindness and asking strangers in the street if the face on his identity card has a mustache. The sudden, small fissure in reality and its corruption of everything real has obvious parallels in the lie at the heart of *The Adversary,* as well as in the themes of Dick's stories and novels: Like the deliquescent physical world in Dick's *Ubik,* which can be temporarily restored but never reliably stabilized by spray applications of the product that gives the book its title, the descent of *The Mustache's* central figure into madness could only be halted if he suddenly believed—really believed—that the mustache he removed at the outset had never existed, or if his social universe acknowledged that it had.

The Mustache is written from inside the hero's refusal to forget what he knows, or thinks he knows; suddenly life stops accepting the image of himself he's carried around, in one stroke banishing him from the external data that define him. His stubborn fidelity to a trivial truth, if it is one, results in a persecution complex as self-destructive as Michael Kohlhaas's quest for justice in Kleist's novella. Carrère's sentences and paragraphs resist any whisper of digression, scanning like a fable worn smooth by repeated telling. It's a radically concentrated text, though at 200 pages, not a remarkably short one.

Class Trip, more replete with physical incident and possessing the episodic quality of a novel, is surprisingly briefer than *The Mustache,* and an even more stealthy exercise in delicately paced revelation. The entire novel transpires in the mind of Nicolas, as his father drives him to ski school, and afterward, throughout Nicolas's generally numbed and unpleasant Alpine holiday. The infiltration of Nicolas's gothic dreams and morbid fantasies into the routine of classes, cafeteria meals, and communal bedtimes distorts the tempi of passing time; the crowding of mental events renders real happenings perfunctory and distant, as if the waking life were the dream and the dream a truer picture of Nicolas's experience.

Carrère conveys the desultory tedium of childhood, and the gaps of comprehension imagination fills with make-believe. An especially quiet boy, Nicolas is isolated from the other children even before he arrives at the school: Everyone else goes by bus, but Nicolas's obtusely fretful father, alarmed by a recent school bus accident, insists on driving the few hundred miles to the school himself, only to forget, once there, to unpack Nicolas's luggage from the trunk. Besides his missing clothes, Nicolas's bag, critically, contains a rubber sheet—without it, his fear of wetting his bunk bed while wearing pajamas he's borrowed from Hodkann, the class bully, makes him vulnerable, weaker, less assertive than the other students. Finally, an attack of rheumatic fever excludes him from school activities altogether, creating a solitude filled with feverish, calamitous fantasies.

Hodkann the bully conceives a protective affection for Nicolas, his interest piqued by the discovery that Nicolas's father is a salesman of prosthetic limbs. (The sexual attraction between the two boys, vaguely adumbrated in the book, is more evident in the Claude Miller film of *Class Trip,* for which Carrère wrote the script.) It's expected that the father will quickly discover

Nicolas's suitcase in his trunk and return with it; when he doesn't, the school learns that Nicolas's mother doesn't know his father's itinerary and has no means of reaching him.

Some time later—time contracts and expands mysteriously—a local boy goes missing. Soon after, his mutilated body is discovered hundreds of miles away. Nicolas, who has invented for Hodkann a tale about a kidnapped sibling whose kidney was removed by organ thieves, reveals that his father is on a private mission to catch the body snatchers. The charmed complicity of the boys, between whom Nicolas's fantasies develop a play-narrative elaboration, has an undertaste of something real hidden inside it. The most unsettling aspect of Nicolas's violently surreal stories is his own passive relation to them. He's spellbound, emotionless at mental pictures of terrorists storming the school, of his father's bleeding body twisted in a car wreck, of the story "The Monkey's Paw" coming to life. Nicolas's waking nightmares substitute for repressed knowledge, easier to consciously accept than what they cover up.

The revealed secret of *Class Trip* raises even darker questions than it answers, and like much of Carrère's writing to date seems written *around* those elements of consciousness that remain unquantified and inexplicable, though they certainly exist and may only be accessible by inference. We "know" more about each other and ourselves than we think we know, more than we can bear knowing—our perceptual scanning pattern registers the disruption of a lie, whether we recognize it as such or not, and the cues by which we assemble a consensual reality also broadcast our secrets, which others, in turn, may reconfigure in ways that mitigate their horror.

In this sense, Nicolas knows what his dreams mean, even as they protect him from unassimilable terrors. A mustache can be the missing outward sign of something essentially false in our transpersonal arrangements. The family and friends of Jean-Claude Romand must always have known that his illnesses and quirks and prevarications were the effluvia of something infinitely worse. Carrère is perhaps the preeminent poet of slippages between what we agree to recognize as the world around us and "the world inside this one." His characters, both real and imaginary, are people who tumble down a rabbit hole to a place very few of us would characterize as Wonderland, but it seems a wonderfully well-observed place, where we meet up with ourselves in the dark and discover that the arrangements we've made with ourselves have been canceled.

P A R T

IV

AND THE FOG
COMES ROLLING IN

THE EXCREMENTAL REPUBLIC

WHEN THE US presidential contest of 2004 began to be widely framed as "the most important election of our lifetimes," a statistically unmeasured number of Americans registered this claim as the stubborn, nostalgic residue of progressivist optimism, an appealing but futile, empirically baseless belief in the indestructible fairness and moral decency of "the American people"—essentialist qualities, thought to be embarrassingly violated by such shockingly un-American phenomena as conspiracy and fraud at banks and energy companies; insider stock trading; piratical trade practices at pharmaceutical corporations, insurance companies, manufacturing conglomerates, and utility providers; rampant bribery of judges and legislators; revenue-skimming from domestic programs by government appointees; grotesque civil rights abuses; promiscuous use of military force; and deployment of "intelligence services" to overthrow legitimately elected, reform-minded governments in parts of the world considered possible sources of future resource exploitation.

The official accounts of such lapses, equally firm in the belief that corruption and reckless disregard are un-American, typically lament the "unintended consequences" of tax code loopholes, failure to spot loose cannons in the bureaucratic morass of government agencies, misfiled secret documents, wrongly interpreted telexes, distracting personal emergencies, excessive apprehension on the part of one or another faction of advisors, failure to switch off the office coffee machine before leaving for the weekend, and other circumstances synonymous with "accident."

Note that "unintended" and "accidental" are always the favored constructions. American governments do not make mistakes, hence cannot admit any, and therefore can never learn anything from them. The deepest and most lingering quintessence of this fantasy, the Vietnam War, remains for many Americans, all these decades later, what the Versailles Treaty represented to Germany's extreme right wing during the Weimar Republic. The atrocities Americans committed at My Lai and in countless "strategic hamlets" have been monstrously relativized as "unfortunate incidents" of a type that happened "on both sides." (In this connection, Noam Chomsky has noted that the only war crimes prosecuted at Nuremberg were actions the Allies hadn't also committed themselves—if we do it, it's acceptable warfare; if they do it, it's a crime against humanity.)

While most countries indoctrinate their schoolchildren in exalting national myths, the United States is unique among advanced nations in its cartoonlike educational dogma of America's unblemished history of noble intentions, global altruism, heroic vigilance in pursuit of universal justice. The magnetic allure of its boundless freedoms accounts for the envied magnificence of its economic system and the perfection of its institutions. In short, this farrago of preposterous homilies and infantile clichés constitutes the average American's entire civic education—which, in the absence of credible evidence or any nuanced historical sense, erases fact from the public sphere. It reduces the principle of self-government to a parody of consensus, "elections" that generate no cerebral activity but instead spawn endlessly iterated, meaningless bromides and the touting of numbingly irrelevant "issues" instilling a collective sense of unreality.

From a strictly constitutional perspective, the most important election of our lifetimes was not, in any meaningful sense, an election at all, but the judicial travesty of a per curiam Supreme Court opinion, issued only in written form (traditionally, important rulings are first delivered orally) at ten in the evening on December 12, 2000, which halted the Florida recount and thus awarded the American presidency to George W. Bush.

The ruling itself, for legal scholars and jurists, was an astonishing corruption of judicial practice: "Per curiam" is a term applied almost exclusively to unanimous decisions on matters of such untroublesome triviality that the customary written opinions of the individual justices are considered unnecessary. None of the Court's nine justices were identified by name on the December 12 document. Yet the opinion that decided *Bush v. Gore* was far from unanimous, and the issue at stake was one of profound and repercussive national importance.

Moreover, the wording of the *Bush v. Gore* opinion stipulated that the Court's "consideration is limited to the present circumstances, for the problem of equal protection in election processes generally presents many complexities." This caveat, disclaimer, whatever you want to call it, was unique in the history of American and Anglo-Saxon law, and in fact nullified the foundational basis of the entire legal system, which is, of course, the understanding that any ruling by a court, unless reversed on appeal, establishes a precedent to be invoked in subsequent rulings. In the case of the Supreme Court, there is no higher venue for appeal, and hence no possibility of reversal. In effect, it now became the law of the land that one of the Court's most historically controversial decisions immunized itself from becoming the law of the land, on one hand deciding who would occupy the nation's highest office, on the other hand eradicating itself from legal history. The opinion virtually acknowledged its illegality.

It was assumed by media pundits and politicians alike that the fury ignited by the obviously partisan character of *Bush v. Gore*—even taking the case proved the Court majority's bias in favor of Bush—would quickly subside, and recognition of a fait accompli would "unite" Americans in conciliatory acceptance of the new president. For a time, actually, it seemed superfluous to dwell on the new president's illegitimacy, since his manifest incompetence and surpassing ignorance were embarrassingly clear even prior to his swearing-in ceremony. He was, perhaps, the only chief executive in history presumed to be fated for a single term before his inauguration, even by most people who had voted for him.

But, as history teaches us, shit happens.

A week after this mush-mouthed, dyslexic, perpetually vacationing cipher hit an unprecedented nadir of public approval, Condoleezza Rice, conferring with staff a mere 12 hours after the attacks of 9/11, perceived them as a providential "opportunity" for Bush and his administration. The adage that every disaster is someone's stroke of luck is a central article of faith for Ms. Rice, and can equally apply to her government employment vis-à-vis the disaster of Bush's presidency-by-fiat.

The events of 9/11 brought violent death to almost 3,000 people and a chance for George W. Bush to posture like a painfully constipated fire marshal in the London Blitz, costumed as a rescue worker perched atop the smoking wreckage of the World Trade Center, whining a litany of vapid solemnities through a megaphone that seemed surgically implanted in his voice box ever after. His "resolve" to avenge the dead and hunt down "the evildoers" (in more recent Bush Ebonics, "suiciders") who "hate America for its freedoms" moved hearts and marginally sentient minds in every trailer park and industrial bidonville across America. Our country had, after all, suffered a deep wound, and though this wound was only more visually ubiquitous than America's seldom-broadcast, indiscriminate slaughter of civilians—in far greater numbers than the 9/11 fatalities, all over the world, in "conflicts" that never involved actual declarations of war, in promiscuous bombings of select infrastructural targets within sovereign nations, and un-countable violations of international law—the United States squeezed a Niagara of sympathy from much of the world, even from countries it had itself terrorized for entire generations. Having no moral aversion to violence him-self, Bush interpreted this sympathy as a global endorsement of his own terrorist agenda.

Declaring a "war on terror" and himself a "war president," Bush instantly reactivated long-standing plans to invade Iraq while intimidating Congress into passing the Patriot Act, a malignant assault on numerous constitution-ally guaranteed civil liberties. The Bush administration seized the "opportu-nity" of 9/11 and the panic it created so adroitly that the administration itself might as well have planned it. The consolidation of power after 9/11 allowed by a president elected with the questionable mandate of fewer than 200 votes bore an eerie resemblance to the political aftermath of the Reich-stag Fire.

The "war on terror" facilitated a concurrent war *of* terror on the citizenry, waged with cynically manipulative, fake warnings of imminent attack, the discovery of "sleeper cells" in various backwater communities, proliferation of "security measures" in every conceivable public location, sweeps and arbi-trary arrests in certain ethnic neighborhoods, incarcerations—without spe-cific charges, indictments, trials or right to legal counsel—and harassment of political activists, as well as Nixonian investigations into the private lives of journalists, intellectuals and dissident entertainment figures. Bush's cos-tume switch from ranch hand overalls to military uniforms from the Home-land Security wardrobe department enabled the presidential hologram to unleash his congenital belligerence, his use of language as a tool of decep-tion, and a view of human existence as a "faith-based," apocalyptic clash be-tween good and evil. Decades of drink and subsequent embrace of religious psychosis made him the ideal transmitter of "values" epitomizing the death instinct. The type of divine guidance Bush asserts at every opportunity lost its totalitarian grip on the Western mind during the 15th century. Its re-crudescence in 21st-century America says less about religious faith or "a personal relationship with Jesus Christ" than it says about a power structure that systematically cripples public education, demonizes the concept of a national health system, flatly denies scientific proof of global warming, considers the poisoning of our air and water insignificant side effects of economic expansion, and jails an aberrantly high percentage of African Americans for victimless crimes as a method of disenfranchisement.

The kill-or-be-killed ethos of contemporary America presents itself as, variously, free trade, healthy competition, individual self-empowerment, liberation from "big government," meritocracy, whatever. Its practical effect is the total dismantling of an already vestigial social safety net; its goals are the erasure of every social welfare program instituted since Franklin D. Roosevelt's New Deal, elimination of Social Security, and the fusion of government with global corporations. The result will be peonage for the vast majority of the population, enslaved to international business entities for the basic necessities of existence; the "securities" provided will be privileges bestowed on disposable servants, instead of rights ensured by the government.

By the final days before the 2004 voting, of course, how much was still at stake had become clear. The poll figures narrowed to a virtual tie, reactivating the calamity of 2000 as portent of something even more crippling to the practice of self-government. This time several states might have thrown the election into chaos. Armies of lawyers were deployed to polling places. Testing of electronic voting machines proved them to be unreliable, defective and simple to hack into, their memory cards easily removed and replaced with counterfeits. Republican intimidation of black voters proliferated in every state. Election observers from other countries spread through the South and many northern states as well. It was, at last, clear to at least half of America how much damage had been done to the electoral process in 2000, how many of our institutional foundations had been compromised, how little that had seemed immutable, even in the darkest crises of the past, remained.

On the Republican side, the campaign was unquestionably the filthiest and most unscrupulously conducted in American history. The Democratic side made the usual reductive compromises with its largely ceremonial pandering to its supposed "base" of minority citizens and progressives (which it had not served with any credible efficacy even when the Democratic Party

held power under Jimmy Carter and Bill Clinton), while both underesti-
mating and overestimating, with astoundingly bad timing, the extent of the
public's surrender to reductive catch-phrases, buzzwords, perceptual reshap-
ing by television commentators, and primitive opinions drawn from the fa-
cial expressions, tones of voice, and body language of politicians, from
baseless warnings of imminent catastrophe, from patently false assertions,
and so on. The miniaturization of important things into trivia practiced by
mass media became the public's imitative reflex. When a verifiable, damning fact emerged—for example, the looting of an unsecured weapons depot
in Iraq—the outrage such information once would have generated was
deftly refocused on accusations that a proven fact was reported "for political
reasons," that its "timing" was suspect. The novel questioning of why news
was reported replaced the content of factually reported news.

Another innovation in the media discourse, one I find difficult to elucidate, may have less to do with partisan sparring than the intrinsic inanity
and feigned reflectiveness of many American journalists. It appears in opinion columns (and, increasingly, in reportage itself). The columnist, rather
than speculating on the meaning or consequences or implications of the reported event, places the event "in context." The event is likened to many
other events, often events of the very distant past, or likened to events whose
similarity to this event is either specious or superficial. Or the comparison itself reduces to virtual parity a large event and an event of such smaller magnitude that it amounts to saying that an ant and an elephant carry around
the same body weight.

This species of opinion writing often involves a deftly insinuated pretense of vast historical knowledge or some other expertise in a highly cerebral activity. A harmless enough fakery in itself, but the actual effect of the
column is its assurance to the reader—whose moral, ethical and intellectual
reaction to the news story might otherwise produce alarm, and, cumula-
tively, among many such readers, civic action—that the news is actually
"nothing new." It has happened before. It happens all the time. It will happen again.

At its most ludicrous, this barbecue of something new into nothing new
compares a current event of terrifying barbarism with an event, or series of
events, that occurred in the era of barbarism that followed the era of savagery
and evolved over centuries of agonizing, brave, persistent struggle against

brutality and ignorance into civilization. And it is at this ludicrous juncture that the opinion columnist most witlessly collaborates with the trivialization of civilization's regression to barbarism. The inability of a badly educated generation to reason becomes a change of styles, tastes, slang, attitude, etc., a superficial matter that "always happens." An election fraud in 2000 is "nothing new" because "it happened before" a century ago. A loaded gun fired into a person's brain has always been fatal. Lemmings have always thrown themselves off cliffs.

The words "always" and "never" should be closely scrutinized when they appear in political discourse of any kind. Neither is automatically credible, nor often used to tell the truth in modern journalism.

But I am wary about blaming George Bush's 2004 victory on the media, submental political rhetoric, and other mind-softening external forces. Leftist and liberal journalists have the habit of flattering the public's irrationality and abdication of responsibility by citing irresistible, demoralizing influences that render it powerless. Trick us once and you're the fool. Trick us into fooling ourselves and we're idiots. The world is everything that is the case, begins Wittgenstein's *Tractatus Logico-Philosophicus.* If the existence of persistent, principled, rationalist resistance to barbarism ceases to be the case in the time ahead of us, the world will belong to any tyrant who claims it.

ÜBERDOLLS

VALLEY OF THE DOLLS, reprinted a few years ago by Grove Atlantic, was one kind of quintessential trash novel of the '60s (another kind was Terry Southern and Mason Hoffenberg's *Candy*), written with an insider's eye on the showbiz of the '50s. Its Ike-era prototype, Grace Metalious's *Peyton Place,* describes the adulteries and out-of-wedlock pregnancies of a small New England town; in Metalious's sequel, *Return to Peyton Place,* heroine Allison Mackenzie writes a book very like *Peyton Place,* finds a New York publisher, and enters a swirling cesspool of Manhattan glamour and corruption. Like Allison, *Valley*'s Anne Welles eschews her bucolic New England roots in favor of the big city and falls hard for a powerful man, experiences heartbreak and learns some bitter lessons. *Valley* author Jacqueline Susann seized on Metalious's Harlequin-romance-meets-Zola formula and brought it forward into the early years of megapublishing, a task for which she was infinitely better equipped than her predecessor.

Metalious was a deeply troubled hick who, only a few years after success struck, sabotaged her career with booze and pills, becoming a dreadful problem guest on talk shows and later a cirrhosis fatality. Susann, by contrast, was a seasoned survivor long before setting crayon to paper. Married to publicist Irving Mansfield, Susann had acted on Broadway and been a jacqueline-of-all-trades in the early television industry. She came from a sophisticated family of Philadelphia Jews (her father was a prominent society portrait artist), and had mixed with the entertainment world's elite throughout the '40s and '50s. She knew intimately the slick, sentimental, sordid world of Walter Winchell, "21," and *The Sweet Smell of Success* that developed out of vaudeville and radio after World War II. *Valley of the Dolls* wrapped that world up and delivered it to the '60s like a coroner's report.

The foreward to the last edition of Barbara Seaman's *Lovely Me: The Life of Jacqueline Susann* locates *Valley of the Dolls* in the mid-'60s cultural mix of The Beatles's *Revolver* album, Capote's *In Cold Blood* and "the high period works of Andy Warhol," but it was not so much the novel itself as its prodigious, innovative marketing campaign that belonged to that specific moment. The pop-ness of *Valley* was its inexorable momentum on the best-seller lists, and the Amazonian campiness of its author's gaudy, Pucci-clad personal appearances. Susann was middle-aged by the time the Rolling Stones appeared on the Ed Sullivan Show; her characters were squares who slopped martinis while their kids dropped LSD.

At the same time, author and book became vastly popular as homosexual kitsch, and as powerfully energized throwbacks to a fading era. They belonged to the strain of '60s pop exemplified by Vegas, Nancy Sinatra, and the Hell's Angels, an antipsychedelic death-trip strain of hedonism trackable to England's Teddy Boys and the Mods-vs.-Rockers division of what was called, in 1960, "Generation X." (Incredible as it may seem.) *Valley*'s downfall portraits of fag-hag divas Judy Garland and Ethel Merman won fans among the then-clandestine gay community; for the first time in pop fiction characters openly referred to "queers" and "fags" in the entertainment industry. At the same time, the rampant drug-taking in *Valley* signaled an outlaw affinity with the chemical revolution of the Love Generation, though Susann's sensibility was more aligned with the discreet nonconformity of Rockefeller Republicanism. (The purest representation of this vanished libertinism can be found in Jack Warden's and Lee Grant's performances in *Shampoo*.) Barbiturates (and amphetamines, before the Warhol set popularized speed) may have been square drugs, but they were still drugs; the glazed housewives and hyper executives who popped them asserted the same bleary personal autonomy, differing merely in style from the average hippy on psilocybin.

In *Valley of the Dolls,* it is Neely O'Hara's hysterical insistence that she needs her pink and yellow "dolls" to keep going—fuck the studio, fuck her career—that elicits our keenest sympathy. Jennifer's breast cancer is tragic, and Anne's romantic disillusionment makes us sad. But Neely's robotic lunge for the pill bottle in stressful moments is what sold *Valley* to a mass audience of Americans, whose coping mechanisms broke down in the social chaos of the '60s. *Valley* was a uniquely unnostalgic anachronism that knew all about "Mother's Little Helper" and the bleak interiority it kept at bay.

The film version of *Valley* was no less an anachronism than the novel. The presence of Dory Previn (soon to lose her co-composer, André Previn, to Mia Farrow, who played Allison Mackenzie in the *Peyton Place* TV series) on the soundtrack, and Sharon Tate in the role of Jennifer, eventually lent the movie a kind of retroactive contemporaneity, after Previn became an early hip-feminist solo performer and Tate was murdered by the Manson Family. (The Tate-LaBianca killings ended the '60s, and in some respects vindicated the plastic straight world's emphasis on rules and decorum. Youth culture had taken everything too far. And this was, of course, the lesson *Valley of the Dolls* winkingly taught about an earlier style of being modern.)

As an icon, Jacqueline Susann belongs to a small pantheon of indomitable superwomen in whom the regressive elements of a given age find near-complete expression. Susann's will to power was a free-floating trait that attached itself to myriad activities before finding its ideal vehicle in the drugstore novel. Once her proper métier had been established (with the publication of *Every Night, Josephine,* an extended mash note to her poodle), Susann pursued world domination with a single-mindedness worthy of Napoleon. When JFK was assassinated the week *Josephine* appeared, she famously blurted, "Why the fuck does this have to happen to me? This is gonna ruin my tour!"

Before Susann, Leni Riefenstahl exemplified the butch, micromanaging female artist succeeding in a man's world. However specious Riefenstahl's memories of "struggle" in the Third Reich, it remains a provocative anomaly that a woman was chosen to direct *Triumph of the Will* and *Olympia.* Some psychopathic quality of will must have struck a sympathetic chord in Hitler, who admired Leni's acting in Weimar-era alpine epics like *The Holy Mountain* and enabled her "purely artistic" directing endeavors even in the Gotterdammerung ambiance of 1944. A half-century later, Leni continued to describe her activities in the '30s as apolitical: She merely seized the opportunities provided by fascism to realize her artistic goals. Like Susann, Riefenstahl viewed self-aggrandizement as a supreme value in itself, an obvious good without ideological implication or negative impact on artistic culture.

This state of mind demolishes distinctions and connections that have characterized a rationalist mainstream of intellectual life since the Enlightenment. A cruder, blockier form of thought monumentalizes the achievements of a Riefenstahl, a Jacqueline Susann. However destructive or puerile the product, its emanation from a woman (or a gay, a black, a pre-op trans-sexual or whatever) represents an advance in the general good. The super-woman exception invites us all to live in the moment, take a bath in the mainstream of our time, and celebrate our newfound visibility in the form of one or two celebrity stereotypes.

Jackie's books outsold contemporary literary novels, and also outsold Flaubert, Proust, even Dickens: In her own mind, that put her up there with Proust and Dickens, and a surprising consensus of postmodern literary theorists would readily agree. The *reception* of a work is what gives it signif-icance in the era of mass affect. In this connection, in the rise of Martha Stewart's magazine, TV, and household-marketing empire (chronicled in the ghastly, unauthorized biography, *Just Desserts*) we see a refinement of the superwoman archetype: the feminist over-achiever as anal-compulsive housewife. While the off-screen Martha, with her shrewd business manipu-lations, carries on the Riefenstahl-Susann tradition of Woman as Corporate Ball-Buster, on-screen Martha is an unflappable, soft-edged, obsessive re-proach to the working mom, the career woman, and the less-than-driven housewife alike. You *can* decorate that birthday cake and restore a barn full of broken furniture and cultivate your own orchids all at the same time, *any woman can.*

Just as *Valley of the Dolls* met the challenge of the '60s with the feminine stereotypes of the '50s, as Leni Riefenstahl applied the testosterone-worshipping, fascist aesthetics of the '30s to her African native portraits of the '60s and '70s, Martha Stewart has reinvented the high school home economics major for nouveau riche women of the '90s. But schizo-Martha, whose dualism presents the alternating images of country kitchen and cor-porate boardroom, is the Janus-faced superwoman ne plus ultra: purveyor of impossibly confining, prescriptive images of women *and* steel-willed proprietress of the image factory.

THE GEARWORKS OF DOOM

IN "THE MANIPULATORS," an episode of the 1972 British TV series *The Fright-eners* written and directed by Mike Hodges, a trainee at an unidentified organization is obliged to spy on, and make harassing phone calls to, a young couple with a baby. He observes the nerve-wracking effects of his calls, and much else, from the windows of a flat opposite theirs, as he is himself being monitored by a supervisor. Via wiretap and the fragmented window view, we see or hear the couple bickering, the husband falling apart under mounting stress, attacking his wailing infant, then strangling his wife when she comes in from work.

The trainee's every impulse is to intervene. There is ample time after the baby's death to keep its mother out of harm's way. The supervisor forbids this. The trainee becomes hysterical as he hears, and partly sees, the worst happening. Finally, the supervisor picks up the phone, dials the flat, and tells the person on the other end to show himself in the window. The man appears, holding up the perfectly unharmed baby, followed by his equally unharmed "wife." It has all been a test, which the trainee, alas, has failed. The supervisor then shoots and kills him.

This tightly wrought drama has a tickling comic undertone, with cut-aways to a slide lecture on behavior modification foreshadowing the grue-some climax. "The Manipulators" could serve as a template for Mike Hodges's later films. Its atmosphere of lethal absurdity and its picture of the intolerable as the normal condition of things can be found as easily in his travesty epics, *Flash Gordon* and *Morons from Outer Space,* as in ink-black hyperrealist works like *Croupier* and the director's most recent film, *I'll Sleep When I'm Dead.*

Valery's "machines for creating further anxiety" come to mind in connec-tion with such Hodges movies as *The Terminal Man, Black Rainbow, Croupier* and even the light-headed pastiche of *Pulp*. The anxiety these films generate is the fear of manipulation: by computers and science in *The Terminal Man*, by occult and unknowable powers in *Black Rainbow*, by the Mafia in *Pulp*. The apprehension of being controlled by hidden forces, of fate confirming paranoid suspicion, suffuses Hodges's early television films, *Suspect* and *Rumour*, reaching its ultimate refinement in the retroactive poison released in *Croupier*'s closing scene.

I'll Sleep When I'm Dead raises a broader sort of anxiety, as a musing on fate, grief and—inevitably in a Hodges film—the toxic properties of testosterone. Fate is settled as the product of reciprocal misunderstandings and the inevitable end of a logical chain of causality set in gear by a false suspicion. Hodges's film is suffused with imminent catastrophe, a dialectic of inevitability sustained by parallel narratives, their connection kept in abeyance for the viewer to puzzle out. A fluid temporal structure flashes slightly behind or ahead of the story piecing itself together. As nothing gratuitously digressive ever occurs, each scene rewards sharp attention to minor details and almost inaudible bits of dialogue.

I'll Sleep When I'm Dead begins on the last night in the life of Davey (Jonathan Rhys-Meyers), an instantly winning young man-about-town who deals small quantities of cocaine. Davey's evening is intercut with cryptic glimpses of a shaggily bearded man (Clive Owen) living in a caravan up north. Davey moves through the London night, followed by a black car. He delivers some blow to a stoned woman at a swank party, later goes home with a pick-up, makes love, gets dressed, and flags a minicab.

Inside the black car are three men: one, silver-haired, imperious, clearly in charge. The woodsman brings a beating victim he's found in the forest to a remote cottage indicated on the man's driver's license. The next morning he's laid off his forest-clearing job. He eats breakfast in a diner. He heads for London in his white van. Meanwhile, Davey has been seized on a dark street, dragged into a warehouse, and raped by Boad (Malcolm McDowell), as Boad's accomplices hold him down.

Come morning, Davey staggers back to his flat in a sickened daze, ignores the greeting of his landlady (the indomitable Sylvia Sims) as she departs for work, lurches into his bathroom, vomits, fills the tub with water, and sinks down into it fully dressed. Soon the tub is full of blood.

Even getting this far in describing *I'll Sleep When I'm Dead* really needs a storyboard, or an ambidextrous shifting of tenses. Each scene's amplitude of detail and nuance seems complete in crisp, unanticipated ways; its apparent disconnection to the one that follows resembles the polymorphic set changes of a dream.

We learn, eventually, that the woodsman is Davey's older brother, Will Graham, who once controlled a gang in the London district where the film plays out; he was married to, or living with, Helen (Charlotte Rampling), who now owns an upscale restaurant; he suffered a breakdown three years earlier, abandoned Helen, Davey, and his associates, fled north, and kept constantly on the move, finally breaking off all contact. What we don't learn, since fate implies the endemic gaps in life-as-narrative, is how Boad and his cohorts foresaw Davey's cab sputtering to a stop where it did, forcing Davey to walk the rest of the way home; or that a broken-into warehouse would handily exist in the nearby alley where it appears. Similarly, when Helen asks Will why he is suddenly there, he answers that it's "because of Davey," though he couldn't have known when he headed south that his brother had committed suicide, or was going to.

These are magical operations of a kind Hodges's films offer as a compliment to the filmgoer's imaginative process: Buñuelian pleats in a doom-weighted picaresque. The black car incarnates Fate—malefic by nature, the undoing of all expectations. Fate is a mechanism for making corpses, like existence itself. Will's beat-up van, a serendipitously claustral box containing remnants of a life, has the traumatized look of a sacrificial offering. It propels him southward on its own volition, an essential pawn in an inessential game.

Scattered inside and between the alternating threads of the same story, almost imperceptible clues, hints, puzzle pieces stick in memory like a mote in the cornea. A subplot follows Davey's friend Mickser (Jamie Foreman) as he discovers Davey's corpse, goes to Helen's restaurant demanding her help in finding Will, clocks his anger when she tells him, truthfully, that she doesn't know where he is. He's shown cornered by Turner (Ken Stott), the current mob boss, who cautions him that if Will turns up, he should bury his dead and clear off again.

What follows has a different opacity: the dream behind the dream, more disturbing than the film's atmosphere of violence. Will wants to know why Davey killed himself. Why must he know? Because he is guilty, because he possesses conscience, and because he's an unregenerated thug whose effort to transform himself will come to nothing: Take your pick.

He makes contact with Helen and with his former crew. Helen has nothing for him. His old crew want him to reclaim his gang territory from Turner. What begins as a story of brothers becomes a trap for the living set by the dead. It's an essential feature of Hodges's bleak and bemused view of things that Will's fate is sealed by his friends rather than his enemies, that Helen's fate is sealed by Will, that nothing goes right that can possibly go wrong.

Hodges has much to show about the class system, about the waste of human possibilities intrinsic to the capitalist order, and the interchangeable nature of victims and victimizers. He indicts the uselessness of moral feeling in a world gone dead, a place that has no fixed center and everyone in it is a moving target. Yet Will's effort to understand himself, to understand what has happened to "a life wasted," as he describes his own, is its own kind of redemption, one that cannot save his life but might afford it a glimpse of sense.

Hodges is among the last of the great directors: by which I mean directors who try to discover reality through film, in the spirit of exploration, rather than proceeding from a set of fixed assumptions and foregone conclusions. Aside from Barbet Schroeder, I can think of no contemporary filmmaker whose work so thoroughly refuses to strike the familiar poses we've come to associate with "the auteur," and more redolent of flexibility and the willingness to be surprised characteristic of an authentic artist. Both directors make astounding movies—not signature "Hodges" or signature "Schroeder," but rather, open-ended investigations that end in a different place than where they began.

For this reason alone, Hodges can't entirely credit the notions of Fate that his films illuminate with such sardonic knowingness. Existential freedom, as Sartre points out, is contingent on the world in which we exercise it: Hodges's characters have "free will" to the degree their circumstances grant them, and hence seem caught in an endless loop of willing, judging and failing to include the reality beyond their own volition in their calculus of wishes. Yet it remains possible to thwart inevitabilities we create for ourselves, even in the face of death.

There is always something we don't know, and in Hodges's work that element behaves like the chemical equivalent of Fate—Hodges's universe is logical, but often proceeds from a flawed assumption, a factor overlooked or an emotion mistaken for a fact. Life is not about feelings, as Céline so coldly and correctly put it: but if we all knew that, to paraphrase another great novelist, we would have paradise on earth.

I'll Sleep When I'm Dead holds up a distorting mirror to Hodges's first feature, *Get Carter,* which remains his best known. Both feature a man searching out the truth about his brother's death, determined to wreak vengeance on the person responsible. In *Get Carter,* this figure goes north from London to Newcastle, where he once operated as a heavy; in *I'll Sleep,* the movement is reversed. In both films, the return of the exile sets off fatal consequences, planting them down in worlds that have become alien despite their familiarity, and where their current modes of life cannot be comprehended by those they've left behind.

The oblique procedures of *I'll Sleep* make its differences from the much earlier film more compelling than its similarities. They reflect a much thicker psychological soup than existed between Hodges's characters in the early seventies. *Get Carter*'s brutality remains logical and true to Hodges's ideas about the dusting of contingency that turns freedom into fate, but fate has become more overtly and intimately linked to chance. In *Get Carter,* the people Carter hunts turn out to be his former associates. In *I'll Sleep,* the revenge object has no connection to the protagonist's abandoned underworld. While both films might be read as meditations on inevitability and the inescapability of the past, *I'll Sleep* offers a small window of escape, a narrow passage between inexorable forces, only to shut it as an aesthetic or ethical option. Hodges invests this version of fate with the full weight of tragedy, although to a certain eye it could also appear an extremely dark farce, turning on the notion of unintended consequences following from seemingly honorable intentions.

Carter remains a hard case in his new London life. However affected he may be by his brother's death, he hasn't undergone any inner transformation since his Newcastle days. He has become more professional, more sociopathic, and more, one could say, himself. (As various characters tell him throughout the film, he's "a real bastard.") Will's nature will always have a reflexive brutality available to it: Wiring is wiring. But as we see from his hesitant impulse to help the beating victim in the forest, he mistrusts his own bad instincts, cursed with conscience that keeps him human, and vulnerable. Abjection clings to him like a wet sheet. He has, in a manner of speaking, been cornered into self-consciousness, by what he tells Helen is "grief for a life wasted." Will's slouching posture, the resigned way he ignores the taunts of Turner's bodyguard, signal to his former rivals that he's broken down, a threat to nobody. But Turner refuses to believe it. The latter belongs to the thoughtless quick instead of the contemplative dead.

Turner's paranoia is mirrored by Boad, the car dealer who attacks Davey. Turner knows that Will has all the qualities he lacks, and therefore needs to destroy him; the same is true of Boad with respect to Davey. This is, strangely, underscored by the fact that Will's voiceovers, which bookend the film, use exactly the same phrases to evoke Davey, albeit in different cadences, that Boad uses to snarl his contempt for him. It's true that Hodges sometimes returns to a film's point of origin, but the place itself has changed beyond recognition.

It's possible that London, the ever-masticating maw of all modern cities, automatically plugs Will into its lethal mechanisms, reduces him to the promptings of instinct, though it's more likely that only the inexplicable— i.e., Davey's rape—has the power to override the self-control he has achieved in solitude. Simply by showing up, however, he becomes a menacing presence in the underworld's zone of exaggerated masculinity and its futile rituals of threat and violence.

Hodges finds this realm endlessly, repulsively fascinating. In *Get Carter* and *Pulp,* the absurdity of violence is inferred from its surplus, with beatings and gunshots as punctuation. The loony militarism depicted in *Flash Gordon* and *Morons from Outer Space* reflects Hodges's acid disdain for the institutionalized violence of the larger systems in which figures like Carter float about like pieces of enraged lint.

Both *Croupier* and *I'll Sleep When I'm Dead* approach this theme in a more contemplative, not to say strangled, way. Little overt violence occurs in either film, only enough to show how deeply embedded it is in the protagonist's background. In both films, the voice of calm sanity emanates from a female character, Marion (Gina McKee) in *Croupier,* Helen in *I'll Sleep.* (In *Get Carter,* women are brainless playthings and soulless chippies.) Helen warns Will to "forget the funeral," that unless he leaves he'll be destroyed—an accurate prediction. She will be destroyed as well, though Will "transforms" himself shortly before discharging his rage, shaving off the beard he sprouted in the north, dressing up for the funeral, retrieving a stash of money and a slick car, planning his exit with Helen. But by this time, there's really no exit.

A mournfully submerged tone, an exasperated weariness over an endless cycle of cruelty fueled by the will to power, inflect Hodges's recent work as a kind of negative grandeur, as if the suppurating wounds of modern consciousness have at last become simply "what we have to live with" as we come to recognize how very brief the game is and learn to value what we have instead of what we want. Even good luck is contingent on the ever-changing parameters of chance. This is represented most cogently in *Croupier* with shots of the spinning roulette wheel, in *I'll Sleep* by the image of Davey's shoe tip slowly floating up to break the surface of his bloody bathwater.

Hodges's films engage two distinct narrative approaches, each in its way undermining linearity. The first, which occurs in *Croupier* and several other films, is the implicit or explicit framing of the action within the point of view of a character reporting to an imaginary audience. Jack Manfred (Clive Owen), in *Croupier,* is writing a novel and telling it to us. For the most part, his voiceover agrees with what we see onscreen, merely turning the image's eternal present into the past tense. But Jack's novel also shapes our perception of him beyond what we see, interposing a fictional persona who may or may not coincide with the Jack we observe.

In the TV film *Rumour,* Hodges uses the urgent voice of a Fleet Street hack (like Will, also dead before he finishes narrating) as an overgloss that often works against the image. The parodic hard-bitten prose on the soundtrack often has a purely adhesive relation to what's onscreen. This also happens in *Pulp,* in which the dime-store novelist played by Michael Caine is less an unreliable narrator than one whose apprehension of what's occurring is continually undermined by whatever happens next. *Morons from Outer Space* also features a reporter who becomes hopelessly entangled in his "story."

While many films use the trope of a journalist solving a mystery while pursuing a scoop, Hodges's are often layered by this device to question a manufactured, consensual reality. At the outset of *Black Rainbow,* for example, Tom Hulce's newsman believes he finally sees the vanished medium he has been tracking down for years, that he photographs her, even talks to her. At the film's end, the developed photos reveal an abandoned house overgrown with kudzu.

Hodges's other favorite narrative strategy informs *I'll Sleep When I'm Dead* and involves a warping or looping effect vis-à-vis temporality, not entirely unlike the editing style of Nicolas Roeg, though Hodges's reasons for

using it are both more legible and more aesthetically persuasive than the al-
most-aleatory approach Roeg's films take. The malleable rendering of
chronology in *I'll Sleep* echoes several of Hodges's films, notably *Black Rainbow,* which uses time itself as a metaphysical conundrum. (We never exist
entirely in the present but live partly in the past and perhaps partly in the
future, too.) Technically, *I'll Sleep* is "narrated," at both ends, by Will's
voiceover. Something of *Black Rainbow*'s slithery, paradoxical elusiveness
persists in *I'll Sleep,* given that by the end Will is dead by implication,
within an hour or so of the film's internal time, yet "alive" via the voiceover
thought-bubble. Hence his spoken thoughts about Davey ("What's there to
say he was ever alive?") are also the film's thoughts about Will.

In effect, it's hard to tell which parallel events are simultaneous, which
are premonitory, which are "past," and which are imaginary. The film's internal time, unless I've missed something, extends only from the night of
Davey's attack to the day before (or, perhaps, the day *of*) his (scheduled,
undepicted) funeral—three or, at most, four days, and more probably two
or three. Assuming that Will has gone to Boad's house a second time, alone,
after his first surreptitious visit with Mickser—something I infer because (a)
a party is taking place the first time and (b) Will still wears a beard on the
first occasion, and in the film's penultimate scene he's beardless—then time
has been carefully bent out of shape in order to throw the "reality" of this
scene into question. And, by extension, the reality of everything we've seen.

In the hands of a director less ingeniously skilled and pointedly skeptical
about the reality of anything, this kind of ambiguity might read as an expedient trick. *I'll Sleep When I'm Dead* registers as anything but: It is, rather,
the self-consuming artifact par excellence, a consummate work of art that
tears itself to pieces as it moves along and reconstitutes itself, in the end, as
an impossible object worthy of repeated contemplation.

DON'T BUY US WITH SORRY
AFTER BURNING DOWN THE BARN

I WILL first reveal, without embarrassment, that I fell asleep five times during a morning press screening of Errol Morris's *The Fog of War*—which received its U.S. premiere at the New York Film Festival last September and is currently playing in theaters around the country—and I left the auditorium with precious few impressions besides that of the spectacularly bad dental work that Robert S. McNamara, the former secretary of defense, exposed each time he was featured in close-up. Having now viewed the documentary three additional times, while fully awake, what ultimately seems most impressive about Morris's skewed framing, Philip Glass's brooding, ominous score, the cutaway montages of stock military footage from World War II and Vietnam, and the random clips of media moments from the era of McNamara's cabinet tenure under Kennedy and Johnson is how well they are deployed to contrive an illusion of deepening insight and imminent revelation while dispensing entirely with the factual glue necessary to place McNamara's role in either administration into any legible context.

Much of Morris's oeuvre to date (from 1976's *Gates of Heaven,* his documentary on pet cemeteries, to his 2000 TV series *First Person,* whose episodes bore titles like "Mr. Personality" and "The Smartest Man in the World") has consisted of a geek's-eye view of subjects only slightly geekier than the director himself—a view that is almost invariably glacial and contemptuous of both his subjects and his audience. Yet now and then, Morris's technique of staring "objectively" at the human oddities he collects achieves a transcendently hideous rendering of the lame and the halt in human nature, very much in the spirit of Francis Bacon's portraits of shrieking popes and lumps of human meat writhing about in barren interiors: While Morris's visual sense is rather quotidian and hardly as exalted as Bacon's

iconic genius, he has a definite flair for turning humans into talking sea cu-
cumbers obsessed with philosophical or historical matters clearly beyond
their intelligence. That they also seem beyond the director's intelligence
accounts for the quirky hilarity that rescues much of Morris's work from
being taken seriously.

In McNamara, Morris has at last found a subject whose callow, self-
serving evasions and stridently complacent banalities have a deep affinity
with Morris's insufferable delusion that his work digs deep below the surface of things, enlightening the public in ever-more innovative ways.

Here the trope of audience improvement, spelled out in the film's subtitle, consists of "Eleven Lessons from the Life of Robert S. McNamara,"
which range from clichés as old as von Clausewitz ("Empathize with your
enemy"), to specious dicta ("Rationality will not save us"), to secular mysticism ("There's something beyond one's self"), to corporate-training-manual
exhortations ("Maximize efficiency"), to McNamara's personal notions
about how warfare should be conducted ("Proportionality should be a
guideline in war"), to pseudo-profundities ("Belief and seeing are both
often wrong"), to blatant cynicisms epidemic among governments everywhere ("In order to do good, you may have to engage in evil"), and, pen-
ultimately, to a "lesson" routinely spouted by film stars, retired politicians,
seasonally traded athletes, grocery checkout clerks and uncountable other
Americans who've acquired it through cultural osmosis: "Never say never."
Last, and least, is the bromide "You can't change human nature."

This final "lesson" is demonstrably the case where McNamara himself is
concerned. At the time of filming, he appears convinced that something
that seemed the right thing to do in, say, 1962, though history has proven
it to have been the wrong thing, was nevertheless the right thing because it
seemed the right thing when he did it: "You don't have hindsight at the
time," he astutely observes. And precious little foresight sight, either, judging by the vast historical literature on the Cuban Missile Crisis and the
Vietnam War. There is nothing resembling an apology, a mea culpa, anywhere in this film: McNamara admits that his role in the firebombing of
Tokyo would probably have been considered a war crime if America had
lost World War II, yet seems oblivious to the fact that he committed many
war crimes over the course of a war we did lose, even at one point admitting
that he can't remember if he was the person who authorized the use of

Agent Orange. When asked who was responsible for the Vietnam War, McNamara unhesitatingly says "the President" but softens this pronouncement by kissing Johnson's ass with his very next breath, lingeringly enough that even LBJ would have been mortified by it.

The film blithely skips over the routine doctoring of military budget figures and outright lying about casualties that was McNamara's specialty—connivances that made him LBJ's favorite inherited cabinet member—as the Johnson administration plunged deeper into a war that neither Johnson nor Kennedy before him believed could be won from its very inception, and glosses over the intense antagonism between McNamara and the Joint Chiefs of Staff (in this, at least, McNamara seems to have had the right idea, albeit in the wrong brain). In one of the few unobsequious moments in Morris's fogbound movie, we at least get to see McNamara jauntily asserting, at a press conference, that the war is going very well indeed, at a moment when even the business community had soured on the whole sordid enterprise, the Quaker peace activist Norman Morrison had incinerated himself directly below the window of McNamara's office at the Pentagon, and 50,000 antiwar demonstrators had descended on Washington. (McNamara praises himself for refusing to allow the military guard around the Pentagon to load live rounds in their rifles; we then see footage of demonstrators getting clobbered with rifle butts—which proves that Morris can still work himself up to a sense of irony, if not actual humor.)

Unhelpfully, the filmmaker allows McNamara to repeatedly, with fervor, remind us that the world came "that close" to nuclear war during the Cuban Missile Crisis—often emphasizing the pure luck that saved us from worldwide annihilation by pinching his thumb and forefinger nearly together. This is hardly illuminating. For one thing, anyone over 45 has known this since 1962—and, unlike McNamara, few of us had a nuke-proof bunker at our disposal in which to weather the imminent holocaust.

True, McNamara argued successfully for a blockade and negotiations while JCS mental cases, notably General Curtis LeMay, were truculently lobbying Kennedy to launch a massive air and naval strike against Cuba, which already had over 200 active warheads and the missiles to deliver them. By his account, McNamara applied the "lessons" of Cuba—whatever they may have been—to the war in Vietnam, a culture about which our government knew absolutely nothing. It's perhaps more surprising than it

should be to hear, late in the film, that, at a conference in Hanoi years after
the war's conclusion, McNamara learned for the first time that Vietnam, far
from having been a puppet state of Moscow or Peking, had been fighting a
war of national liberation, that the Vietnamese regarded the American in-
cursion as a new attempt at colonization after the French had been driven
out, and that Vietnam had been engaged in almost perpetual warfare
against China for over a thousand years. McNamara's learning curve apparently works at the same speed as a Martian probe.

Morris's idea of a penetrating question is demonstrated in the film's
epilogue: "Do you ever feel responsible for Vietnam?" he asks. McNamara
refuses to answer one way or the other, though throughout *The Fog of War*
it's abundantly clear that McNamara remains, on the cusp of senescence, incapable of feeling much culpability about anything. At best, he feels rueful
that history has already decisively pegged him as a monstrous bureaucratic
wastebasket. A closing title mentions that after being fired as defense secretary in 1968, McNamara served as the president of the World Bank for
twelve years, until 1981. Curious to learn if his own human nature had
changed even a tad since his years of orchestrating the slaughter of millions
in Vietnam, I phoned the brilliant investigative journalist Roger Trilling and
asked him if he had anything to share about McNamara's tenure at the bank.

"Well, I do know . . . one thing," Trilling, a prodigious geyser of clandestine information, allowed. "When McNamara was handed his sinecure in
1968, he decided to choose a model nation as a testing ground for international development. He chose Thailand, since he was . . . obviously familiar
with the region.

"The primary problem in creating development for the whole country
was the economic discrepancy between the impoverished north and the
economically healthier south. . . . So McNamara proposed the development of a 'leisure industry' that could benefit both areas of the country.
This involved bringing girls from the north to the cities in the south to
work in the sex industry, as a developmental tool." But of course as secretary of defense McNamara had already contributed greatly to the promotion of sexual tourism in Thailand, having negotiated the 1967 "R&R"
treaty that would fill Bangkok's brothels with furloughed American GIs.

Under McNamara's stewardship, the World Bank monitored the entre-
preneurial savvy of aging B-girls over a number of years, identifying which

were capable of developing businesses that would help bring Thailand into the global economy. These country courtesans, on the verge of retirement, were qualified for microlending, enabling them to open messenger services, bridal shops, laundromats and various other small enterprises. As these women turned out to be more adroit and quicker at turning a dollar than the males being groomed for private enterprise by the World Bank, this eventually resulted in a complete reversal of Thailand's traditional gender economics, with women suddenly dominating the economy.

Perversely enough, the system worked, at least to the satisfaction of Westerners like Robert McNamara, who knows that in order to do good, you may have to engage in evil. But the evils involved in sponsoring a Third World sex industry in the interests of globalization are depressingly routine compared with the evil Robert McNamara perpetrated throughout his government career. Concerning which, Errol Morris's *Fog of War* never scratches the surface.

SUBLIME PARIAH
Céline's Voyages into the Whirlwind

[U]nder certain historical circumstances everyone must become a traitor. For example, the entire populations of Norway, Holland, France, Greece, and Yugoslavia consisted of traitors (always in the technical-legal sense of the word) during the German occupation of these countries. No matter which government each individual considered to be his, there existed another in whose eyes he was committing treason.

—HANS MAGNUS ENZENSBERGER,
"TOWARDS A THEORY OF TREASON"

The plain truth, I may as well admit it, is that I've never been really right in the head.

—LOUIS FERDINAND CÉLINE, *VOYAGE AU BOUT DE LA NUIT*

LOUIS FERDINAND Céline was almost 40 when his first novel, *Voyage au bout de la nuit*, known in English as *Journey to the End of the Night,* sent shocks through the Parisian literary nervous system. An explosion of bilious truths and unassuageable rage, a panorama of the class system's rear end as an overflowing toilet in an abattoir, *Journey* flung a hand grenade into the house of fiction and filled the smashed-up structure with ponce argot and working-class vernacular. Céline had previously written a doctoral thesis in medicine more literary than scientific, and two unpublished, unperformed plays, *L'Eglise* and *Progrès/Pericles.*

Journey's author had already lived "a whole life." ("And," he might have said, "if that's all there is, I've been swindled.") Born in 1894—the year of Alfred Dreyfus's arrest and trial before a military tribunal—in Courbevoie-sur-Seine (as he never tired of reminding people), Louis-Ferdinand Destouches, who became "Céline" decades later, really only lived in Arletty's home suburb for three days. He was immediately put out to wet-nurse in Puteaux. During that time, his family moved into central Paris.

In Louis's earliest years, the Destouches survived on thin profits from his mother's lace shop in the Passage Choiseul near the Opéra, and his father's meager earnings (a source of self-immolating bitterness and violent explosions of drunken hysteria) as a low-level employee in an insurance firm. The family lived in the arcade, above the shop, as was common among tradespeople in the declining crafts professions; Céline often transforms the Passage into an opera buffa of petty gossip, commercial rivalries, and surreal pageants of rampaging mobs.

When Céline's fiercely beloved grandmother died, she left an inheritance that provided the family a modicum of security. Céline was sent to private Catholic schools and, later, exclusive boarding schools in Germany and England, to acquire other languages useful for the business career his parents envisoned for him. The disastrous apprenticeships he describes in *Death on Credit* were, in reality, more auspicious positions with jewelers; for a time, he managed the Nice branch of the international firm of Lacloche Frères.

Volunteering for the cavalry on a dare, Céline was swept within a few months into the fantastic carnage of the First World War. While decommissioned for a bullet wound in the shoulder he later mythologized into a shot in the head that necessitated trepanning (an ingenious fib that brought him widely publicized glory as a war hero), he spent a year in Cameroon as a coffee plantation overseer; he subsequently kicked around the squalid underbellies of New York and London before completing his medical training in Paris, on an accelerated schedule available to veterans.

An habitual mythomaniac, nothing Céline said in interviews could be taken at face value. *Death on Credit's* nightly family brawls, his father's volcanic violence, his mother's dishrag submissiveness—much of this fictional exacerbation of the facts has passed for decades as unvarnished autobiographic truth, and Céline nastily stoked the confusion.

Reality: He had mostly affectionate relations with his parents, and, once a doctor, rapidly entered an exalted stratum of material comfort. Under Rockefeller Foundation auspices, he secured an important post with the League of Nations health services, heading "fact finding" delegations to dozens of countries, under the patronage of the League's Director of the Hygiene Service, Dr. Ludwig Rajchman. (It is astonishing how many anti-Semites of all stripes, Nazis, fascist sympathizers, poisonous journalists, murderous politicians, collabos, strutting catamites in SS drag, war criminals and aesthetes—the whole deformed menagerie of hate-mongers of the late '30s—owed their early professional advancement to Jewish patronage. Céline, quite aside from his "Jewish problem," never allowed any good deed done him to pass unpunished. Nothing assuaged his sense of deprivation; benevolence and kindness triggered a perverse desire to reciprocate with betrayal; his paranoia was restive, tireless, free-ranging and, to a degree, democratically unfair, so obviously deranged it nearly qualifies—and many would dispense with "nearly"—as exculpatory, despite its repulsiveness.)

While the League of Nations primarily invented inert committees and supplied caviar and foie gras to torpid diplomats, Céline's transformation of the Jewish Rajchman into a grasping currency speculator in *L'Eglise* was a surpassingly odious slander. Céline bit any hand that fed him. His later books gleefully, maniacally fulminate against his publishers, translators, former friends and benefactors. His letters to Maître Mikkelsen, the lawyer who spent years thwarting Céline's extradition (on charges of collaboration) from Denmark to France after World War II, progress from mild expressions of ingratitude to uninhibited, scatological abuse between 1945 and 1947.

It was when *Journey to the End of the Night* made Céline famous that his "lifestyle" shifted from professional respectability to bohemianism, and his financial security disintegrated. He lived well on his royalties for a time, then less well on shrinking advances. He continued practicing medicine, but the Depression lowered all boats, and, in any case, Céline chose to work in suburban clinics treating the destitute ill.

The epic of transposed, hallucinatory autobiography that constitutes the bulk of Céline's literary production bears to the person Céline a fun-house mirror cousinage to Marcel Proust's "Marcel" in *À la recherche du temps perdu*. Reality and fiction are inextricably merged. The narrator is one of the author's many selves—that is, a literary character constructed from multiple sources, especially himself.

Proust and Céline, stylistic and social opposites, were the supreme literary avatars of 20th-century France. Proust charted the increasingly spectral world of fin-de-siècle aristocracy and its heavily veiled, sordid pleasures; Céline figures as the poet of the lower classes, depicting lives riddled with disease, plagued by alcoholism, debased by an imprisoning scramble for money, trapped in cohabitive hells. The period described in Céline's early novels overlaps that of Proust's epic, although Proust was dead before Céline published anything. Céline lived on to depict the thirties and the Second World War, and his last three novels open in the "present" of the 1950s.

In *Journey to the End of the Night,* Céline's portrait of a brothelkeeper succinctly distinguishes his milieu from that of his only "rival" in 20th-century French literature:

> Proust, who was half ghost, immersed himself with extraordinary tenacity in the infinitely watery futility of the rites and procedures that entwine the members of high society, those denizens of the void, those phantoms of desire, those irresolute daisy-chainers still waiting for their Watteau, those listless seekers after implausible Cythereas. Whereas Madame Herote, with her sturdy popular origins, was firmly fastened to the earth by her crude, stupid, and very specific appetites.

Describing Céline as a "fascist" is like calling an unmedicated manic-depressive a Republican. The Célinean discourse shrewdly impersonates the unchecked verbal torrent of the *délire,* more formally shapely and entirely calculated, its content is no less fantastic than Daniel Paul Schreber's *Memoirs of My Nervous Illness* and its author's imputations of "soul murder" to his psychiatrist, and his penetration by God's "celestial rays."

Céline's nihilism, the cruelty he portrays, his acidic certainty of human worthlessness both invite and repel categorical political inferences. In many ways, his mudslides of invective resemble the protracted arguments Thomas Bernhard's protagonists conduct with themselves. Patrick McCarthy, one of Céline's biographers, notes affinities between Céline's hapless, hopeless characters and those of Samuel Beckett. In both Céline and Beckett, McCarthy identifies a despair so insistently unrelieved that it deliberately mimics the polished routine of a nightclub comic.

For Céline, as for Beckett and Bernhard, the only subject is death. Since death is absurd, it forces us to laugh as well as grieve. Céline's novels are crowded with hilariously pathetic people who don't know how to live, who drag themselves through existences of chronic ailments that become their sole topics of conversation, relieved to relinquish all dignity to the god of disease. Céline's hypochondriacal gargoyles relish the spectacle of other people's misfortunes. Their happiest moments occur when they gather to form a gaping, bloodthirsty mob. Ferdinand's patients revel in the histrionics of their own protracted expiration, discuss their bowel movements and martyrdom to constipation in his waiting room, entertain one another with tales of high blood pressure, cysts and glandular disorders.

In contrast to the sordor and ugliness of poverty and decrepitude, every wretch repines for a moment of beatitude; the express train to hell his characters ride brakes occasionally to afford a glimpse of the beautiful. A landscape, an interlude of piano music, the objects crafted by the Passage's engravers, silversmiths and furniture makers, even the watercolors of sailing boats that Ferdinand's father paints between displays of contemptible, self-righteous intolerance and bottomless self-pity in *Mort à crédit:* The passing instant of grace adds pathos to the claustrophobic shittiness of Céline's cosmos.

His first novels and his last ones run in inverse chronology: *Journey to the End of the Night* begins where the subsequent *Mort à crédit* ends. The grotesque odyssey to Denmark that Céline undertook with his wife Lili and their cat Bébert, through Germany's devastated cities and pulverized landscapes while the final Allied bombing raids continued, amid hordes of shell-shocked refugees and panic-stricken Nazis, unfolds in semi-reverse order in *D'un chateau l'autre, Nord* and *Rigadon.*

Céline was unusually confident of his debut novel's importance, convinced it would win the Prix Goncourt. But for the last-minute defection of two jurors, shifting the ballots in favor of Guy Mazeline's *Les Loups,* it would have, but losing the Goncourt proved more salubrious for Céline than winning it. Literary Paris had recognized and acclaimed a genius, and his name wasn't Guy Mazeline. The Goncourt jury's horse-trading became a scandal the press inflamed for months, sending *Journey's* sales figures shooting through the roof of the Denoël publishing house, its projected 5–7,000 copies mushrooming to 50,000 and beyond.

Journey sweeps like a Steadicam through a carnival of perfidy, betrayal, cruelty, deluded romanticism, amorality, dishonesty, bitterness, degeneracy, psychic mutilation, monstrous selfishness and human viciousness few novelists besides Zola and deSade have taken such withering satisfaction from—a cornucopia of moral and spiritual bankruptcy. It echoes certain events in Céline's life, transposed and bloated into large, malignant shapes, misanthropic, self-flagellating, serenely disenchanted by the entire concept of the wish, and, as perhaps the most demonic features of all, sentimental and romantic. Céline's romanticism is an unaccountably hardy residue of idealism, the doggedly ineradicable regret that the world lacks quite enough will or good faith to make itself a better home for empathy.

Like Céline, the narrator Ferdinand Bardamu experiences some of the bloodiest fighting of the First World War, operates a trading post in a West African colony, wanders for a time through the whorehouses and public toilets, dockside bars and gambling dens of New York and London. Céline wasted less of his own material than most. He eventually found uses for every scrap of experience, like his mother with her leftover lace trimmings. The world he lived in and the one he constructed from it differ little topographically, though Céline himself was both a far better and arguably less palatable individual than any alter-ego he replaced himself with. In any case, the public writer and the private doctor are never the same person. The only quality they consistently share is sadness. Céline's reputation has never lavished attention on the grief that runs like a deep, black river under the more highly painted nihilism strewn across the surface of his fictive landscapes.

From a one-day League of Nations inspection of Ford's Detroit factory, Céline spins a corrosive, accurate description of Ford's grotesquely antihuman Taylorist practice of employing the sick and disabled for piecework. When Bardamu finishes his medical studies in Paris, he finds work in a clinic in Drancy—one of the industrial suburbs being slowly absorbed into the city proper, a cloaca of crime, disease and demoralizing poverty. En route to a house call on the Henrouille family, he asks directions from Bébert, a young boy sweeping the sidewalk. Bébert has "the greenish look of an apple that will never get ripe."

"If you've got to love something," Bardamu reflects, "you'll be taking less chance with children than with grownups, you'll at least have the excuse of hoping they won't turn out as crummy as the rest of us."

Bébert's quick mind and sweet nature inject a tender element into *Journey:* Even the most scurrilous characters are heartbroken when the boy contracts typhus. (It can't be coincidental that Céline's cat, the most famous feline in French literature, was named Bébert—perhaps because "if you've got to love something," you risk even less with a cat than a child.)

The Henrouilles implore Bardamu to commit M. Henrouille's mother, who lives in a shack at the end of the back garden, to a rest home. But after persuading her to see him, Bardamu finds that "Grandma Henrouille was merry; discontented and filthy, but . . . the destitution in which she had lived for more than twenty years had not marked her soul. Her dread . . . was the outside world, as though cold, horror, and death could come to her only from that direction and not from within. She evidently feared nothing from within, she seemed absolutely sure of her mind, as of something undeniable, acknowledged, and certified, once and for all. . . . And to think I had been chasing mine halfway around the world."

In *Journey,* Bardamu repeatedly encounters Robinson, an aimless, world-weary crypto-doppelgnger who, like Bardamu himself, gets entangled with clinging or calculating women. After Robinson breaks up with Madelon, an unpleasant, shallow, exhibitionistic vamp, she begins stalking him. He takes unwelcome refuge in the hospital where Bardamu works. It's basically an insane asylum. When Madelon starts showing up at the front gate, Bardamu hustles Robinson out the back to board with the Henrouilles.

Journey now becomes an elephantine, Célinean version of a Georges Simenon novel. The story becomes Robinson's story, Bardamu the Conradian observer.

Céline detested Zola, and scorned comparisons to him—rightly, from a formal perspective. *Journey* is anti-naturalistic and shatters Zola's linearity into shrapnel. But in its evocation of battlefield chaos, the toxic slum of Rancy and the lethal connivance of Robinson with Mme. Henrouille to murder Grandma Henrouille, *Journey* successively evokes *The Debacle, Germinal* and, most pungently, *La Bête Humaine.* Bardamu's inexhaustible monologue encloses all that happens within his own perception. The absence of coherent transitions and Céline's posthumous tone, as of someone relating what happened long ago, mark a greater departure from Zola's technical methods than from Zola's material.

In *Death on Credit,* Céline's assault on French syntax plays full-out. His famous use of three dots slices the conventionally ordered sentence into verbal musical fragments of tocatta, fugue, capriccio, mazurka, tarantelle. The psychological shorthand of those three dots meshes external reality with the ventriloquial projection of other people's thoughts.

Ferdinand begins his narration as the middle-aged doctor he's become, interlacing his present and earlier selves, transporting us to a previous time, when he grew up in his mother Clémence's lace-mending shop in the Passage des Bérésinas.

Clémence, incapable of quelling the compulsive rages of her husband Auguste, is the archetypal doormat who weeps instead of screaming. (While his mother disgusts Ferdinand, Céline, writing "as himself" in *Féerie pour un autre fois,* reflects bitterly on his own mother's sufferings and recalls heartbreakingly joyful moments they shared.) Like any boy his age, Ferdinand gets into messes while navigating a world he knows nothing much about, but the stress of poverty and his father's paranoia inflate the boy's smallest derelictions into proof of his worthlessness and incorrigibility. His Grandmother Caroline and his worldly uncle Edouard often pacify Auguste's rampages, but the daily tenor of life in the Passage never lastingly improves.

> [H]e pointed across the room at me in my corner. Ungrateful wretch! Sneaky little profiteer . . . getting fat on other people's sacrifices . . . Me . . . with my shitass . . . my boils . . . my insatiable consumption of shoes . . . There I was! All this was about me, the scapegoat for all their misfortunes . . .
>
> "Oh! Goddamit! Goddamit to hell! If it weren't for him! Oh! What's that? I'd clear out so fast. Bah! I can promise you that. I'd have done it long ago . . . long ago. Not tomorrow, see! This minute! Goddamit! If we didn't have this little hunk of shit on our hands!

Uncle Edouard's inspiration to send Ferdinand to England to learn the language lands the boy at Meanwell College, a nightmarish ancient pile out of Sheridan Le Fanu. Here, Céline serves a full menu of bad food, bad weather, Ferdinand's fixation on the headmistress's ass, his unwanted, brotherly caretaking of an imbecile boy who swallows inkwells and cutlery. Unlike Céline, who quickly acquired fluent English, Ferdinand refuses to learn a word besides "hello" during his entire stay at Meanwell.

Death on Credit's claustrophobia is mercifully relieved, 300 pages in, by the introduction of the cracked, fascinating inventor, Roger-Martin Courtial des Pereires. Courtial, whose boundless enthusiasm for scientific experiment combined with a fragile grasp of any kind of science belongs to a long tradition of hare-brained, earnest quackery in France dating back before the Revolution. If Courtial doesn't exactly fill Ferdinand's mind with worthwhile knowledge, he opens it to curiosity; even though *Death on Credit* closes on Céline's inevitable bleak note, the incorrigible kid acquires some incipient intellectual capacity.

Courtial is a quintessentially Célinean character—a scoundrel, addicted to whores and gambling, who hides from creditors in a concealed basement and launches ridiculous competitions for inventors in order to fleece them of their entry fees; at the same time, he's sincerely absorbed by myriad areas of knowledge, by great discoveries, and relentless in his conjuration of pataphysical excuses for his failed experiments. Courtial's long-suffering but formidably domineering wife, whose soliloquies of execration have the tsunami quality of Céline's own authorial torrents of insult, paradoxically worships Courtial. For all Ferdinand's deflative squawking against the old fraud, in Courtial he finds a surrogate father, and continues living with Courtial and his wife even after the inventor's offices are destroyed by the attack of a thwarted contest-loser's gigantic diving-bell. After Courtial sells their sole remaining property in Meudon, they establish a kind of "fresh air school" for problem children in the countryside; their charges quickly become an ungovernable gang of precociously copulating, wily poachers, whose expeditions through the district keep abundant food on the table and incur the violent hatred of the neighbors.

Céline knows nothing of "moderation." Like Dostoevsky, he contrives scenes of byzantine complication and gruesome awkwardness, involving a full complement of human gargoyles. When it seems impossible that anything worse could happen, the author introduces yet another element that surpasses everything previous in antic insanity. The eruption (there is no other word) of Captain Lebyatin into Madame Stavrogin's drawing room early in *The Devils* comes to mind when, after Courtial's suicide, Mme. Courtial and Ferdinand's stunned grief is invaded by the deranged, larcenous, defrocked priest whose mania inspired Courtial's ruinous diving-bell competition in the first place.

Céline planned to follow *Death on Credit* with *Casse-pipe* (*Cannon Fodder*), another novel about World War I, but his second novel's tepid reception sent him into a depression, which he attempted to cure by traveling. He went to New York and Los Angeles. Avoiding Paris, he visited the Soviet Union, where soft-currency royalties from Elsa Triolet's translation of *Journey* could only be spent inside the country. He only visited Leningrad, where the Theater Marinski politely declined to stage his ballets. (Céline wrote several. Dance and dancers intoxicated him; he had a long affair with the American dancer Elizabeth Craig, and later married choreographer Lucette Almansour.)

Céline loathed the U.S.S.R., execrating its workers' paradise as a soulless spiritual privy in *Mea culpa*. As the text was really a short pamphlet, it was combined with the author's thesis on Semmelweiss and issued in book form. Hardly anyone reviewed it. *Mea culpa*'s argument is far from a defense of capitalism; it describes Communism as a reconstituted form of capitalism.

> Materialistic Communism means Matter above everything Else; and when it becomes a question of Matter, in its highest form never conquers, but always in its most cynical, its trickiest, its most brutal. Just look, in this U.S.S.R., how quickly money has been rehabilitated. How money has recaptured all its tyranny right away! and in cubic progression!

Céline's infamous pamphleteering between 1937 and 1941, in *Bagetelles pour un massacre, L'Ecole des cadavres* and *Les Beaux Draps* has been so exhaustively dissected in France since 1945 that it's long been recognized there as the lamentable spillage of Céline's delirium. The pamphlets, excluded from his *Pléiade oeuvres completes,* continue the centuries-old tradition of pamphleteering during political crises. Characteristically, rhetorical excess undermines and refutes the ostensible argument being made. Swift's *A Modest Proposal* pushed the punitive English views of "the Irish question" into an argument for cannibalism; the Dissenter Daniel Dafoe's *The Shortest Way with Dissenters* so violently advocated the High Church's campaign to eliminate dissent that the pamphlet's embrace by church fanatics alienated their constituency.

Céline's pamphlets belong to this dryly comedic lineage, but radically diverge from it in their mixture of ridicule and self-mockery designed to exculpate the author from responsibility for what he's writing. Their satire is indiscriminately aimed, their intentions are convoluted, confused and only unambiguous in effusive anti-Semitic hatred, which was hardly meant to counteract the rampant anti-Semitism of the era. Their anti-Jewish fervor isn't neutralized by the bile Céline vomits at the same time all over the

French, the Germans, the Russians, the British, Hitler, Stalin, Churchill, et al.; Jew-hatred and Jew-ridicule appear on almost every page of *Bagatelles pour un massacre,* interspersed with matchingly offensive philo-Semitic rhapsodies. Céline's comedic genius fails in the pamphlets because his primary victims are chimerical stereotypes of real victims. He echoes the mob mentality he satirizes in his novels, even proposes to lead the mob himself, urging it to violence. Although these books are riddled with contractions that reduce them to incoherence—"his ravings declare their own ridiculousness," as Alice Kaplan observes in her key study, *Reproductions of Banality: Fascism, Literature, and French Intellectual Life*—they were widely enjoyed among "rational" anti-Semitic writers like Drieu de la Rochelle and Lucien Rebatet. In my translation of this passage from *Bagatelles:*

> Everything considered, it isn't just now that I've come to know them, the Semites. On the London docks, I saw lots of them, the Yids. Not Hymie jewelers, but real vicious lowlifes, eating rats together . . . flat as flounders . . . The cop is always an Irishman . . . / . . . fatuous like all the Aryans . . . / . . . Very quickly he softens like a sausage for the Kikes . . . takes pity . . . invites them in for a cup of tea . . .

Even many nonfascist writers saw nothing objectionable about *Bagatelles.* Hannah Arendt, in noting that Brecht's *Dreigroshenoper* had the opposite effect on its receptive Berlin audiences than Brecht intended, encouraging the bourgeoisie "to discard the uncomfortable mask of hypocrisy and to accept openly the standards of the mob," also remarks:

> A reaction similar in its ambiguity was aroused some ten years later in France by Céline's *Bagatelles pour un Massacre,* in which he proposed to massacre all the Jews. André Gide was publicly delighted in the pages of the *Nouvelle Revue Francaise,* not of course because he wanted to kill the Jews of France, but because he rejoiced in the blunt admission of such a desire in the fascinating contradiction between Céline's bluntness and the hypocritical politeness which surrounded the Jewish question in all respectable quarters.

Arendt's conclusion—that "the Nazis always knew [Céline] was the only true antisemite in France"—is valid enough, in the sense that fascist writers like Drieu and Rebatet conceived a Fascist France independent of the Nazis, whereas Céline's nihilism drew no such fussy boundaries. He was just as insane as the Nazis were, though his manias were impervious to any consistency, and eventually useless to any political faction.

He was, as hinted in the above passage from *Bagatelles* (and more emphatically stated elsewhere in the book), contemptuous of the Nazis' "Aryan" ideal, and he once disrupted an anti-Semitic literary conference by shouting that it was "more of the same Aryan bullshit." At a different period, however, he embraced Aryanism and called for the extermination of all Jews. Somewhat like Rebatet, Céline displayed a kamikaze inclination to re-align himself with positions he'd already repudiated, and to repudiate the ascendant tendencies of a given moment—but Céline's schizoid eruptions of verbiage had nothing of Rebatet's poise and tortuous pseudo-logic behind them. His delirium splattered in all directions. At the height of the Nazis' triumph, Céline freely declared to anyone who would listen that "the Krauts" had already lost the war. As Céline biographer Frédéric Vitoux put it: "Impossible to enlist Céline under a banner. The socialist or communist intellectuals in 1932, the fascists in '38, and the collaborators in '40 all found that out very quickly. Céline was not one of them."

Céline's disastrous excursion into "the Jewish question" was the perverted expression of his pacifism as it confronted the certainty of another war, and his need to scapegoat the most vulnerable and persecuted figure, the Jew, as instigator of the looming cataclysm. The hatred Céline inscribes mirrors his self-hatred. He sees the Jews' victimization as a usurpation of his own life-long view of himself as a victim. Céline's supreme moral failure, his unrepentant personal shittiness, is only different from that of such scurrilous survivors of the Purge as Louis Darquier and Maurice Bardèche in one respect: After the Purge, he more or less dropped anti-Semitism as a conspicuous feature of his public manifestations. He dissembled, contradicted himself, spread his execrations over right and left, as if to ameliorate the primary focus of his pamphlets and his rabid participation in various anti-Jewish conferences, congresses, and exhibitions before 1943.

Céline's subsequent works make ample use of his own disgrace, satirize his self-pity while flaunting it, and reveal the disillusioned, nihilified humanist behind the self-constructed monster. The paradox of Céline is that we have to take the monster with the humanist curmudgeon and forget about measuring "guilt" or separating his brilliance from his madness. As with Artaud, brilliance and madness are essentially the same thing. Céline's attempts to rehabilitate his reputation, from the war's final days throughout most of the 1950s, though tacitly acknowledging his "mistake" in promulgating race hatred, never include a straightforward apology, but instead spread guilt over all the parties involved in the war. Céline did, however, resume writing at a level of high literary mastery, and refined the formal innovations of his earlier novels.

In *Guignol's Band I and II,* Céline/Ferdinand recounts his excursions in the London underworld; of *Casse-pipe,* only a fascinating introduction survives; in *Féerie pour une autre fois,* Céline anticipates Thomas Bernhard's technique of surrounding his ostensible story with ever-longer digressions, in this case dealing with Céline's imprisonment in Copenhagen, until the digressive material becomes the story and the original premise becomes the pretext for telling it. *Entretiens avec le Professeur Y* has an implacable interviewer/ interrogator dogging Céline across Paris; it's an extraordinary gloss on Céline's literary method, but remarkable too because Céline and his interlocutor, in physical motion throughout the book, inscribe a map of Paris with the bare minimum of descriptive asides.

These books were only reconsidered on their respective merits after postwar trauma subsided, and more detached curiosity about the war's chaotic finale arose with respect to long-suppressed information about French collaboration with the Germans, especially in Unoccupied Vichy. Céline fled to Germany during the first wave of Allied landings. He spent many months sequestered in a hotel near Siegmaringen, a Hohenzollern castle to which the panicked elite of Vichy (including Pétain and Laval) had been evacuated in German custody. Céline, nominal physician to the castle's occupants, had the goods on Vichy's suddenly powerless, malignant ex-rulers, and had witnessed Reich's End as few others had. He delivered his first-hand account of Germany's collapse in three successive novels that belong among the masterpieces of 20th-century literature. When Gallimard brought out *D'un château l'autre,* the first volume of the trilogy, in 1957, it immediately became a bestseller, and reestablished Céline's unique literary importance.

Castle to Castle juxtaposes Céline's life in Meudon in the late '50s with the deranged atmosphere at Siegmaringen. Among other things, it proves beyond doubt that Céline's vision had never effectively serviced anyone's political programme (even his vilest anti-Semitic outpouring, *L'Ecole des cadavres*, appeared after the German defeat had become a widespread assumption, and, in any case, advertised precisely what the Nazis were by that time trying to conceal), that his view of humanity was as indigestibly negative to the Right as it was to the Left. Of Pétain, for example, Céline's opinion (as noted in *Castle to Castle*) is eviscerative rather than "disillusioned":

> Say what you like . . . I can speak freely because he detested me . . . Pétain was our last King of France. "Philip the Last! . . . " the stature, the majesty, the works . . . and he believed in it . . . first as victor of Verdun. . . . then, at the age of seventy and then some promoted to Sovereign! Who could have resisted? . . . A pushover! "Oh, Monsieur le Maréchal, how you incarnate France!" That incarnation jazz is magic . . . if somebody said to me, "Céline, damn it all, how you incarnate the Passage! the Passage is you! All you!"—I'd go out of my mind! Take any old hick, tell him to his face that he incarnates something . . . you'll see, he'll go crazy . . . / . . . once Pétain incarnated France, he didn't care if it was fish or flesh, gibbet, Paradise or High Court, Douaumont, Hell, or Thorez . . . he was the incarnation! . . . / . . . you could cut his head off . . . he'd go right on incarnating . . . his head would run along all by itself, Perfectly happy, seventh heaven!

One can, by the way, view the fantastic opulence in which the defeated Vichyites clung to delusions of vindication in the second part of Marcel Ophls's *Le chagrin et la pitié,* when Ophls interviews a French volunteer in the Waffen SS as they walk through Siegmaringen Castle. The scene could also serve as a cinematic gloss on the opening of *North* (*Nord*), which covers the first part of Céline's flight, accompanied by Lili, Bébert and the actor Robert LeVigan into the whirlwind of a bombed-out Germany. Their scramble through the wreckage is relieved periodically at the surviving spas where the titled rich have passed the war as if it happened on another planet. Aided by an SS officer named Harris, Céline and his group are quartered briefly in the Simplon Hotel, another nest of Vichyites:

> God knows the guests of the Simplon in Baden-Baden were Gaullists, out-and-out anti-Hitlerites . . . ripe for the Allies! . . . with the Cross of Lorraine in their hearts, in their eyes, on their tongues . . . and none of your small-

time flops, none of your demented down-at-heel shopkeepers . . . oh no! . . .
plush addicts every last one of them, four star, two three chambermaids to
every suite, sun balcony overlooking Lichtenhalalle . . . / . . . I'm speaking of
July '44 . . . very well supplied with food, and very punctually . . . they and
their hangers-on . . . butter, eggs, caviar, marmalade, salmon, cognac,
Mumm's extra . . . airborne shipments, dropped by parachute on Vienna,
Austria . . . direct from Rostov, Tunis, Epernay, London . . . the wars raging
on seven fronts and all the oceans don't interfere with their caviar . . . the
super-squashery . . . Z-bomb, sling, fly-swatter . . . will always respect the de-
likatessen of the high and mighty . . . you won't see Kroukrouzof eating
monkey meat in this world! Or Nixon feeding on noodles or Millamac or
raw carrots . . . the tables of the high and mighty are a "Reason of State" . . .

In *Rigadoon,* Céline's literary voyage comes full circle. Here there is nothing but ruin, as Céline, Lili and Bébert, repeatedly diverted from their
route to safety in Denmark, shuttle from Rostock to Ulm to Hamburg, wit-
nessing the phosphorus bombing of Hanover, and find themselves responsible for 19 retarded children abandoned by the Swedish Red Cross.

Céline's wartime trilogy is a metanarrative, as *North*'s references to Nixon
and Kruschev illustrate. The casual shuffle through time and space begun in
Death on Credit's opening pages permeates *Guignol's Band* and *Féerie pour
une autre fois.* In *Castle to Castle* and *North,* time becomes a free-floating
material available for the bricolage of simulated consciousness and way-
wardly retrieved memories. In *Rigadoon,* Céline partly restores the linear
structure of *Journey to the End of the Night,* but reality itself has now been
overturned in every detail, all solid structures have been twisted, flattened
and smashed into a harrowing fantasia, a hallucination of unbelievable destruction, an indecipherably atomized landscape where the narrator ex-
haustedly slogs toward a safe place while continually getting separated from
his wife, the cat and 19 drooling idiot children who habitually wander off
into the debris. (This reprises the "open air school" of *Death on Credit,* and
clearly influenced the ending of Faulkner's *The Town,* when the evil junior
progeny of the Snopes family are packed on a train to the distant west.)
Rigadoon is pure madness, the clearest reflection of the world as Céline always saw it, and the world's very real horror surpasses the mimicry of its
author's harshest judgments and his darkest fears.

AMNESIA AND ITS DOUBLE

CLIVE JAMES is the quintessential critic-at-large, as popularizers of multiple subjects used to be called. James has also written memoirs, novels and books of poetry. He is familiar to the British public as a television host—pop music shows, talk shows, travelogues. Chat's his game, and when his pen hits paper, call him Deep Chat.

James, like the unjustly forgotten windbag, bon vivant and raconteur Peter Ustinov, is a conventionally but ingratiatingly pompous stereotype of the provincial arriviste set loose in the glittering capital, who knows at least a little about most things and a lot about many. The topographical range of his erudition is often more noteworthy than its depth, but his prose, like his TV work, is lively, nimble and stylish.

I agree with some introductory statements in James's latest book, *Cultural Amnesia:* "It has always been part of the definition of humanism that true learning has no end in view but its own furtherance," for example. James intends his book as a step toward producing a fresh crop of humanists. I'll leave aside the question of whether this is, without qualification, a desirable goal. James uses the least appealing method of pedagogy, in any case, to reach it: the cultic worship of proper names, which function as stop signs to independent thought. James's book even presents his mental hoard of very significant names in alphabetical sequence. In fairness, their owners are not all currently famous, but reviving the currently obscure isn't going to put any glacial shelf back together on your North Pole. James's rescue effort on behalf of a civilization that has already collapsed is, to paraphrase Jenny Holzer, beautiful but stupid.

James's potted lives are sincere attempts to convey ideas that shaped this civilization, but perhaps the snap, crackle and pop approach instilled by a career in television accounts for his habit of miniaturizing figures he disagrees

with, and hyperinflating his personal heroes. James can expound his subjects' accomplishments without oversimplification; what he can't do, apparently, is interrogate his own broad assumptions and, why not say so, his
prejudices.

When he wishes to denigrate a writer, artist, philosopher or what have
you, he refuses them any quarter; he writes more positive things about
Hitler than he does about Cline. That someone can be a shit in private and
one of the world's most formidable writers, concert pianists, philosophers
or anything else in public is one of the many contradictions we have to live
with, hold the humanism on that BLT.

One of James's most firmly asserted and shakiest convictions is reflected
in his mantralike invocation of "liberal democracy" as the ideal arrangement of life on earth, which he conjoins—correctly, in fact, and without
qualm—with free-market capitalism. As Marcuse pointed out, there is such
a thing as totalitarian democracy, and to quote an old detergent commercial, "Madge, you're soaking in it."

Clive James is perfectly entitled to his personal bêtes noires, foremostly
Jean-Paul Sartre, and could make a persuasive argument against many of
Sartre's less inspired efforts on and off the printed page without foaming at
the mouth, if his mental teeth weren't determined to tear out Sartre's jugu-
lar vein. But they are. Sartre has plenty of company in this book, but wins
pride of place as James's Satan Incarnate.

James's loathing of one of 20th-century France's indispensable minds spills
out all over the place, like a trail of candle wax dripped across essays that have
nothing to do with Sartre. It's almost as offensive to Sartre's memory as Henri
Bernard-Levi's admiration. The swipes and insults thicken into such obsessive
preposterousness that when and if the reader gets as far as the "S's" and the
formal grand jury indictment of Sartre, James's bilious "reflections" sound
like a drunken sailor pounding the bar with his fist for attention.

All right, he hates Sartre. Be my guest. But if part of James's project is to
"destroy" people he considers malignant or less wonderful than other
people think, as the jacket of this book asseverates, he should, at least, hire a
fact-checker. It really is inexcusable to reproach Karl Kraus—the magnificent Karl Kraus, in my opinion, so there—for failing to raise his voice
against Hitler's onrushing Anschluss with Austria, if only because this event
occurred in 1938. Kraus died in 1936. (And, by the way, William Faulkner

isn't the author of *Lie Down in Darkness*, and Marshall Pilsudski's name wasn't Pitsudski.)

I suppose if you take on the burden of saving civilization, you're inevitably going to get some little details wrong. Probably the first, largest mistake is to suppose yourself capable of saving a civilization single-handedly, like Clint Eastwood riding into town to take out the trash. The project becomes de trop, in any case, after the civilization in question—ours—has already regressed to barbarism, which seems to me beyond argument. One can exhume parts of a dead civilization, and hope that the essential knowledge it produced isn't lost forever. Forget humanism: We could lose mathematics and physics just as easily as early metaphysical poetry.

That the necessary tools for constructing a civilization can be permanently forgotten was one of Hannah Arendt's most chilling insights. The value of retrieving what can vanish forever, though, doesn't consist of knowing the name of its original discoverer—it's a nice thing if that happens, I suppose, but it isn't the important thing. At the moment, we don't need another hero, unless you mean hero in the sense of sandwich. Slobbering over images and the names attached to them is one of the things that's taken us where we are today. Not a happy place, is it?

Despite its highbrow-for-middlebrows exposition of other people's work and personalities, abrupt flights of shabby moralizing over trivia, and conspicuous impertinences, *Cultural Amnesia* is, for much of its 700-some pages, "a good read," and it may actually gain something from its author having his head in the clouds and his feet in the toilet. Hard to say, however, which is really worse: cultural amnesia or cultural dyslexia.

BLAME IT ON BRIO

NOW THAT she is authentically dead—at 101, felled by a curse from the ghost of Ernst Jünger, who lived two years longer—Leni Riefenstahl has joined the shades she often conjured during a career of ardor, mystification and immutable self-delusion.

What good would it do to apologize? she asks in the 1993 Roy Müller documentary *The Wonderful, Horrible Life of Leni Riefenstahl.* Apologies don't turn the clock back or raise the dead from dust. The sensible tactic, in the face of speeding time and mass amnesia, is to move on and hope that everybody forgets about it. But Leni knew they never would.

The extent, even the exact nature of Riefenstahl's guilt is impossible to quantify. How many people actually joined the Nazi Party after watching *Triumph of the Will* (1934)? Possibly nobody, despite its reputation as the greatest propaganda film of all time. Does it matter? No, yes, you tell me and we'll both know. Sometimes naïve people end up on the wrong side of history. But Riefenstahl wasn't one of them. She was Faust with a riding crop and a mighty stallion she had no idea would ever be put down. She spurred it to the end of the line and got her spurs caught in the stirrups.

Taking the devil's side, *Triumph* is a slightly doctored record of a macabre coven-gathering at Nuremburg, opening with Adolf Hitler's airborne arrival through gauzy clouds, the spiny spires and craggy gingerbread excrescences of the city below reflecting the medieval flavor of the impending toxic saturnalia. It proceeds to highlight revolting public statuary, squat dirndled moms holding chubby brats to gaze at the conquering Charlemagne, torch-lit marches of robotic thugs and nocturnal serenades beneath the Führer's hotel windows, all fairly shrieking that a powerfully nasty dream is becoming wet and repugnant. Add the hoarse baying of lunatics at the Party Congress, and only a werewolf could overlook the grotesque hilarity of this festival of blustering moral imbeciles.

Riefenstahl's postwar notoriety was, career-wise, arguably disproportionate to what she actually did. A self-involved opportunist to the core, she grabbed the chances the age offered. Her compulsive mythomania was a rote and slinking kind any competent researcher could easily deconstruct, though whether her embroideries veiled anything truly damning—besides the obvious—is an open question. Her critics claim to know she didn't believe her own lies. But how exactly do they know? Chronic liars generally wind up believing themselves, and Riefenstahl was the kind of liar who protected her myths with feral conviction.

Over decades of having both her real past and unproved allegations thrown in her face, Riefenstahl's bilious reaction to unpalatable facts hardened into a grout of messily intersecting delusions. When Roy Müller gently contradicts some of her florid assertions, a savage defensiveness bursts from her costume of sagging flesh and winsome smiles. She *never* had dinner at Goebbels's home. That *can't* be in his diaries, even though it is. Vexed by questions about her *first* Party Congress documentary, a sloppier affair than the tautly orchestrated *Triumph,* she actually grabs the director on camera and shakes him. Such outbursts typify the bipolar instability of such Teutonic harridans as Elizabeth Förster-Nietzsche and Winifred Wagner, with whom Riefenstahl shared a capricious cuntishness well into old age.

Some of the facts behind Leni's fictions are hardly glorifying and leave a distinct mud spatter on her ever-grinning persona. What about those Gypsies she pulled out of Maxglan concentration camp to play extras in *Tiefland*? Riefenstahl's detractors claim these bit players went directly to their end after filming; her memoirs assert that they all survived, and occasionally sent her affectionate greeting cards. (At the age of 100, while under judicial investigation for "denying the Holocaust," Riefenstahl publicly recanted these claims and promised never to repeat them.)

Still, after 50-some years, one can't avoid the thought, "So what?" It wasn't Riefenstahl pouring Zyklon B into the Auschwitz death chambers—it was I. G. Farben, a corporation that continues to flourish in today's Germany. It wasn't Riefenstahl who facilitated the Final Solution by supplying the Nazis with business machines and the magnetic punch cards whose numbers would be tattooed on death-camp victims' forearms—it was Thomas Watson and

IBM's micromanaged European subsidiaries. The truly powerful, and monstrously culpable, are far more often the beneficiaries of public amnesia than the morally blinkered and less directly guilty public celebrity.

And there is a special odium reserved for the female celebrity of less than bleach-white character. Consider the snowmelt once known as Martha Stewart, another indefatigable narcissist, reduced to a puddle of cake frosting for a mingy bit of insider trading while the gnomes of Enron have (so far) gone scot-free for the biggest robbery in U.S. history. The impervious smugness of a Leni, a Martha, gooses scads of public glee when they slip off the trapeze. This merriment evaporates, for many of us, at the thought of the various sociopathic pirates who have been showered with favor for looting the world's wealth and slaughtering its peasants.

What did Riefenstahl do, in the end, that is so unforgivable? Many directors of Reich-time racist melodramas went on working in the postwar film industry almost without interruption, including Veit Harlan of *Jud Süß* notoriety. Most were insignificant mediocrities; it's the exceptional artist, or, in Riefenstahl's case, adroit technician, whose meretricious decisions hound him or her to the grave.

Nevertheless, time eventually issues a kind of pardon for an exemplary artist's stupidities. In the '30s, Louis-Ferdinand Céline expectorated four surpassingly insane book-length tracts urging the extermination of the Jews; he is, quite justly, revered as the greatest French prose writer of the 20th century besides Proust. Ezra Pound, Knut Hamsun, Curzio Malaparte, and even Gottfried Benn (whose "Answer to the Literary Emigrants" [1933] remains the most eloquent excuse for political blindness ever written) have long been embraced by the literary canon.

The question a Riefenstahl provokes can't really be answered: What culpability attaches to the lesser type of artist who lands on the wrong side of history? And how to regard those unlucky enough to long outlive their mistakes? Riefenstahl's case is complicated by the fact that her filmic mastery is solely displayed in her Nazi propaganda efforts, and in *Olympia* (1938), a film commissioned as propaganda despite its lack of overt ideological intent. She could never entirely disown these corrupt technical achievements, since they also contained her only innovative work.

However, Riefenstahl's postwar projects, and arguably her pre-Nazi work as well, don't neatly mesh with the notion that she was a consistent purveyor of "fascist aesthetics" in some estimations. Slavoj Žižek has recently argued that *The Blue Light* (1932) can be read as a social pariah's destruction by the mob, rather than an allegory of mystical Nazi strivings. Helma Sanders-Brahms, director of *Germany, Pale Mother,* interprets *Tiefland* (1954) as an anti-Nazi parable advocating tyrranicide. These interpretations are what they are.

The primary feature of "fascist aesthetics" is the monumentalization of kitsch. *Triumph of the Will* observes a lot of bloody-minded histrionics, but the film itself is not kitsch. Nor is *Olympia,* where the mealy-faced, taxidermical Hitler falls into inescapable contrast to the splendid physique and luminous physiognomy of the black American track star Jesse Owens—adored by Leni's camera in overt defiance of Nazi racism. Owens is the *punctum* of *Olympia,* the heroic racial Other despised by the Aryan claque in the bleachers. His prominence in the film may have been exploited by the Reich to project a sham internationalism, but the images themselves don't suggest that Riefenstahl's intentions were anything but aesthetic. While an adoring lens on the Führer was de rigueur in *Triumph, Olympia* more fairly reflects Riefenstahl's instinctive understanding that a movie star is someone a great many people would like to fuck, and none but the blind-folded could possibly prefer Adolf to Jesse.

It may be a tonic exercise to suspend the usual verdict on Riefenstahl as an unregenerate Nazi, impelled by some tangle of mental wiring to produce dangerously seductive, authoritarian-minded visuals, and to disconnect the voluptuous, muscular bodies competing for Olympic medals from ash-coated Africans engaged in ritual wrestling matches whom she photographed extensively in her later years, producing miles of unedited film footage and two gorgeous coffee-table books, *The Last of the Nuba* (1973) and *The People of Kau* (1976). If the Nuba ash decoration can be polemically used as evidence of a "death cult," it might also be explained as a simple way to keep the wrestlers from slipping on each other's sweat.

The demonization of Riefenstahl overshadows the fact that she was an obsessive, technocratic artist and a political groupie, hardly a formidable intellectual or ideologist. She would have been thrilled to see her influence at work in Calvin Klein underwear billboards and the normative look of the average Chelsea gym queen. If her preoccupation with visual fireworks and eroticized bodies blinded her to the political implications of her films, it also immunized her from deeper complicity with the ideological agenda of her sponsors. She never joined the Nazi Party and, as far as anyone knows, never publicly made anti-Semitic remarks. The thrice-denazified Leni's haunting sin was a common, hubristic one: the constitutional inability to admit that anything she did was wrong-headed, ill considered, harmful, deleterious or stupid. For many reasons that are both legible and problematic, including a harsh obduracy I can't find despicable but merely obnoxious and depressingly common, it was impossible for her to repudiate the steps she took to get ahead, or to apologize for taking them.

It could be that Riefenstahl, who never completed a feature after *Tiefland,* spent half a century trying to dissipate, through mediocre artistry, the odium she'd acquired by riding the worst possible political horse when she was too naïve and unscrupulously ambitious to imagine where the finish line actually was. Her long sojourns in impoverished zones of rural Africa provided escape from a revised social order that held no respectable place for her. Photographing the Nuba, the Masai and other tribes, she found equivocal salvation, in her own mind, by winning the trust and affection of the most elemental and hermetic people she could find. They didn't judge her past, because they had no idea who she was.

Her final completed movie, the 45-minute-long *Underwater Impressions* (2002), was filmed after Leni learned scuba diving in her eighth decade. The interview that precedes the film shows a Riefenstahl we have never seen: relaxed, genial, reflective in an undefensive way, and genuinely likable. Rather like the giant toad who has, at last, eaten its fill of flies and can't see any buzzing in her immediate vicinity. The movie itself is an almost aleatory succession of meaninglessly beautiful images, an unfolding of gorgeously bizarre, teeming life forms inhabiting coral reefs. It's a majestic display Riefenstahl's insatiable visual curiosity, her eye for spectacular detail, her editing mastery, her indomitable physical tenacity. And that's all it is, not quite a work of art, but the best iMax presentation the world will ever know.

Underwater Impressions leads one to the disturbing speculation that the defectively brilliant Leni Riefenstahl suffered from an aesthetic autism focused on the beautiful to the exclusion of any other artistic criteria, that beautification of whatever she beheld, whether it was Adolf Hitler and masses of Nazi banners, athletes swanning off diving boards, painted African bodies or the lacy forms of a coral reef. (She even managed to make herself look like an absurd parody of Rita Hayworth's Gilda in several shots in *Tiefland*.) In this respect, *Underwater Impressions* can be considered Riefenstahl's most revelatory film. Depressingly revelatory and ravishingly beautiful.

This final exile into the deep was Leni Riefenstahl's last—and, as she well knew, futile—attempt to make peace with a world that was determined never to afford her any. Now that she is gone, perhaps we can give some credit to her best work, her rejection of the quotidian, her steely focus on the task at hand, her willingness to abandon projects that didn't meet her fanatically high standards. We don't need to pretend the lady herself was someone we'd greatly like spending time with or wish to emulate. To slightly tweak Marlene's famous line in *Touch of Evil,* she was some kind of woman; anyway, what does it matter what you say about people?

NO SUCH THING AS PARANOIA

ON THE CULTURE OF CONSPIRACISM

Like conspiracies themselves, conspiracy theories are as old as gossip and politics. To understand the world one inhabits, it is impossible to credit the idea of contingency or chance as the root of all weirdness. Just as any psychotic tends to utter something true in the process of saying something crazy, there is usually a kernel of reality in even the most far-fetched conspiracy theory. While it is easy to distinguish a belief that aluminum foil wrapped around one's head filters out alien brain waves from rational but dissident ideas, some modern writers on conspiracy theory tend to conflate nonconformity with the most bizarre and cognitively defective extremes of it. So-called "consensus historians," following the lead of Richard Hofstadter's famous 1964 essay, "The Paranoid Style in American Politics," have effectively pathologized any suspicion of active conspiracies, however defined, into a synonym for "nut job" in public discourse.

Our mass media, its ownership consolidated among a handful of billionaires whose interests are identical with those of corporate cronies (globalized "free trade" for the wealthy nations, peonage for the third world, Chomsky's "manufacture of consent" via a constant torrent of propaganda for the status quo), reflexively dismiss the most obvious or credible explanations for ugly phenomena as the perfervid fantasy of "conspiracy cranks"—for instance, the idea that successive "preemptive" wars might be launched against demonized enemies in order to award reconstruction contracts to corporations formerly helmed by, say, the vice president of the United States and other exalted government employees, or that the strategic purpose of one such war might be the economic colonization of former Soviet republics rich in oil and mineral resources, and to guarantee a secure pipeline for the exploitation of said resources. Instead, the altruism and democracy-spreading goodness of the American power elite are portrayed as self-evident, taking all other motives off the media table.

The necessary proof of such a conspiracy, if we choose to call it that, often turns up 25 or 50 years after the fact, when the release of classified documents churns up no public outcry or indictments. Such was the recent case with the declassified revelation that the late Connecticut senator Prescott Bush, grandfather of the current president, along with his law partner W. Averill Harriman, a former governor of New York, managed a number of concerns on behalf of Nazi industrialist Fritz Thyssen. These included the Union Banking Corporation, seized under the Trading With the Enemy Act on October 20, 1942 (Office of Alien Property Custodian, Vesting Order No. 248), Seamless Steel Equipment Corporation (Vesting Order No. 259), and the Holland-American Trading Corporation (Vesting Order No. 261).

The Union Banking Corporation financed Hitler after his electoral losses in 1932; the other Bush-managed concerns have been characterized as "a shipping line which imported German spies; an energy company that supplied the Luftwaffe with high-ethyl fuel; and a steel company that employed Jewish slave labour from the Auschwitz concentration camp." Fuller details are documented in *George Bush: The Unauthorized Biography,* by Webster G. Tarpley and Anton Chaitkin; in Kevin Phillips's *American Dynasty: Aristocracy, Fortune, and the Politics of Deceit in the House of Bush;* as well as in the colorful, conspiracist history *Fleshing Out Skull & Bones,* by Anthony Sutton et al., and further confirmed by John Loftus, a former prosecutor in the Justice Department's Nazi War Crimes Unit. Since only the Nazi partners in the Bush-Harriman interests were permanently deprived of their frozen stock, Prescott Bush and his father-in-law, George Herbert Walker, waltzed off with $1.5 million when the Union Banking Corp. was liquidated in 1951. (This was, in effect, the foundation of the Bush family fortune: once a Snopes, always a Snopes.) Briefly picked up by the Associated Press and buried deep in the pages of American newspapers, this half-century-late disclosure led to no media follow-up and left no impression on the potential electorate for the 2004 US presidential contest.

Contingency theorists would declare that the activities of one Bush 50-some years ago have nothing to do with those of subsequent Bushes. Yet the story confirms a pattern of corrupt profiteering through abuse of power that runs continuously through the Bush family dynasty. They would like-wise find nothing "conspiratorial" about the duck-hunting trip Vice President Cheney took with Supreme Court Justice Antonin Scalia during the week of 4 January 4 2004, "three weeks after the court agreed to take up the vice president's appeal in lawsuits over his handling of the administration's energy task force," according to the *Los Angeles Times*. "I do not think my impartiality could reasonably be questioned," Scalia hilariously told reporters, perhaps believing they had already forgotten his sordid role in fixing the 2000 presidential election for George W. Bush. Perhaps the brazen lack of ethics and truthfulness displayed by everyone in or associated with the Bush administration shouldn't be characterized as "conspiratorial," since this implies a secrecy that Cheney et al. believe unnecessary, given the monumental apathy and programmed ignorance of at least half the American public. (Cheney may not want to release transcripts of who said what, but that isn't a secret—it's a crime in defiance of American jurisprudence. There are no secrets, only things we know about that we don't know all the little details of.)

Hofstadter's essay, written in the aftermath of the McCarthy witch hunts and the Kennedy assassination, with an eye on the then-marginal but scary realm of right-wing plot-weavers, has been eerily assimilated by a certain idling pedantry, which rummages through the historical debris of arcane conspiracist subjects (the Knights Templar, Jesuit intrigues, Freemasonry, the Illuminati, alien abductions, the Rothschilds, the Bilderberg meetings, the Knights of Malta), often recounting the same narratives at numbing length, with little fresh insight. Only a few contemporary writers drastically depart from Hofstadter's historical itinerary, or his parochial vision of America as a "pluralist democracy," whose institutional framework is essentially benign and immutably fair, rational and systemically mistrusted only by paranoid schizophrenics. "One need only think of the response to President Kennedy's assassination in Europe to be reminded that Americans have no monopoly on the gift for paranoid improvisation," Hofstadter declared, 15 years before the US House of Representatives' Select Committee on Assassinations concluded that Kennedy's murder was indeed the result of a conspiracy.

Hofstadter's prescience is amply evidenced in Michael Barkun's *A Culture of Conspiracy: Apocalyptic Visions in Contemporary America* (2003). Barkun

has ingested Hofstadter's imperious tome whole, and his book does little
more than regurgitate its polemical eurekas. Barkun informs us that the
"essence of conspiracy beliefs lies in attempts to delineate and explain evil."
Ergo Christianity, Judaism, Islam and most other organized religions qualify as conspiracy beliefs, though Barkun neglects to say so. Barkun identifies
three principles "found in virtually every conspiracy theory," to wit: *Nothing happens by accident. Nothing is as it seems. Everything is connected.* Clearly
Freud, Plato, Leibniz and Einstein all suffered from at least one symptom of
conspiracism; fortuitously, without mentioning any of them, someone has
finally exposed these thinkers as mentally ill.

Writers like Barkun are fond of inventing buzz concepts like "improvisa-
tional millennialism," "the cultic milieu," "agency panic" and "stigmatized
knowledge claims." The latter, according to Barkun, are "claims to truth that
the claimants regard as verified despite the marginalization of those claims
by the institutions that conventionally distinguish between knowledge and
error—universities, communities of scientific researchers, and the like." Few
besides the amply tenured and remuneratively institutionalized would be
likely to endorse Barkun's tweedy self-flattery as descriptive of American
academia—as Jane Jacobs points out in her new book *Dark Age Ahead,* our
colleges and universities have largely degenerated into mere credentialing
factories—and what political scientists consider a science tends to be more a
recruitment pool for think tanks, few of which trouble to separate knowledge from error, but simply bend data to suit the particular tank's ideological
orientation.

The same impossibly murky entities are combed over in most books on
conspiracism, though some of the literature and related nonfiction have begun to deviate considerably from consensus historicism and the Hofstadter
school. The traditional conspiracist books look backward through the jumbled mythologies of nebulously interwoven secret societies, usually beginning with the Bavarian Illuminati (currently a hit topic with the rerelease of
Da Vinci Code author Dan Brown's 2000 novel *Angels & Demons*), though
some point back to the Knights Templar, an order of monks and knights
founded by Hugh de Payens in 1118. The Templars originally occupied the
Temple of Solomon in Jerusalem and later went in for money lending; in
October 1307, on Friday the 13th (a charged date ever since), the Inquisition arrested the leader and 123 other Knights Templar, who were promptly

tortured into confessing blasphemy, black magic, devil worship and homosexual sodomy. It's believed by some that rather than disbanding, the Knights reorganized themselves sub rosa and continued to influence events and the activities of other cults.

The Illuminati are another historically shape-shifting bunch. Historians generally date their foundation as 1 May 1776, in Ingolstadt, Bavaria, by a former Jesuit and future Freemason, Adam Weishaupt. Supposedly the Illuminati infiltrated Masonic lodges and came to dominate the movement for pro-democratic secularism. The Illuminati were shut down in 1785 by the Bavarian government, but the group allegedly reconstituted itself, like the Templars, under other names, and is still active today. It's unclear what the Illuminati are active in: satanism, control of international banking, anarchism or Communism, depending on which conspiracist you read.

Early fears of an Illuminati conspiracy were widely disseminated via Abbé Barruél's four-volume *Mémoires pour servir à l'Histoire du Jacobinisme* of 1797, in which the author, a Jesuit expelled from France with the rest of his order, claimed the French Revolution had emanated from a conspiracy of Masons, Illuminati and "anti-Christians." A contemporaneous screed by a Scottish scientist, John Robison, *Proofs of a Conspiracy Against All the Religions and Governments of Europe, Carried on in the Secret Meetings of Free Masons, Illuminati, and Reading Societies,* advanced the same idea. The book became wildly popular in America, where, it is often pointed out, several Founding Fathers belonged to the Masonic order.

Hofstadter cites Federalist fears of "a Jacob-inical plot touched off by Illuminism" in the early years of Jeffersonian democracy. An anti-Masonic movement swept the country in the late 1820s and early 1830s, slightly overlapping a wave of anti-Jesuit hysteria. "It is an ascertained fact," one Protestant minister wrote in 1836, "that Jesuits are prowling about all parts of the United States in every possible disguise, expressly to ascertain the advantageous situations and modes to disseminate Popery."

Freemasonry, whose date of origin is somewhere in the 16th or 17th century, purports to be (according to its adherents) a benign organization, albeit with a mystical element, which served for much of the 19th century to disseminate rationalist learning among its members in the days before public education: geometry, architecture, astronomy and similar subjects. Its members aren't allowed to discuss politics or religion within the Lodge. As

Brother Roscoe Pound, a Mason and current professor of jurisprudence at Harvard, puts it, "Every lodge ought to be a center of light from which men go forth filled with new ideas of social justice, cosmopolitan justice and internationality." All the same, Masons have been periodically accused of satanism, manipulation of global finance and secret influence among the world's movers and shakers. Robert Anton Wilson, in *Everything Is Under Control,* reports that the P2 society in Italy, founded in the 1970s (purportedly as a subsect of the CIA's Gladio operation), which allegedly engineered the Bologna railway bombing in 1980 and financed itself by fraud and drug running, "recruited exclusively among third-degree members of the Grand Orient Lodge of Egyptian Freemasonry."

Mumia Abu-Jamal, the death-row activist, reports in his column that the "CIA hid massive stockpiles of weapons and explosives throughout Italy. They amassed an army of 15,000 troops in something called Operation Gladio . . . to strike vital targets and overthrow the elected Italian government if they dared to vote against Washington's will."

Well, who knows?

OPUS HEYDAY

Conspiracy theories emanating from both the left and the right, along with the many that issue from the Planet Debby, almost invariably rely on scapegoating as a core methodology. The interdigitating shadow organizations that fill so much of conspiracy history invariably involve the Jews or the Jesuits or both. What right-wing conspiracy theory could be complete without *The Protocols of the Elders of Zion,* and what secularist or Protestant conspiracy theory without the Jesuits thrown in? (The extreme left has its own menu of the automatically culpable, which I won't elaborate on here.)

The Jews are routinely blamed for everything (their menacing worldwide financial reach epitomized by the Rothschilds) and held to be responsible for heartless capitalism and godless Communism simultaneously. Neil Baldwin, in *Henry Ford and the Jews,* writing of this hero of American business mythology, describes a 1922 article from Ford's column in the *Dearborn Independent:* "Within four paragraphs, the word 'control' recurs five times, most often in connection with the Jew's annoying propensity for business. . . . He is the perpetual alien, 'a corporation with agents everywhere'—a reference that brings to mind the structure of the Ford Motor Company itself." Let's not forget ZOG, the secret Zionist world government, a favorite fantasy of American survivalists and neo-Nazis everywhere. While anti-Semitism (as distinct from anti-Zionism) is a mental illness most virulently spread today by Semites, namely Arab Islamists, there has always been a sinister air about the Jesuit Order. Judaism discourages proselytizing; the Jesuits were founded on Ignatius Loyola's determination to spread Roman Catholicism all through the world. It is doubtful, though, that Jesuits masterminded the French Revolution, as their enemies claim.

Madame Blavatsky, founder of Theosophy, stated in a letter to A. P. Sinnett that the "greatest statesman in Europe, the Prince Bismarck, is the only one to know accurately all their secret plottings. . . . He knows it has ever been the aim of the Jesuit Priestcraft to stir up disaffection and rebellion in all countries to the advancement of its own interests." The Sarah Bernhardt of Occultism went on to accuse British statesman W. E. Gladstone of having been "privately received into the R.C. Church by the Pope himself." She continued: "W.E.G. precipitates his own temporary retirement from office, in order to get . . . an overwhelming majority from the votes of the newly emancipated laborers at a General Election. . . . He still thinks he can, perhaps, contrive to carry a dashing scheme for handing Ireland over so much further into the hands of the unscrupulous agitators, so that the next agitation will complete the severance and dismember the British Empire—which has long been the darling scheme of the Jesuits." Perhaps relatedly, in *Lord George Bentinck: A Political Biography* (1851), Benjamin Disraeli warned the House of Commons about secret societies in France, Italy and Germany.

There also exists an anti-Jesuit organization that itself qualifies as a conspiratorial cult, the Catholic lay group Opus Dei, recently flushed from its lair of secrecy by Dan Brown's bestseller, *The Da Vinci Code*. Founded in Franco's Spain in 1928 by Josemaría Escrivá de Balaguer y Albás, Opus spread worldwide; its current membership is estimated at 80,000. It was soon recognized by the Catholic Church as its first "secular" religious institution: In the early 1980s, Opus Dei was declared by Pope John Paul II to be a "personal prelature"—that is, a church entity headed by a "prelate" under no control by local bishops and dioceses. Since its founding, Opus has had only three successive leaders: Escrivá, Alvaro del Portillo, and, currently, Bishop Xavier Echevarria, a native of Madrid. Each has promoted a cult of personality.

To the horror of many Catholics, particularly the Jesuits, Escrivá was beatified in May 1992 and canonized as a "saint" in October 2002. This follower of Franco was believed to have cured a doctor of radiodermatitis caused by prolonged exposure to X-ray machinery, a "miracle" that could very well have been the result of natural healing—Pierre Curie suffered the same sort of ailment after handling radium, and it cleared up in a few weeks.

Opus members go in for self-flagellation and other rituals of self-inflicted pain. The organization has its own list of banned books and a hierarchy of membership levels, and is virulently opposed to abortion and gay rights. It endorses most of the other lunatic phobias of the ultra-right Christian Coalition. Opus Dei would not merit all that much attention were it not for the fact that Robert Hanssen, the FBI agent/Russian spy, was revealed to be a member, and that there have been plausible allegations that Louis Freeh, the former FBI director, along with Supreme Court justices Antonin Scalia and Clarence Thomas, belong to Opus Dei too.

One could go on, into alien abductions and the legendary UFO crash site at Area 51, or Groom Lake, 90 miles north of Las Vegas (Michael Barkun, in *A Culture of Conspiracy: Apocalyptic Visions in Contemporary America,* finds it suggestive that Timothy McVeigh visited the former a year before blowing up the Oklahoma City federal building); anticipation of the Rapture by various religious psychotics; expectation of the Antichrist's arrival, recently announced by Jerry Falwell on national TV (he noted that the AC would be a Jew); belief in humanoid reptiles inhabiting vast underground tunnels; and so forth. But the current analyses of eccentric belief systems inevitably have had to take into account that the 20th century, and now the 21st, have seen myriad authentic conspiracies unravel or partly unravel, sometimes leaving piles of dead bodies in their wake. The Kennedy assassination, Iran-Contra, Watergate, the CIA-sponsored overthrow and/or assassination of Arbenz, Allende, Mussadegh, Sukarno, Lumumba and dozens of other democratically elected or potentially electable progressive leaders, the Enron scam, B.C.C.I., the sinister workings of the Carlyle Group—there is too much of the real stuff around for a thinking person to dismiss certain apprehensions as "paranoid." Especially since 9/11, the consensus model of thinking about America as a Norman Rockwell painting with a few unsightly threads dangling from the canvas has reached a nadir of popularity and credibility.

In an introductory essay, Peter Knight, editor of the 2002 collection *Conspiracy Nation: The Politics of Paranoia in Postwar America,* attributes modern conspiracism to "the pervading sense of uncontrollable forces taking over our lives, our minds, and even our bodies." He writes that "conspiracy thinking has become not so much the sign of a crackpot delusion as part of an everyday struggle to make sense of a rapidly changing world." In effect, individuals are losing their sense of agency in a period of political chaos and technological overload, compulsive consumerism and fear of the future, experiencing a loss of self and a sense of interchangeability with other digitized and horrifically surveilled humans, unable to get the big picture into focus and hence fixating on an idea of the world itself as a vast, impenetrable conspiracy. The worst thing about the above catalog of alienation effects is that it seems irreversible and inescapable.

Knight's book is well worth reading, as its contributors differentiate critical inquiry and skepticism from "paranoia." They problematize the friction between conspiracism and contingency theory, and the way these opposites interpenetrate; they deal with American pop culture far more knowingly than Barkun; their references encompass Lacan, Jameson, Althusser and Žižek, among others. Especially worthwhile are Skip Willman's "Spinning Paranoia: The Ideologies of Conspiracy and Contingency in Postmodern Culture," Ingrid Walker Fields's "White Hope: Conspiracy, Nationalism, and Revolution in *The Turner Diaries* and *Hunter*" and Eithne Quinn's "'All Eyez on Me': The Paranoid Style of Tupac Shakur." The tendency to pathologize vigorous opposition to the status quo crops up here and there more as a reflex than a position.

Similarly, Timothy Melley's 1999 *Empire of Conspiracy: The Culture of Paranoia in Postwar America* illustrates "agency panic" as woven into postwar American fiction and nonfiction—Joseph Heller's *Catch-22,* Thomas Pynchon's *The Crying of Lot 49* and *Gravity's Rainbow,* and works by Burroughs, Ishmael Reed, Don DeLillo and many others. He acknowledges the establishment bias of traditional conspiracy critique, yet often brings to mind Mary McCarthy's remark that criticizing Burroughs's style is like criticizing the sartorial manifestations of someone banging on your door to tell you your house is on fire.

"Because the convictions I have been describing usually arise without much tangible evidence," Melley sensibly writes, "they often seem to be the product of paranoia. Yet they are difficult to dismiss as paranoid in the clinical sense. . . . As Leo Bersani points out, the self-described 'paranoids' of Thomas Pynchon's fiction are 'probably justified, and therefore—at least in the traditional sense of the word—really not paranoid at all.'" While dutifully noting the wide influence of Richard E. Hofstadter's seminal 1964 essay "The Paranoid Style in American Politics," which rather broadly identified conspiratorial thinking as a misreading of chance and contingent events, Melley is loath to automatically apply Hofstadter's axioms to the more complex realities of postmodern culture. Still, he invokes them ambiguously, enough so that *Empire of Conspiracy* becomes an exercise in ambivalence about consensus politics and a meandering soliloquy about what is and isn't pathological.

Mark Fenster's 1999 *Conspiracy Theories: Secrecy and Power in American Culture* is easily the best recent addition to the literature of what radio and TV host Long John Nebel used to call the Way Out World. (Nebel's wife, Candy Jones, revealed under hypnosis that she had been brainwashed by the CIA and operated for it as an assassin without her wet work leaving any conscious residue in her memory.) For starters, Fenster tears much of Hofstadter's Cold War assumptions about the vitality of the American mainstream to shreds, noting that Hofstadter "applied a theory of individual pathology to a social phenomenon—an interesting, perhaps productive exercise for an analogy, but problematic if . . . one is attempting to produce a concept that can be used across history to explain, for example, populist political dissent in the 1990s." In Fenster's view, conspiracism is a direct effusion of the failures of the political system, which are at least as much "conspiratorial" as "contingent" or unintended.

There is, of course, another way of considering this: Contingency and lack of intention may often constitute an unplanned, collective conspiracy dictated by historical events and their inevitable repercussions. The essential guide to this notion can be found in Eric Hobsbawm's 1994 Amnesty International lecture, "Barbarism: A User's Guide." Hobsbawm doesn't call the historical process conspiratorial, but many of the opportunities it activates certainly are.

DISORGANIZED CONSPIRACY

It's important to recognize that words like *conspiracy* and *paranoid* have limited credible application in political analysis or in everyday life. Fusing them into a single concept vanquishes malign motives behind political and business decisions that affect the lives of ordinary people. In the Gilded Age, which produced a golden age of journalistic muckraking, the public knew that amoral greed resorts to subterfuge and conspiracy, as the press was not monopolized by people feeding at the same trough as the robber barons.

"Pirates are commonly supposed to have been battered and hung out of existence when the Barbary Powers and the Buccaneers of the Spanish Main had been finally dealt with," wrote Charles Francis Adams Jr. in *Chapters of Erie*. "Yet freebooters are not extinct; they have only transferred their operations to the land, and conducted them in more or less accordance with the forms of law; until, at last, so great a proficiency have they attained, that the commerce of the world is more equally but far more heavily taxed in their behalf, than would ever have entered into their wildest hopes while, outside the law, they simply made all comers stand and deliver."

Adams's two reports of the Erie wars of 1868, like his brother Henry's account of the New York Gold Conspiracy (inserted between them in *Chapters of Erie*), are so meticulously detailed as to seem irrefutable. He unravels the intricate plotting of Cornelius Vanderbilt to wrest control of the Erie Railroad and its branches from Daniel Drew, James Fisk Jr., and Jay Gould, no slouches in the conspiracy department themselves. *Chapters of Erie* uncovers depths of corruption and conspiracy undreamt of in America before then and unparalleled until the G. W. Bush administration. Players in the Erie drama manipulated the stock market like a rigged slot machine, liberally purchased judges and legislators, and in one spectacular instance staged a rail collision in a tunnel north of Albany.

After an injunction issued in downtown Manhattan ordering the Drew party to cease any actions in "furtherance of said conspiracy," the Drew attorneys obtained a counter-injunction from another jurisdiction and dumped 50,000 shares of Erie stock on the market, which were instantly bought up by Vanderbilt before he learned their source; to avoid arraignment on contempt of court charges, the Drew minions fled the financial district at 10 in the morning for the safety of New Jersey:

[T]he astonished police saw a throng of panic-stricken railway directors—looking more like a frightened gang of thieves, disturbed in the division of their plunder, than like the wealthy representatives of a great corporation—rush headlong . . . in the direction of the Jersey ferry. In their hands were packages and files of papers, and their pockets were crammed with assets and securities. One individual bore away with him in a hackney-coach bales containing six millions of dollars in greenbacks.

Adams's account conjures images of the so-called perp walk that some of Wall Street's most egregious recent knaves have taken for the cameras, though contemporary financial scandals have produced little authentic reform. The agencies entrusted to cleanse the system have been as tainted as their targets. The revolving door between government jobs and corporate board seats, rampant looting as corporate S.O.P. and the Orwellian duckspeak of a conglomerated media system are symptoms of a failing democracy.

While Adams could write frankly about the true state of affairs within America's power elite ("Mr. Justice Sutherland, a magistrate of such pure character and unsullied reputation that it is inexplicable how he ever came to be elevated to the bench on which he sits . . . "), "investigative reporting" in our era has become a desk job involving a few phone calls and the endless quoting of "anonymous sources" who are, invariably, government officials rather than ordinary citizens fearing retribution from these same officials.

Since Michael Barkun's *A Culture of Conspiracy* typifies the "one bad apple" approach, its opening anecdote is worth recounting:

> On January 20, 2002, Richard McCaslin, thirty-seven, of Carson City, Nevada, was arrested sneaking into the Bohemian Grove in Northern California. The Grove is the site of an exclusive annual men's retreat attended by powerful business and political leaders. . . . McCaslin . . . was carrying a combination shotgun-assault rifle, a .45 pistol, a crossbow, a knife, a sword, and a bomb-launching device. . . . [He] told police he had entered Bohemian Grove in order to expose the satanic human sacrifices he believed occurred there.

The interesting detail here isn't a thwarted massacre by one of those deranged loners responsible for all political assassinations, but Barkun's bland characterization of Bohemian Grove: Inexplicably, he implies, the place is a magnet for conspiracists, some of whom also suggest "that the Grove's guests include nonhuman species masquerading as human beings."

In last year's *Where I Was From,* Joan Didion provides a more textured and provocative description of Bohemian Grove:

By 1974 . . . one in five resident members and one in three non-resident members of the Bohemian Club was listed in Standard & Poor's Register of Corporations, Executives, and Directors. . . . The summer encampment, then, had evolved into a special kind of enchanted circle, one in which these captains of American finance and industry could entertain . . . the temporary management of that political structure on which their own fortunes ultimately depended.

It's no mystery that citizens of a country methodically eliminating its social services, waging "preemptive" wars on behalf of corporate interests, defunding education and building more prisons than hospitals view the prevailing power structure as a public menace; that many of those citizens who can't afford health care, whose jobs have been exported to countries where slave wages and child exploitation are endemic, spill over the edge, embrace bizarre cultic notions and believe there are "aliens among us."

One smells a metaphorical truth in McCaslin's belief that "human sacrifices" occur in Bohemian Grove's exclusive covens, typically attended by Henry Kissinger, Colin Powell, James Baker III, Bush père et fils, the Bechtels, George Shultz, the heads of the World Bank and the IMF—none, as far as I know, even vaguely troubled by human sacrifices produced by the pursuit of their own enrichment.

The word *conspiracy* reduces logical thought to paranoia, and it's misleading in a different sense too: Little of what we ought to know about the dealings of power is especially secret anymore. Much of the public doesn't have the ability to make obvious connections between available facts. Remove education from the public agenda and you replace the capacity for analysis with an atavistic belief in horoscopes and astrology, alien abductions and Zionist imperialism.

Everyone in an authoritarian society understands what lies beyond the pale of consensual reality. Skepticism is demonized as "conspiracy theory," evidence of real conspiracies ridiculed by mainstream media. Any rejection of received ideas is misrepresented to burnish absurdist images of conspirators as Dr. Mabuse-like lunatics gathering in dark basements and Masonic lodges.

Actual conspiracies do not involve interplanetary visitors, pod people and the other fantasies conspiracist analysts call "stigmatized knowledge." They involve money and power, and the manipulation of appearances by powerful interests. Conspiracies can evolve over time, without highly organized or explicit planning. Indeed, the "disorganized conspiracy" transpires in increments over generations, with no consistent personnel, and requires only a continuity of anti-populist, authoritarian ideology.

Ted Nace's *Gangs of America: The Rise of Corporate Power and the Disabling of Democracy* charts the insidious, century-long accumulation of precedents constructed around a glaring judicial error, arising from the 1886 *Santa Clara County* v. *Southern Pacific Railroad* case, that has ultimately resulted in the extension of "equal protection" under the law to corporations, and the bestowal of "civil rights" and "immortal personhood" on economic entities, including the First and other Bill of Rights amendments intended to protect human individuals. This lethal absurdity has now become extraterritorial, as GATT and WTO measures enable corporations to file suit against sovereign states whose labor or environmental laws inhibit corporate profit-taking.

Nace cites the perversion of the Fourteenth Amendment, intended to guarantee due process and equal protection of the law to the slaves newly freed under the Thirteenth Amendment, into an instrument for "the empowerment of the corporation." Per Nace: Justice Hugo Black noted that in the first 50 years of the Fourteenth Amendment's existence, "'less than one-half of 1 percent' of cases in which it was invoked had to do with protection of African Americans, whereas 50 percent involved corporations." Nace further notes that "the person who did more than anyone else to bring about this [corporate] empowerment was Supreme Court Justice Stephen J. Field . . . [whose] older brother David . . . served as counsel for the notorious railroad barons Jay Gould and Jim Fisk."

Christian Parenti's *The Soft Cage* follows another "disorganized conspiracy," one that begins with the written physical descriptions on passes required for plantation slaves to travel off their owner's property, and charts the gradual extension of obligatory identification documents into the lives of virtually all citizens. (An elegant exposition of the pre-photographic methods used in 18th-century Britain to identify fugitives can be found in William Godwin's spellbinding 1794 novel *The Adventures of Caleb Williams.* Happily for many Southern slaves, who had secretly acquired literacy and could forge these passes, the passes themselves were usually inspected by illiterate Southern whites; British fugitives had no such luck.)

Parenti's book ends, or rather continues, with the gradual morphing of mandatory ID into interface media for the panoply of visual and electronic surveillance technologies now used to amass data on virtually every individual on earth. One could say, contingently, that these temporally spaced, individually smallish corrosions of individual rights and privacy "just sort of happened," though the structural contradictions between capitalism and democracy they reflect, and the manufactured belief that the two things are identical, seem hardly the products of pure chance.

Economist Loretta Napoleoni provides an exhaustively researched account of one recent conspiracy in her book *Modern Jihad*:

> Just as Worldcom was able to use accountancy techniques to tamper with its books, bin Laden's associates succeeded in utilizing sophisticated insider trading instruments to speculate on the stock market prior to September 11. . . . [O]n 6 September . . . around 32 million British Airways shares changed hands in London, about three times the normal level. On 7 September, 2,184 put options on British Airways were traded on the LIFFE (London Futures and Options market), about five times the normal amount of daily trading. Across the Atlantic, on Monday, 10 September, the number of put options on American Airlines in the Chicago Board Options Exchange jumped 60 times the daily average. In the three days prior to the attack, the volume of put options in the US surged 285 times the average trading level. . . . Ironically, in attacking one of the symbols of Western capitalism, bin Laden may have masterminded the biggest insider trading operation ever accomplished.

According to *The Independent on Sunday* of 14 October 2001, "To the embarrassment of investigators, it has also emerged that the firm used to buy many of the 'put' options—where a trader in effect bets on a share price fall—on United Airlines stock was headed until 1998 by 'Buzzy' Krongard, now the executive director of the CIA. . . . There is no suggestion that Mr. Krongard had advance knowledge of the attacks."

This information isn't "secret," but indicates a more coherent motive for the September 11 attacks than the conjuration of insane Islamists who "hate our democratic freedoms," and who can therefore serve as pretexts for a "war on terror" that has so far done little to protect American citizens but has grossly enriched the corporate sponsors of the Bush administration, such as Halliburton, Bechtel and myriad other interests whose emissaries revel round the campfire every summer at Bohemian Grove. And because it reveals what modern conspiracies are really all about, you are likely to find some garbled, discrediting version of it on page B27 of your daily newspaper rather than above the fold on page 1.

PART

V

UTOPIA'S DEBRIS

BARBET SCHROEDER'S
TERROR'S ADVOCATE

SINCE THE events of 9/11/01, the Hollywood cinema (to say nothing of stage and television) has prodigiously embarrassed itself with dramas and documentaries about something vaguely identified as "terrorism": maudlin, elegiac "personal" stories about lives lost, tasteless re-creations of the horrors inside the doomed planes, stories of miraculous survivals, civic heroism, with wall-to-wall flag-waving and blustery avowals of revenge as mise-en-scène and ideological given; instead of hard thinking, exercises in grief management and demonization have defined the American response to the first attack on the country's "soil" (as it's always, and only, referred to in militaristic verbiage) since Pearl Harbor. (I just came in from grocery shopping on American soil, by the way.)

There have been the portmanteau films, those intricately plotted, densely interwoven narratives that leap from terror cells in Beirut or some other mysterious foreign place, to figures on mobile phones in New Jersey delicatessens, to nonexistent government "command centers" stuffed with the latest in surveillance equipment; intrepid investigators, ultrasecret military bunkers, glimpses of "the Arab street" in Karachi or other teeming, alien cities; plots about "ticking bombs," fantasies woven from whole cloth about "how terrorism operates," and how duplicitous and undercover movie stars manage to save civilization from the rabid fanaticism of a few bad apples in the otherwise wholesome religion of Islam.

A few films, mainly documentaries, have bravely attempted to expose these meretricious products of the culture industry as the chauvinistic unreality they represent, but have rarely taken a long, systemic view of what modern terrorism is, how it evolved, and what it actually portends for the coming years. In reality, 9/11 is simply one, spectacular, but otherwise unremarkable event in a succession of atrocities committed by both sovereign states and freelancers.

Anyone hoping to understand the reality of terrorism should first of all stop viewing it through the lens of Americanism (or anti-Americanism), as if terrorism only became "real" on September 11, 2001.

Terrorism, or asymmetrical warfare, has a long modern history, dating at least as far back as the Decembrist movement in Czarist Russia. A terrorist assassination triggered World War I. But terrorism as practiced today—"blind terrorism," in which the identities of the victims are irrelevant—has its salient point of origin in French Algeria, and it is there, in 1945, that Barbet Schroeder's *Terror's Advocate* really begins. As one of Schroeder's recurring witnesses, FLN founder Bachir Boumaza, informs us, on the very day when France celebrated its liberation from the Nazis—V.E. Day, 8 May 1945— French forces launched a bloodbath in the Algerian town of Sétif, where demonstrators waved the Algerian flag and sang (Algerian) patriotic songs.

A substantial percentage of French combat forces in WWII had in fact been Algerian, and the demonstrations in Sétif and other Algerian communities were as much celebrations of the German defeat as assertions of Algerian nationalism. Yet at least 15,000 Algerians were massacred; some estimates run as high as 45,000.

This was the beginning of the French-Algerian War, though French repression maintained an uneasy peace in Algeria until 1954. While France relinquished its colonial claims on Indochina after the defeat at Dien Bien Phu in 1953, and granted autonomy to Tunisia and Morocco, Algeria had been "incorporated" into France itself, and was considered inseparable from the rest of the nation. Many Algerians were themselves conflicted between considering themselves "French" or "Algerians," for among its positive contributions to Algeria, France had instituted a highly effective educational system, built roads and communications networks on a par with those of France proper, and French had become Algeria's dominant language. French culture was deeply interwoven with the daily life of Algeria—as, to a considerable degree, it still is today.

But the memory of the Sétif massacre, and the punitive disproportion of Algerian representation in the French parliament, the second-class treatment of Arabs, Kabyles and Berbers by French settlers, and the routine expropriation of arable land from Algerians by French viniculturists and farmers, brutal methods of social control and the racist arrogance of colonial rule had created the ideal conditions for a full-scale revolt, which erupted on All Saint's Day, 1954, under the general auspices of the Comité Révolutionnaire d'Unité et d'Action, or C.R.U.A. This took the form of attacks on French militia and police, public installations, the colonists' private property and Muslim collaborators.

The French-Algerian War lasted from 1954 to 1962, one of the longest in modern history, marked by continual escalation of civilian casualties, the French use of torture and bombings by both sides. The Algerian side was organized and led by the Front de Libération Nationale, or FLN. It defeated the superior numbers of French troops and the morale of the French settlers through the selective bombing of bars, nightclubs and casinos patronized by French vacationers and *grand colons*.

One of the best-known episodes in this campaign, the bombing of the "Milk Bar" in Algiers in September 1956, was carried out by Djamila Bouhired, a Casbah seamstress recruited by the FLN's military strategist, Yacef Saadi—who later wrote his memoir, *The Battle of Algiers,* and produced the celebrated film by Pontecorvo, in which Saadi plays himself.

Djamila was put on trial for her life, and became the symbol of Algerian liberation. The lawyer who defended her and, after her conviction, obtained her pardon by mobilizing world opinion in her favor, was Jacques Vergès—the ostensible subject of Schroeder's film.

Vergès appears throughout Schroeder's movie, pictured invariably behind his desk, in his well-appointed office, smoking an enormous cigar. Yet despite his centrality, Vergès also serves as a sort of punctuation mark between the testimony of many others: terrorists, investigative journalists, lawyers, former political prisoners, politicians and even the top echelon of the Khmer Rouge.

After Djamila's eventual release from prison, Vergès married her; the couple had two children. As novelist Lionel Duroy, one of this film's most engaging "talking heads" puts it, "Djamila was never Vergès's wife; he was Djamala's husband." In Algeria, Vergès's moment of heroism and the story of a great love brought him a practice as a small-time divorce attorney. As a man somewhat devoted to a grandiose notion of himself, Vergès did something entirely unexpected: He disappeared for eight years, leaving his family, dropping (almost) entirely out of sight.

Where was he? The possibilities include Libya, Yemen, Jordan, Moscow, South Africa, Cambodia, East Germany, China, Algeria and Cuba. If, as both Duroy and Claude Faure, the historian of the French Secret Service, manage to suggest, Vergès may have been an agent of both the STASI and French Intelligence, it would have been easy for Vergès to have circulated through all these places, as he was always able to return to France. Will we ever know? Probably, in time. Several eyewitnesses swear they ran into him right in Paris, and Vergès himself, in hypothetical mode, speaks of living in cheap hotels under assumed names.

If *Terror's Advocate* were only concerned with Vergès's "missing years," or with Vergès himself, for that matter, it would simply be an interesting documentary. But Schroeder's film is a gripping, suspenseful drama, replete with a symphonic musical score, neither ploddingly "factual" nor "fictional" in the invented sense—its fictional aspect derives from the ambiguities inherent in what its large cast of witnesses say, and leave unspoken.

Meanings and counter-meanings are telegraphed by still photographs, snippets of footage, a few quoted scenes from *The Battle of Algiers,* and the like; remarkably, most of its shots are fixed-frame interviews, in highly expressive, static backgrounds, of single individuals, juxtaposed in a polyphonic montage that opens up a world of questions, and answers others in surpassingly shocking ways.

When Vergès resurfaced in public, he had, in Duroy's view, abandoned all political solutions. Vergès himself was a "colonized" person, whose mother was Vietnamese, his father from Reunion, and he had been prominent among the anti-colonial student movement at university (where he became friendly with, among others, Saloth Sar, later known as Pol Pot). In his "second skin," so to speak, Vergès became something quite different than the champion of victims. He assumed the role of "all-purpose lawyer," taking on the defense of such monsters as Moise Tshombe—the man responsible for the murder of Patrice Lumumba, one of Vergès's heroes—as well as numerous African dictators; Carlos Ramirez Sanchez ("the Jackal"), perpetrator of countless murders and terror attacks; Carlos's future wife, Magdalena Kopp, jailed for attempting to plant bombs in the Paris subway system; most reprehensibly of all, Vergès took on the defense of Klaus Barbie, "the butcher of Lyon," who tortured and killed Resistance leader Jean Moulin, and ordered 44 Jewish children deported to their deaths.

Vergès has ready rationalizations for all these decisions. He would, he told the genial illustrator of "Charlie Hebdo," Siné, use the Barbie trial to expose the French atrocities in Algeria. Behind the narrative, another, uglier narrative emerges.

Tshombe's family had agreed to pay off a huge loan Vergès owed an Algerian bank, if Vergès got Tshombe released from prison. (As the latter died in jail, Vergès still owes the equivalent of a million dollars.) Barbie's defense—and, depressingly enough, much of the funding for the FLN, the defense of Carlos and Magdalena Kopp, among many of Vergès's clients—was underwritten by François Genoud, a former Nazi espionage agent, implemental in the ODESSA "underground railroad" of Nazis escaping to South America after the German defeat, literary beneficiary and executor for the writings of Hitler and Goebbels, and founder of a Swiss bank. Genoud's bank paid the defense fees for innumerable airline hijackers and other practitioners of "blind terrorism"—terrorism with a political pretext, conducted strictly for profit.

Barbet Schroeder has uncovered the dirty secrets behind contemporary terror, including the "Islamic fundamentalist" variety: After the liberation of Algeria, for which one can justify some, though hardly all, instances of FLN terrorism, virtually all notable terrorist actions have been contracted to a core of professionals like Carlos, from the OPEC kidnappings in Vienna to the bombings in Bali and the World Trade Center attacks. There has always been a financial motive behind these atrocities, whether the ruin of the Balinese tourist industry or the windfall of put options produced by careful stock betting in the days before 9/11. The cadres of religious dupes sometimes used to carry out these operations get their reward in Paradise; the contractors and their clients reap the profits here on terra firma.

Terror's Advocate weaves a spellbinding web connecting events that seem unrelated and prove to be "all of a piece." Schroeder's particular genius for getting people with everything to hide to chat freely about their secrets on camera is an art in itself—an art of persistence, of assuming a neutral stance, of letting reality speak for itself, without tendentious commentary, voice-over exegesis or editorializing.

Schroeder leaves it up to us, the viewers, whom to believe, what to conclude, to decide whether someone is lying part of the time and telling the truth at other times, dissembling, or being totally candid. Some of *Terror's*

Advocate's richest moments are the pauses, hesitations and guarded locutions of certain witnesses, the ambiguous vocabulary that often comes into play, contrasted with the spontaneity and candor of speakers like Duroy, Oliver Schrom (a journalist who has written a book on Carlos's network), Patricia Tourancheau (author of *Le Gang des Postiches* and reporter for *Libération*) and Tobias Wunschik, an expert on the STASI archives.

Some of Schroeder's subjects are just plainly convincing—surprisingly so, for example, in the case of Horst Franz, former STASI agent and East German overseer of surveillance on the Carlos group. Others, like Magdalena Kopp, seem so self-involved that their expressions of regret over their past actions sound perfunctory and unreal. Carlos, whom we only hear via telephone from his French prison cell, sounds like a psychopath, and he undoubtedly is.

If *Terror's Advocate* could be said to have a hero, it is hardly Jacques Vergès, whose pronouncements from behind his cigar seem progressively more hubristic, more complacent and more deluded: Yet Schroeder has unerringly nailed Vergès own psychopathology, and it is astonishingly like that of Jimmy Stewart's in *Vertigo*, and the "false replacement" of the fictionalized Fernando Vallejo, in *Our Lady of the Assassins*, of one lover for the slain original. Vergès lived a moment of real heroism, real nobility, and a great love, once upon a time, when he moved heaven and earth to save Djamila Bouhired from the guillotine. Since then, he has tried to recover that moment, accomplishing only its grotesque parody and the ruin of his former nobility of purpose. He retains his charisma, his eloquence, his cleverness. But there is "something missing."

Perhaps we might find that something in Hans Joachim Klein: former bodyguard of the lawyer Klaus Croissant and participant in the OPEC kidnapping of the oil ministers in Vienna, Klein was shot in the stomach, flown to Algeria, and after his recovery gradually withdrew from "the movement." He vanished for 20 years after writing his confession, sending it, with his gun, to *Der Spiegel*. Klein renounced violence, repented his terrorist past and, after his arrest in 1998, served six years in prison. He is a free man today, in every sense: free of the past, free from the hypnotic delusion that violence begets anything except further violence.

Thus Schroeder's film is not without a note of hope, though what it illustrates about "blind terrorism" portends nothing especially hopeful about the time ahead of us. Every American should see this movie before uttering another word about "terrorism": It's absurd to speak of it without understanding a thing about its working mechanism, and Schroder has provided a complete blueprint.

And in any foreseeable future, we will never be rid of it. Too many sovereign states, including the USA, practice it with the full force of arms. And too many freelancers are employed by them for clandestine activity, or have set up shop on their own. There are far too many fools on this earth willing to murder in the name of God, and too many hucksters and profiteers eager to turn a dollar on their madness.

SUSAN SONTAG
(1933–2004)

LIKE MARIA Callas's voice, Susan Sontag's mind, to borrow a phrase from the great filmmaker Werner Schroeter (one of countless underappreciated artists Sontag championed), was "a comet passing once in a hundred years." In a dauntingly, often viciously anti-intellectual society, Sontag made being an intellectual attractive.

She was the indispensable voice of moral responsibility, perceptual clarity, passionate (and passionately reasonable) advocacy: for aesthetic pleasure, for social justice, for unembarrassed hedonism, for life against death. Sontag took it as a given that our duty as sentient beings is to rescue the world. She knew that empathy can change history.

She set the bar of skepticism as high as it would go. Allergic to received ideas and their hypnotic blandishments, she was often startled to discover how devalued the ethical sense, and the courage to exercise it, had become in American consumer culture.

Sontag had impeccable instincts for saying and doing what needed to be said and done while too many others scrambled for the safety of consensus. Hence the uproar when she declared, at the height of Solidarity's epochal crisis in 1982, that "communism . . . is fascism with a human face." Hence also the depressingly rote indignation mobilized against her response to a *New Yorker* survey about the 9/11 attacks, published on 24 September 2001—a survey that most respondents used to promote themselves, their latest books, the depth of their own "feelings."

Of course it was, and still is, easier for many Americans to pretend the events of 9/11 were inexplicable eruptions of violence against American virtuousness, perpetrated by people who "hate us for our freedoms." Indeed, the habitual assertion of the American way of life's superiority is probably what persuades supposedly serious writers to weigh in on a civil catastrophe by promoting their own narrow interests, dropping in news of their current travel itineraries, their marriages, their kids—oh, and how shaken they were by the tragic events.

It takes unusual bravery to cite, in a large media venue, cause and effect as operant elements in a man-made emergency—especially when the programmed pieties and entrenched denial mechanisms of society run in the opposite direction.

Sontag drew her own better-than-well-informed conclusions about what happened on 9/11. The habit of independent thought has so little currency in 21st-century America that dissent is the last thing most Americans consider worth protecting.

What Jean Genet referred to as "the far Right and its imbecilic mythology" have already been activated in several "obituary" pieces, including one fulminating, hateful dismissal of Sontag's entire lifework. It's lowering to realize how terminally bitter the American right really is: Even in its current triumphal micro-epoch, it needs to demonize somebody.

Sontag's political "lapses," cited even in sympathetic articles, are in fact the public moments one should most admire her for. She was usually right, and when she hadn't been, she said so. It's customary these days to damn people for "inconsistency," as if it's somehow virtuous to persist forever in being wrong. Sontag interrogated her own ideas with merciless rigor, and when she discovered they no longer applied, or were defectively inadequate or just plain bad, she never hesitated to change her mind in public.

Certainly she felt the same revulsion and horror at the atrocity of 9/11 that any New Yorker, any citizen of the world, did. But she also had the moral scruple to connect the attacks to generally untelevised, lethal American actions abroad, to the indiscriminate carnage that has typified both state policy and terrorist violence in the new century. Where, exactly, does the difference lie?

Unlike our government's loudest warmongers and their media cheerleaders, Sontag put her own life on the line, many times, in defense of her principles—in Israel during the Six Day War, in Hanoi during the American bombardment, in Sarajevo throughout much of the conflict there. Like Genet, she was willing to go anywhere, at a moment's notice, out of solidarity with people on the receiving end of contemporary barbarism.

The range of her talents and interests was no less impressive than her moral instincts. She once told me that "every good book is worth reading at least once" (in her case, it was usually at least twice). Her appetite for cultural provender—opera, avant-garde theater, film, dance, travel, historical inquiry, cuisine of any kind, architecture, the history of ideas—was inexhaustible. If you told her about something she didn't know, she soon knew more about it than you did. She routinely went directly from a museum to a screening, then to a concert; and if there was a kung fu movie playing somewhere after all that, off she went, whether you were still ambulatory or not.

I know I'm in a minority, but I remain a fan of Sontag's early novels *The Benefactor* and *Death Kit*—Sontag herself cared little for them in later years. Not enough people have seen the films she directed: *Duet for Cannibals* and *Brother Carl* in Sweden, *Promised Lands* in Israel, *Unguided Tour* in Venice. These early and middle works could be considered noble experiments, operating on a high level of fluency and daring.

None of these works are as sumptuously realized as her best essays, or her later novels *The Volcano Lover* and *In America*. At times, her reverence for the European modernists who influenced her eclipses her own seldom mentioned, American gift for absurdist black humor. (*Death Kit* has anything but a reputation for hilarity, but it's one of the most darkly funny narratives written in America during the Vietnam War.) Many of Sontag's essays, for that matter, have threads of Firbankian whimsy and manic satire running through them—and no, I'm not referring to "Notes on Camp."

There's no way to summarize her restless cultural itinerary and her immense services to "the republic of letters" in the space of an obituary. What I can speak of, here, again, is the indelible example she set as a moral being, citizen and writer. She sedulously distinguished between the merely personal and the insights personal experience generated. "I" appears less frequently in her writings than in those of any other significant American writer I can think of. If Sontag was less averse, in recent times, to saying "I," it could be that she at last realized she'd earned the authority for "I" to mean more, coming from her, than it does coming from most people. (In America, "I" isn't simply a pronoun, but a way of life.)

It's my guess that growing up in Arizona and Southern California, among people who placed no special value on intelligence and none at all on its cultivation, Sontag's first line of defense against being hurt by other people was the same thing (aside from physical beauty) that distinguished her from ordinary people—that awesome intellect. She could be ferociously assertive, and at times even hurtful, without at all realizing the tremendous effect she had on people. In some ways, like any American intellectual, she often felt slighted or underappreciated, even when people were actually paying keen attention to her.

Her personal magnetism was legendary. Even in later times, she had the glamour of a film star. She almost never wore makeup (though she did, finally, find a shade of lipstick she could stand), and usually wore black slacks, black sweaters and sometimes a black leather jacket, though occasionally the jacket would be brown. She had the body language of a young person: She once explained to me that people get old when they started acting like old people.

I never heard her say a dumb word, even in moments of evident distress. She did, from time to time, do things that seemed quite odd, but then, who doesn't? Her will to keep experiencing, learning and feeling "the old emotions"—and, sometimes, to make herself empty, restock her interiority, break with old ideas—came with a project of self-transcendence that Sontag shouldered, like Sisyphus's stone, cheerfully, "with fervor."

She once told Dick Cavett, after the first of her struggles with cancer, that she didn't find her own illness interesting. She stipulated that it was moving to her, but not interesting. To be interesting, experience has to yield a harvest of ideas, which her illness certainly did—but she communicated them in a form useful to others in ways a conventional memoir couldn't be. (To be useful, one has to reach others on the level of thought, not only feeling—though the two are inseparable.)

In light of her own illness, she set about removing the stigma then attached to cancer, dismantling the punitive myths this fearsome illness generated at the time. We don't look at illness in the same way we did before *Illness as Metaphor* and the widespread examination of our relationship to medicine that it triggered.

Her detachment in this regard was a powerful asset. Many years ago, I went with her one morning to her radiologist. The radiologist had gotten back some complicated X-rays and wanted to discuss them. On the way uptown, Susan was incredibly composed, long resigned to hypervigilance as the price of staying alive.

At the clinic, she disappeared into the doctor's office for a worryingly long time. When she came out, finally, she was laughing.

"She put the X-rays up," Susan told me, "and said, 'This really doesn't look good.' So I looked them over, and thought about it. Then I said, 'You're right. These don't look good. But you know something, these aren't my X-rays.'"

They weren't her X-rays. Her most recent procedure had left a temporary, subcutaneous line of staple sutures running from her throat to her abdomen. The tiny metal clamps she knew were there would have glowed on an X-ray.

For some reason this was the first memory that flashed to mind when the sad news came that she was gone.

ROBERT BRESSON
Hidden in Plain Sight

I HAVE an unusually convenient way of remembering when I first became fascinated by Robert Bresson's films. *Pickpocket* was the first one I saw, at the old Orson Welles Theater, in Cambridge, Massachusetts, in my late teens; it was also the first movie I saw on LSD. (Even on acid, I was never one to enjoy *Snow White and the Seven Dwarfs.*)

Since I hadn't absorbed the truisms about Bresson that even then encased his work in a gelatin of spiritually heroic clichés, I was, after *Pickpocket*, skeptical about the thematic platitudes critics and film writers routinely and confidently attached to Bresson. Some of them were plausible, some undoubtedly true, but many just sounded convincing: Once art becomes a religion, you can say any high-minded nonsense about it with utter impunity.

As per standard critical note, *Pickpocket* is, obviously, "inspired" by Fyodor Dostoevsky's *Crime and Punishment.* A man commits forbidden acts, gets caught and goes to prison, where his suffering is ameliorated by the steadfast love of a good woman.

But *Pickpocket*'s central character, Michel (played by the Uruguayan nonactor Martin LaSalle), with his watery, feebly asserted version of Raskolnikov's Nietzscheanism, is merely a petty thief, conspicuously lacking the will to monstrosity of Dostoevsky's ax murderer. His crimes never rise above the level of common, small-time transgression. They are only enlarged to epic scale by his neurasthenic imagination. His decision to tempt exposure and shame on a daily basis is a difficult one, but not because he wonders, terrified like Raskolnikov, whether he's truly capable of it. It isn't monstrous to steal. Often it is necessary, and its drastic punishment is more wicked than the crime. *Les Misérables,* after all, is about a man implacably hounded by the law for stealing a loaf of bread.

True, Michel could get a job. But stealing has a specific psychosexual meaning for him, beyond fulfilling the simple need to eat. Michel is like a man who knows he can cop an orgasm if he manages to be in the right place at the right time, and rubs against the right partner. His fears are more logistical than spiritual, and also function as aphrodisiacs.

It's unlikely that Michel steals because he considers himself a "superman," in a class of hypothetical, extraordinary beings whose unusual gifts place them above the law—though he posits such a theory, abstractly, in his sour, unengaging encounters with the police detective played by Jean Pélégri. Michel steals because it is the only act that makes him feel alive in a world becoming dead; not only dead to pleasure and unprogrammed emotions but, as later Bresson made ever more explicit, organically dead. Theft reconnects Michel to the flow of life around him, from which he otherwise feels desperately isolated, and that he perceives as pathetically limited in its possibilities.

When he refuses to see his dying mother, and answers his friend Jacques's sarcastic reproach "And you say you love your mother" with "More than myself," Michel says the literal truth. This is not because he can't access a profound love he really feels for her, but because he feels nothing at all, and loves her as much—in other words, as little—as anything or anyone else. A prisoner of coercive social forms, like all of us, Michel "feels" he should feel what he can't feel, but since he doesn't, he can only offer the empty verbal assurance that he does.

Michel is more like Albert Camus's Meursault than Raskolnikov, but this likeness is nearly as superficial. Meursault's only important act in *The Stranger* is the unmotivated killing of an Arab on an Algerian beach. Michel's thefts, on the other hand, produce an income, require continual refinement, and relieve him of the wage-earning regimentation of the Parisian subbourgeoisie. He sets a trap for himself, but the forces of order that close it on him have no intrinsic worthiness; they simply defend a mediocre status quo that governs the circulation of capital.

The erotic center of *Pickpocket* is not Michel's growing love for Jeanne, the young woman neighbor looking after his mother. Indeed, the shrewdly chosen visage of Marika Green emits expressions of overdrawn humility and neurotic dutifulness. If she wishes to "save" Michel, whose disjointedly angular beauty so closely resembles that of Egon Schiele, this may be the effusion of saintly purity, but if you ignore the austerity of Bresson's cinematography, you can also assume that she wants to save Michel for herself, to secure an attractive breadwinner for her fatherless children, "redeeming" him for a future life of dreary convention.

Far more romantic than his dealings with Jeanne are Michel's encounters with the professional thief identified in the film's credits by the single name Kassagi. Distinctly reptilian, as comfortable in criminality as a rubber duck in a bubble bath, Kassagi is like the lover who, after you've had a few quotidian partners, reveals the astonishing range of pleasures available from someone who actually knows what he's doing.

The "redemptive ending" of *Pickpocket,* cannibalized whole in any number of movies, is also, from a certain angle, specious. Jeanne may well repine while Michel's in prison, sustained by the exalting power of love; Michel, on the other hand, given his good looks and fragile physique, will probably find dozens of lovers in jail to refine his talents as a criminal, and emerge a hardened, masterfully seductive, charmingly predatory thug.

Yes, it's comforting to think otherwise. We would like to believe, contrary to everything we know, that a hopelessly corrupt world offers endless opportunities for rehabilitation. But as the protagonist of *The Devil, Probably* (1977) would put it, rehabilitation to what? Belief is just as toxic as cynicism. Redemption has become a business, a commodity, a lucrative premise for launching an Oliver North or a G. Gordon Liddy as a talk show host. Bresson had to have known this well in advance of the fait accompli, given that *Pickpocket* was made long after Guy Debord and the Situationists had described precisely how our emotions were being turned into products.

The Catholic right loves to claim Bresson as a sort of "Christian atheist," yet his work is remarkably fixated on the death of feeling and the uselessness of Christian faith. To find in it a lamentation for the absence of God is to cheapen the existential toughness of its core. While Bresson adapted material from a protofascist Christian like Georges Bernanos, his version of *Diary of a Country Priest* (1951) presents its clergyman as an insipid admirer of his own earnest masochism. Bresson's real subject is not the priest, but the poisonous malice of the provincial imbeciles who constitute his "flock."

Furthermore, before anyone awards Bresson a Jean Hersholt Humanitarian Award for his so-called belief in spiritual redemption through suffering, and in the ennobling, Tolstoyan honesty of peasant ordinariness, we should consider his first great work, *Les dames du bois de Boulogne* (1945), and his final masterpiece, *L'argent* (1983). In the former, Bresson shows us Maria Casarès wreaking an intricate and ingenious revenge, à la Choderlos de Laclos, on a once potential lover she never wanted in the first place, and only desires after she ruins him; frequently described as an anomaly in Bresson's oeuvre, this film is anything but. Tolstoy's story "The Forged Coupon" illustrates through the metaphor of counterfeit currency how the inauthentic spreads destruction through a society; in Bresson's adaptation, *L'argent,* he bends this tale into a straightforward, horrifically brutal depiction of money itself as humanity's ultimate self-annihilating invention.

Pickpocket, like all of Bresson's films, records the expiration of humane feeling in the modern world, the impossibility of decency in a universe of greed. This is amply illustrated in *Au hasard Balthazar* (1966), a film about the sufferings of a donkey so painful to watch that if you can see it through without weeping, you deserve to be hit by a Mack truck when you leave the theater. For Bresson, the casual destruction of life, any life, is the damning imperative of the human species. As William Burroughs put it, "Man is a bad animal." This message is spelled out in boldface in *The Devil, Probably,* with its copious footage of man-made ecological disaster.

Critics frequently link Bresson with Carl Dreyer, which is a bit like pairing August Strindberg with Henrik Ibsen. Like Ibsen, Dreyer has a seamless lack of humor and a solemnity that gives his films the gravity of a cancer operation. In Bresson, however, the absurdity that delicately fringes Strindberg's dark dramas echoes in whole passages of deliberately idiotic dialogue, in actions that speak volumes about nothing but feel uncomfortably textured like real life. Dreyer boils life down to its pivotal moments; Bresson shows that most of our lives are consumed by meaningless routines. This can be startlingly funny, just when you thought a Bresson movie couldn't become more grim.

In *Pickpocket,* the society whose laws Michel breaks is far more criminal than he is—not technically, not legally, but spiritually: This is Bresson's archly comic irony, heavily veiled in nocturnal chiaroscuro. His film's tragedy, which is finally more important, is that Michel would like to feel guilty for his crimes, and would even like to love his mother, or Jeanne. But like the humans of the future that Bresson so clearly envisioned, who are already living among us, Michel can't feel a thing, and couldn't love anyone if his life depended on it. The sad truth is, it doesn't.

SIMENON L'INCROYABLE

G EORGES SIMENON (1903–1989) was the 20th century's Balzac. He wrote pulp by the wagonload before producing his serious works: 70 or so Inspector Maigret novels, an ever-darkening franchise in which justice, of an approximate, perverse sort, usually prevails, and well over a hundred *romans durs,* or "hard novels," undertaken between Maigrets (for which they were thematic sketches), in which ordinary lives of quiet desperation suddenly jump the tracks. Justice has no existence in the world of Simenon's *romans durs*—when it occurs there, it's by accident.

No less gluttonous a researcher than Balzac, Simenon spent years wandering France's rivers and canals in small boats. Later, when Maigret made him rich, he greedily roamed the planet collecting material. He soaked up regional physiognomies and accents, the fine details of commonplace trades and livelihoods, the distinguishing features of port cities and provincial towns—though he knew Paris and his native Belgium inside out, Simenon wanted a much bigger working map. He became so familiar with the world's variety and sameness that he could paint atmospheres, landscapes, distances, faces, as well as states of mind, with unparalleled compression. Simenon needs fewer words than any other prose writer I can think of to bring a situation into being, a setting into life, a character into legibility.

Simenon found bourgeois convention suffocating, yet necessary for the clockwork production of his novels. These were written fast, in a state of complete isolation, "by the calendar," and their composition squeezed so much out of him he needed to consult his doctor before starting one, and again when he finished. A devoted husband and father at home, he had a vast, ever-expanded network of lowlife and criminal connections, countless affairs and sex with thousands of prostitutes (also necessary for his production), with Mrs. Simenon's blessing.

Balzac spares us nothing of what he's learned (Witold Gombrowicz once compared him to an exquisite soup someone had squeezed a tablespoon of toothpaste into), but Simenon's genius is the art of reduction, making things appear without mentioning them. He can teach you how to run a restaurant in a few sentences lightly sprinkled across a novel, and how to poison your spouse in even fewer lines—in the same skinny book (*Dimanche*), no less.

Some of his characters turn into murderers, others dump their families and jobs and disappear to chase obsessions they didn't know they had. Sometimes these prove to be false obsessions, desires Simenon's creations think they must satisfy, only to discover they've imitated someone else's, in an effort to make themselves more interesting to themselves and/or present an invented identity to other people. (Patricia Highsmith explored this theme in some of her least characteristic stories, among the many recently gathered in *Nothing That Meets the Eye*.) A man or woman may simply break loose from a tedious existence, inhabit a new persona for a while, then return, changed or not, to the safety of former habits and routines.

Simenon, who never outlined his plots in advance, generates continuous tension by keeping a novel's many possible outcomes immanent until the final few pages, or even, often, the last page. Like Highsmith, he grasped the psychopathology of the 20th century at its gnarled, fatally diseased roots; the century began with alienation, and ended with alienation and sociopathy, its legacy to the time we live in now. Our era seems depressingly certain to reduce the dessert menu to collective suicide. (Consider how ludicrous we find earnest efforts to produce small, salubrious changes in the negative patterns our species has established. Everything seems too small, too late, too contingent on a presumption of intrinsic goodness in human nature: The ultimate revelation of consciousness, itself an accidental development of evolution within a single biological phylum, may turn out to be that there is no human nature—or at least, none that is necessary, ineradicable, or informed by any inherent morality.)

Simenon's radical economy of language, using almost no adjectives or adverbs, is more extreme, and far more involving, than the eloquent white space in the works of Ernest Hemingway. A month of reading Simenon inevitably makes a writer like Raymond Carver look utterly bogus, and one like Cormac McCarthy seem terminally precious. (The latter has always struck me as "Faulkner without content," a novelist only short story writers and minimalist poets could find worthwhile.) Simenon didn't fetishize the supposedly heroic ardor of searching for the perfect, startling word, a cause of literary acne that runs rampant in the work of writers like McCarthy and E. Annie Proulx. He thought the approximate word was quite good enough. Looking for the perfect one would have slowed him down. Finding the perfect one is often a repulsively masturbatory accomplishment. Life isn't words, and the quickness of life can only be suggested by language. This may not be news that writers like to hear, but it's true all the same.

NYRB, the publishing wing of *The New York Review of Books,* has been rescuing out-of-print literary treasures for several years, among them several of Simenon's best non-Maigret novels: *Three Bedrooms in Manhattan, Monsieur Monde Vanishes, Tropic Moon, Dirty Snow* and *The Man Who Watched Trains Go By.* A recent addition to this collection, *Red Lights,* takes us inside the head of a man "going into the tunnel" as he and his wife, Nancy, leave Long Island to fetch their kids from a summer camp in Maine. (*Feux Rouges* was made into a remarkable film in 2004 by Cédric Kahn, starring Jean-Pierre Darroussin and Carole Bouquet.)

"The tunnel" is a place in Steve's mind where Nancy's better job, her occasional asperities and his feelings of inferiority grow uglier as he bolts double whiskeys, to Nancy's disgust, in bars along the traffic-clogged highway. It's a typically shrewd Simenon touch that Steve is explicitly *not* an alcoholic, indeed hardly ever drinks heavily. Moreover, he loves Nancy and their children. Yet his behavior en route becomes almost demonic. Nancy disappears while Steve visits another bar. He finds a note that says she's going to catch a bus.

He gravitates to another saloon. Another customer rebuffs his attempts to start a conversation. When he leaves the place, Steve finds the same man sitting in his car. The stranger has just escaped from prison—a jailbreak has been announced on the radio all evening, and Steve instantly comprehends who his new companion is, accepting his presence without fear, indeed welcoming the opportunity to feel, by osmosis, an outlaw himself, eventually referring to the two of them in conversation as "men like us."

The nightmarish traffic and lashing rain, the glaring sunlight on a gas station and a diner the next morning, the desuetude of the seaside town where the rest of the novel occurs—these shifting venues have such convincing presence that Simenon makes a sagging porch emanate almost unbearable emotion. I know how he does it, but have no idea how he *can* do it.

Among other things, *Red Lights* is one of the scariest literary renditions of how wrong things can turn on too much alcohol—a sobering companion, so to speak, to Dostoyevsky's "A Nasty Incident" and Hans Fallada's *The Drinker.* It's one of Simenon's more tentatively hopeful novels as well.

A hopeful Simenon pulls you through hell before much hope comes into it (*Three Bedrooms in Manhattan* does for romantic love what this book does for drunk driving). But he isn't interested in passing moral judgments, or interfering with his characters' decisions, and he doesn't mind if things occasionally come to a tolerably positive end.

WEILL, BRECHT, *MAHAGONNY*

*T*HE RISE AND FALL OF THE CITY OF MAHAGONNY was originally presented in a truncated, 25-minute cabaret version as *Mahagonny-Songspeil,* at the Deutsches Kammermusikfest in Baden-Baden in 1927. Brecht and Weill expanded it into a full-length opera over the following two years. A radical reconception of opera that used the sounds and vulgar popular melodies of the music hall, along with lyrical ballads and operatic arias uncoupled from Verdian or Wagnerian tradition by *Mahagonny*'s scabrous social critique, the work foregrounded instruments that were sparingly if ever used in traditional opera: alto saxophone, banjo, elements associated with jazz and be-bop. The instrumentation was even more radical than *The Threepenny Opera*'s.

The staging includes a boxing ring, where Trinity Moses kills Alaskawolf Joe. The audience at Baden-Baden was mystified and insulted, as the show, in the words of Weill biographer Foster Hirsch, "reveled in bad taste and had the effrontery to ask the audience to join in." Some forward-minded musical avatars attending this performance, notably Otto Klemperer, as radical in his way as Brecht and Weill, welcomed *Mahagonny*'s demolition of the wall between opera and contemporary musical and dramatic forms.

Brecht and Weill, in their collaborations on *Threepenny Opera* and *Happy End* as well as *Mahagonny,* sought an opera form in which discrete elements would in a sense undermine each other, the opposite effect of the Wagnerian *gesamtkunstwerk,* which Brecht particularly disliked because of its mesmerizing appeal to a passive, emotionally overwrought, easily manipulated audience. Brecht's distaste for what he considered superannuated in theater and works of art generally was more didactic than Weill's. Weill was committed to progressive challenges to the audience, but not keenly invested in alienating it.

He recognized Brecht's genius. He considered Brecht himself almost un-endurable. All their work together was contentious and personally brittle, as Brecht contrived always to have his own way. Weill especially prized *Mahagonny* because, for once, he was able to manipulate Brecht into giving him the upper hand; it is more Weill's opera than Brecht's play set to music.

The finished work, when presented in 1930, encountered less hostility than the *Songspiel* had from much of its audience, eliciting less virulence than expected from more dangerous quarters than conventional opera lovers—a deceptive indifference, as truly drastic cultural strictures were being quietly and meticulously worked out, and needed only sufficient political momentum to impose themselves overnight.

By the time Brecht and Weill offered *Mahagonny* for the Kroll Opera's season in Berlin, the Kroll's acting director, Otto Klemperer, who had calmed Lotte Lenya's nerves after the edgy reception of the *Songspiel* in Baden-Baden three years earlier, now, after much agonizing and prescient appraisal of the political atmosphere, declined to book it, uneasy about the brothel scene in Act 2.

No other Berlin opera would take it. It was accepted at the Leipzig Opera only on condition that the brothel scene be revised. Brecht and Weill altered the scene to give it a "scientific" rather than erotic flavor, as anything scientific still retained some cachet of authority.

As a brutal sign of rapidly changing times, the 9 March premiere in Leipzig was disrupted by a contingent of Hitler's Brownshirts, which turned *Mahagonny* into a political rather than artistic provocation.

For the sake of their careers, which they knew didn't have copious running time ahead in Germany, and to keep the other bookings already set up (let's not forget that Brecht and Weill both worked within the structure of commercial theater—despite Brecht's Marxist utopianism, he and Weill both wanted to transform what could be done within that structure), they further neutralized *Mahagonny*'s ending, removing any suggestion that the climactic demonstration was "communistic." As Weill wrote to his music publisher, *Mahagonny* "perishes because of the crimes of its inhabitants, the wantonness and general chaos . . . We show clearly that anarchy leads to crime and crime to ruin. You can't get more moral." This was not, as Weill fully realized, an argument destined to go anywhere. For one thing, it was transparently insincere. For another, anarchy, crime and ruin were arguably the unconscious goals of Nazism itself, dissembled by a cosmetic, overbureaucratized facade of social regimentation.

Despite the changes, the play's subsequent performances in Leipzig and then in Branschweig were violently disrupted, not only by uniformed Hitlerites but by Brundhilde-type upper-class Germans and their husbands who considered themselves prototypes of the Master Race that the decidedly un-Aryan, flat-faced little colonel from Linz was screeching about in his speeches.

Seven performances in Kassel came off without incident, but *Mahagonny*'s contract was canceled in Essen, Dortmund and Oldenberg.

The work had a briefly recuperative success in Berlin during the Nazi's electoral setback in 1932, positive reviews coming from both the leftist and the reactionary press. In any case, few Berliners thought of themselves as Nazis, culturally or politically, even after Hitler installed himself in the capital as Ghengis Khan of the Thousand Year Reich. Berlin was Germany's New York—reputedly a glittering cesspool of crime, subversion and immorality, which the rest of Germany viewed with a mixture of salacious envy and pious contempt.

Even in the depths of the Hitler years, Berliners remained indifferent to Hitler's ravings and eluded much of the Reich's worst oppression with ingenious ease. Drag clubs like Lutzower Lampke continued operating with only honorary harassment. Moreover, the Lampke's entertainers (many, as nonogenerians, still going strong in the late 1980s) and those of many other clubs kept songs by Brecht-Weill in their repertoires, and other anti-fascist songs. The extent of "internal exile" throughout Germany has been greatly underestimated: I have never seen it estimated by region or state, but will venture to guess that such figures would differ dramatically from city to city, province to province, and economic class to class.

One eloquent irony worth mentioning: Throughout the war period, the most popular piece of music in Germany was the Spring Song of Mendelssohn, with lyrics by Heinrich Heine—a 100 percent Jewish product, which even a totalitarian regime couldn't prevent its subjects from singing and playing. (And, as bombs fell on Hamburg and Dresden, the number one hit was by Zarah Leander, singing of the chaos and mayhem laying waste to the Third Reich, and to hefty numbers of its civilian population: "because of that, the world doesn't crumble, tomorrow the skies will be himmelblau!"—heavenly blue.)

The Weimar Republic, which had survived the inflation of 1923—the year of Hitler's first attempted putsch—had stabilized the currency and maintained its continually embattled legitimacy with the introduction of the Rentenmark in 1924, and its replacement with the Reichmark in 1925. Since its establishment in 1919—the year that Rosa Luxemburg and Karl Leibernicht were murdered (in retrospect, as a metaphor, Alexander Kluge suggested to me that "the Berlin Wall was Stalin's memorial for the murder of Rosa Luxemburg," as the Wall ran through the Canal where Rosa Luxemburg's body was thrown in)—in 1919, Weimar had accelerated the growth of Berlin into a world cultural capital, a laboratory for radical experiment in the arts—in film production, painting and, preeminently, in architecture.

The Bauhaus ideal of architectural lucidity, the rejection of decorative excrescences and the Wilhelmine style of neoclassical monumentality replaced the notion of the street as an aggregate of static facades concealing interior spaces. The kinesthetic flow of the new architecture opened the inside to the outside. A fresh emphasis on functionalism incarnated what Adolf Loos advocated in the manifesto-essay "Ornament and Crime" and his other writings on the design of household objects, machinery and clothing: The paring away of useless fringe and filigree that Loos had applied to small commercial spaces like the American Bar in Vienna informed the design of factories and private housing commissions.

The revisionist expressionism of Paul Scheerbart and Bruno Taut's Berlin housing projects ran along a continuum of so-called pure design in buildings by Bernhard Sehring, for example in the Tietz department store; Paul Mahlberg in the construction of Tempelhof Airport, and the melding of facade and window display exampled in the KaDeWe department store (which still features what has to be Europe's largest meat department); the Wertheim emporium on Leipzigerstrasse designed by Alfred Messer. Retail as well as industrial construction used glass as its visually dominant material, as per Scheerbart's visionary theories; the gleaming new forms of the city center frequently served as decor and backdrop for Festivals of Light that transformed nocturnal Berlin into an enthralling spectacle, akin to the pyrotechnical displays that reached their pinnacle of sophistication and complexity during the fin-de-siècle.

Though Loos's functionalism was a strategy of resistance to commercial seduction, its application in Weimar Berlin and other German cities promoted exactly the opposite effect. Ingeniously alluring displays of merchandise behind store windows at street level multiplied throughout Berlin's center and commodified the activity of the flâneur, the solitary urban explorer who used the street for the pleasures of surprised observation and oneiric contemplation, or who, like Edgar Poe's cipherlike Man of the Crowd, dissolved in the shifting flow of pedestrian traffic. The enshrinement of the commodity, and its flashing presence everywhere through electrically lit advertising, transformed this meditative figure into the desiring-machine of the compulsive shopper.

German critics of this phenomenon referred to the spread of advertising as "Americanismus," as if all of America could be extrapolated from Times Square. In the Weimar years, Berlin acquired a seething, mottled skin of advertising, from street-level display boxes to electrically lit columns and clock-towers ablaze with product logos. This electrification of the night street created a thrilling mixture of illuminated product promotion and varicolored, throbbing signage directing the consumer to restaurants, nightclubs and bars. Barely clandestine establishments offered onstage sex exhibitions, cocaine and other fun in exchange for hard currency.

Berlin was also the locus of a multi-faceted sexual revolution unprecedented in the industrialized West. Hundreds of gay and lesbian bars, strip clubs, bathhouses, massage parlors, s&m clubs, peep shows, dance halls, transvestite cabarets and brothels catered to all sexual appetites and fetishes. Tiller Girl revues and chanteuses on the game were complemented by a ubiquity of outdoor cruising areas, sex parks and other spots where one encountered a Nirvana of prostitution, doll-boys, minettes, line boys, grasshoppers, half-silks and boot whores. Efforts to curb this libidinal eruption were met with contempt and indifference by most Berliners and were in any case alien to the secular spirit of the age and the ungovernable scale and diversity of the metropolis. The spread of prostitution had begun during the scramble for foreign currency during the inflation period, and continued through the years of stability as Berlin's unique menu of tourist attractions.

This sexualized Berlin, and the Weimar Republic itself, have somehow become conflated with the "decadence" of the Nazi period, despite the ideological puritanism and selective persecutions of sexual minorities the Nazis used to control the general population. The real flowering of sexual expression as well as scientific inquiry into human sexuality was strictly Weimar.

In New York, a similar desublimative free-for-all transpired, under the rose, right after V-J Day, into the years of Alfred Kinsey's first researches— and, decades later, reprised itself, completely openly, during the heyday of The Toilet, The Hellfire Club, and similar venues. One can attribute part of this saturnalia to the city's desperate fiscal crises of the 1970s.

Both periods are bracketed at either end by repressive social forces—in Germany before Weimar by rigidly patriarchal family structures (which included the bizarre child-rearing rules and disciplinary devices invented and promulgated by Dr. Daniel Gottlieb Moritz Schreber, the father of Judge Daniel Paul Schreber—the generation of children raised in conformity with Dr. Schreber's sadistic practices became the adults who voted for Hitler); after Weimar, a resurgence of Dr. Schreber's doctrine of "total submission" to authority may have enabled Nazism's bizarre theories of eugenics and racial purity to infect the society unchecked.

The National Socialist anti-modern regression to nature worship and the athleticism of paleolithic Goths, important features of official dogma, was refuted in practice by the Nazis' pragmatic, highly effective adoption of new technologies, industrial production and sophisticated advertising techniques, very much like the fundamentalists of the three major monotheistic religions today, some of whom may live in caves and embrace "beliefs" of prehistoric simplemindedness, but also rely on satellite phones and Internet access.

In New York before World War II, the traditional values enshrined in Norman Rockwell's covers for the *Saturday Evening Post* were more or less the unregenerated mores that veiled dissonant social realities under the surface; at the end of the 1970s, a drastic historical shift was effected by an unexpected resurgence of Christian fundamentalism as a politically powerful influence. Not on the city itself, but the big, dumb country around it.

In Weimar, as the 50-hour work week was reduced to 41 hours, thus creating "the weekend," proletarian amusement settings such as Luna Park flourished as commercial enterprises that afforded the new industrial worker relief from the monotony of manufacturing labor. The mechanized rides and attractions were an anarchic parody of the factory, useless circular or spiraling movements of "fun machines" that produced physical thrills rather than industrial commodities. A very special place in this glitzy Berlin was occupied by its elaborate new film castles, many of which still survive;

the German-American film treaty of 1928, which resuscitated UFA, enabled the German film industry to revive at its earlier prolific pace. Even before, American film had flooded the cinemas and drawn audiences away from stage theater into immense dream chambers. The cinema palace looked at the time like a fantasy exaggeration of the modernist aesthetic holding sway over housing design and retail construction, architectural cousins of Luna Park, though today their ruins have the aura of much older specialty buildings. The Ufa-Palast-am-Zoo opened in 1925, followed in 1926 by the Gloria-Palast and Capitol movie theaters. Eventually there were hundreds, including the Urania, named for Magnus Hirschfeld's term for homosexuality.

Commercial expansion from 1924 onward took its visual inspiration from the credo of Neue Sachlichkeit functionalism, the New Sobriety as it was sometimes known, or the New Objectivity, with emphasis on geometrically precise, bold surfaces realized in modern materials. This sensibility also prevailed in design, photography, painting and sculpture.

Berlin's population reached 4.24 million during its transformation into a fast-paced urban center ringed by an outlying belt of heavy industry. The machine culture that kept it running had its raison d'être in the Taylorist theories expounded in Henry Ford's autobiography, which in Janet Ward's words viewed "the holistic entities of community and individual personality into a merely functioning 'tiny piece of the mass.'" (Another book by Henry Ford, *The International Jew,* perhaps enjoyed even greater popularity in the post-Weimar period.)

By 1930, the fragile hegemony of the Weimar Republic disintegrated rapidly in the aftermath of Black Monday on Wall Street and its devastation of world currencies. Weimar continued to decline as escalating disruptions from both the Communist Left and the Fascist Right fractured the final two years of its existence.

Few Berliners thought the Nazis could seize control. Most considered Hitlerism an aberrant fringe phenomenon that would subside with the march of progress, much as Parisians regarded the perverse rise of Le Pen as a political phenomenon decades later. The average citizen did not believe the clock could truly be turned back, that *ressentiment* over the Versailles Treaty and the mouthings of a deranged agitator could reverse the core values of civilization. The allure of the irrational was vastly underrated in those times as well as these. Capitalism and its double, Soviet Communism, had not raised all boats on the tide of scientific progress, Kafkaesque bureaucratic organization and the enrichment of the upper classes. Nor had secular ideologies taken into account the deeply rooted spiritual need of the working classes to domesticate their fear of death by belief in an invisible realm where something fills what Sartre termed "the God-shaped hole" in modern existence, incarnated in a charismatic demagogue, who promised them a less miserable life.

We can jump ahead here 40 years, past the era of Brecht's grouchy exile in the "city of nets" in California, his later escape from the McCarthy Committee's inquisition to East Berlin, and the founding of the Berliner Ensemble; past Weill's less grandiose adaptation to Broadway and the commercial theater of the U.S.; to the New York City of 1970–1980, the years in which Harry Smith labored on his astonishing, aleatory and, frankly, endlessly protracted, often soporific but gloriously excessive film, *Mahagonny*. Perhaps I can raise some questions about how the New York of Smith's film can and cannot be compared, except metaphorically, to the city of Mahagonny, and to the closing days of the Weimar Republic.

In thinking about this I have been haunted by the title of the second novel of Sartre's trilogy *The Roads to Liberty,* "The Reprieve." *Mahagonny* is probably the most complex and challenging collaboration, as well as the penultimate one, that Brecht and Weill created. It is possible to view the entire Weimar period, through the lens of *Mahagonny,* as one of reprieve— a long one, relatively speaking, that produced an immense outpouring of superior creative work.

In America, in the years 1970–72, a decade of civil revolt had ended in a diminution of countercultural energies, the demoralization of a collective youth rebellion that had been murderously squashed by our own National Guard at Kent State, routed during the Chicago Convention in 1968, and hopelessly fragmented after Nixon's electoral victory, though resistance was still an active wish, so to speak. Mass demonstrations continued, with diminishing impact. Added to COINTEPRO's infiltration of virtually every leftist group in the country, the systematic assassination of the Black Panthers by police and FBI, Nixon's deployment of the IRS as a weapon against the names on his ever-expanding "enemies list," etc., the Revolution, whatever it may or may not have had the possibility of incarnating, was effectively dead, though nonconformist youth continued opposing the Vietnam War and American adventurism; but while it's been mindlessly reiterated a million times since that long-ago moment that America's Viet veterans were "spit on," ridiculed, treated like pariahs and never "honored" for their blind obedience to criminal orders from higher up the military food chain, the truly stigmatized "veterans" of a blatantly racist and illegal war were the many, perhaps millions, of young people who'd obeyed their consciences, and were no longer welcome in the places they came from, where, even if a majority of Americans had soured on the war, those who had opposed it in the first place were considered traitors, an inference derived from depressingly trivial criteria: their hair, their music, the way they dressed, their refusal to follow the safe paths laid out for them by their families, their choice of personal freedom over patriotic sacrifice or security, summed up beautifully in Grace Slick's quotation from James Joyce, "I'd rather have my country die for me."

Naturally, many for whom rebellion was more than a rite of passage into a tight white collar, or an experiment in sexual opportunism, gravitated to New York City, or just washed up there, like Fatty and Moses and Lady Begbick when their truck breaks down, and founded their own Mahagonny inside a city where you indeed had to find the next little dollar to survive—but only a *little* dollar at the time, if the accumulation of money and objects was not your overriding ambition in life.

For instance: State rent control laws, which had been in effect since World War II, were turned over to the city in 1964, while rent stabilization had gone into effect in 1961. It was therefore possible to rent an apartment for a very small amount of money, and if you were an artist you could hole up in your cheap apartment or residence hotel for 20 years, developing your art without interference or an overriding imperative to make large sums of money simply to pay rent. Survival was a struggle, but it was not an impossible struggle to survive at a modest level.

As it happened, New York City was experiencing a reprieve from the schemes of urban planning that had shaped a great deal of the city's outlying infrastructure into a visual and experiential nightmare. The trigger for this reprieve was probably the demolition of the old Pennsylvania Station in 1963, over the protests of America's most eminent architects, writers, artists, city historians and activist citizens. The wonderful columns and facade sculptures of Penn Station were unceremoniously dumped into Seacaucus Meadows, a New Jersey swamp familiar to many of us as an occasional body dump used in *The Sopranos*—this coincided with the spreading influence of a book published in 1961 by Jane Jacobs called *The Death and Life of Great American Cities.* Jacob's argument was an eloquent and commonsense plea in favor of distinct neighborhoods, generous sidewalks and the unregimented diversity of the city, and against the blight inflicted by urban planning. Jacobs especially targeted the depredations of Robert Moses, who had shaped New York since the early 1920s. Moses had mainly attacked the most vulnerable boroughs and communities, the minority enclaves, ripping out so-called slums, concentrating their inhabitants into high-rise housing projects. At the time of Penn Station's destruction, Moses planned to criss-cross Manhattan with a series of elevated expressways. Like Henry Ford, he viewed people as undifferentiated quanta whose lives should be shaped and determined by urban renewal schemes that, as Jacob's book eloquently demonstrated, did nothing to improve the quality of city life, but made it more dangerous, inhuman and alienating.

Moses's "urban renewal" was carried out under funds for New York from the congressional act of 1949 known as Title I, which Moses had wrested exclusive control over. What he'd done as Parks Commissioner epitomized his virulent racism and his vision of the city as a business center that people left at the end of the day for suburban pockets accessible via Moses's "parkway" system, which connected a patchwork of outlying greenery inaccessible to working-class families without cars.

A rebarbative feature of Title I was a clause stipulating that none of its funds could be used to preserve or restore existing communities, but required the city to raze them. When community groups presented viable alternatives to deal with urban blight that would minimize the destruction of existing housing, Moses responded by zoning vast areas for removal; in his construction of the expressway system he had done the same. The Cross-Bronx Expressway is one of the most hatefully clogged and ugliest patches of urban roadwork in the country. Diverting a small part of it by a quarter mile would have required pulling down only five buildings. Instead, Moses sliced the Cross-Bronx through the most densely clustered housing in the area and displaced tens of thousands of people who ended up incarcerated in housing projects.

The idea was that Manhattan would be a business center whose white middle-class personnel disappeared every evening, while the service industry catering to it, consisting entirely of blacks and Puerto Ricans, would be housed in project islands.

This transformation of New York into a metastasized Minneapolis slowed appreciably when John Lindsay, a proponent of Jane Jacob's ideas, was elected mayor in 1965, though the decay of minority neighborhoods continued. Jacob's argument in favor of the sidewalk and street as the loci of the city's liveliness and diversity and its sense of shared living space became the prevailing philosophy of city government, with one tardy manifestation being the preservation of landmark buildings—the Chelsea Hotel, by the way, is one of them, and is currently rumored to be, like so many other "landmark buildings," surreptitiously passing into ownership by one of New York's handful of professional city-rapists calling themselves "hoteliers"— and, until fairly recently, the common sense, humanistic decency of Jacob's vision restrained, to a greater or lesser degree, successive city administrations. Civic scruple is the last thing anyone currently holding public office in New York City would dream of stooping to, when whole armadas of Asian and European money launderers zip into town every day bearing goodie bags of campaign money and some extra traceless income for a new limo, a mink for the wife and an iPhone that eliminates nasal hair and induces strainless bowel movements while picking up stock quotations, e-mail, and can even be jerry-rigged to function as a telephone.

So we could say much of the '70s was a time of reprieve. A reprieve that's come to its end, as developers like Donald Trump have devised elaborate methods of buying up blocks of Manhattan real estate through shell companies and accomplished through subterfuge the right to demolish large quadrants of cityscape to put up whatever ugly, gigantic clusters of luxury housing or commercial space they want.

With the Reagan '80s, the civic opposition to such developers declined, as the city's voting population became less economically diverse, despite an ever-expanding demographic of working-class and underclass citizens. These were demographically disenfranchised by the incarceration of a large percentage of its male youth under the draconian Rockefeller Drug Laws. Mayors Koch and Giuliani were both generous in handing out zoning variances to large corporations, and the end of rent control and rent stabilization is being carried out in advance of its legal dismantling by landlord "buyouts" of sitting tenants. In Jane Jacob's day, the middle class could keep skyscrapers out of its backyards by organizing; today only the very rich are able to preserve the characters of their neighborhoods (which generally have none), while the poor, of course, have never had a voice in architectural planning in New York.

One hapless irony attached to the city's phase-out of Robert Moses is that the last gigantic architectural defacement of Manhattan was engineered by the very people who got rid of him. It was a routine stratagem of Moses to threaten resignation from his various innocuous-sounding official posts, knowing the offer would be routinely rejected; in 1968, Governor Nelson Rockefeller ambushed the old thug by accepting his bogus announcement of retirement, thus ridding New York of his control. However, Governor Rockefeller then conspired with his brother, David, President of Chase Manhattan Bank, to use the Port Authority as their personal fiefdom in order to clear hundreds of landmark cast-iron buildings in downtown Manhattan in order to put up the World Trade Center, perhaps the ugliest structures erected in the 1960s in Manhattan besides the Pan Am Building.

Now, this says nothing about the destruction of the Trade Center any more than the metaphor that the Berlin Wall is Stalin's monument to the assassination of Rosa Luxemburg says anything about the Berlin Wall. It should be understood as an architectural fact, and not a celebration of the towers' violent destruction.

I have described what Weimar was like and what New York was like when Harry Smith merged these two eras into a metaphoric synthesis of nonlinear imagery and the linear musical saturation of *The Rise and Fall of the City of Mahagonny*, without speaking directly of the film Harry Smith devoted so much of his life to assembling.

I have thought about the eight years of editing Smith devoted to this film, and how its images convey, albeit haphazardly, the spirit of *Mahagonny*, which is a somewhat contradictory procedure: Mahagonny is suckerville and paradise at once. The question, which is ambiguous enough in the opera, is even more ambiguous in the film: Suckerville or Paradise for whom? In the opera, Lady Begbick and her cronies are the entrepreneurs, whose moral attitudes are determined by whatever brings revenue to their newfounded city, or drains it away. But the builders of Mahagonny-inside-

New York were eccentric, noncapitalist types whose fortunes in a nonmaterial sense flourished precisely as the city's financial fortunes declined. In 1975, New York was teetering at the edge of bankruptcy, its municipal bonds had become almost worthless, and the hatred and envy the city's cultural richness and racial diversity inspired in the rest of the country was neatly summarized in a *New York Post* headline: FORD TO CITY: DROP DEAD.

This rhetorical absurdity was necessarily followed by a federal bailout that carried New York through a period that could indisputably be characterized as one of extreme "decadence" for those who find this word meaningful, and, not unrelatedly, a period of almost unprecedented artistic ferment, where aesthetic forms and practices meshed in new ways: We experienced a reinvention of pop music, a renaissance of poetry, a variegated use of film and video as artistic media outside the commercial system, an explosion of mixed-media experiment and performance art and innovative uses of photography, and an overthrow of the normative clichés of painting and gallery art as the spontaneous effusions of the artist-as-gifted-child: In other words, New York in the 1970s was a time of extreme civic distress that produced a revolution in art instead of despair, an assertion of private liberty instead of resignation and conformity, experiment, synthesis, a complete redefinition of cultural practice. OUR Mahagonny drove many over the edge into oblivion; but it gave a new generation the sense that it too could carve its own path, that an individual could become a writer or a musician or a filmmaker, look how he or she wanted to look, dress as he or she wanted to dress, and all could ignore the mindless blandishments of consumer society.

That Mahagonny began its decline as the surrounding tides of so-called conservatism swept the outlying provinces; its devastation was furthered by the AIDS epidemic, an unchecked hypergrowth of corporate power and by the wildly disproportionate influence on mass media by religionists, militaristic patriots and an unquestioned ethos of capitalism in its most primitive and punitive forms. The amplified noise of capitalism's coercive voice drowned out the music of rebellion and the discourse of reason, it demonized altruism, reified greed, and drove from Mahagonny both its edgy dangerousness and its creative spark. In effect, Mahagonny has been destroyed, it is gone, and much of the demolition has in fact been accomplished in the name of God. (I mean in the name of money: in Mahagonny, they're synonyms.)

From this perspective, Manhattan-Mahagonny of Smith's movie somewhat shakily parallels the arc of New York City's history as well as Weimar's Mahagonny, though Smith's film reached its completion before the unhappy end of the city's long reprieve.

Many know the story of the Brecht-Weill opera, and in fact you can almost infer it from the songs that have become standards: Mahagonny is founded by three fugitives to lure goldminers returning from Alaska and relieve them of their cash by stocking the new city with whiskey and whores; for reasons that are never clear, for all opera has some of the illogic of dreams and fairy tales, prohibitions on behavior are eventually introduced, the inhabitants become bored, many people leave. One of the original arrivals, Jimmy Mahoney—Johann Ackerman in the original—decides, at the moment that Mahagonny is threatened by a typhoon, the forecast sometimes lessened to a hurricane, again for no logical reason—that these DON'Ts that the matriarch Begbick has unaccountably instituted—don't sing, don't dance and so on—are the very reason for Mahagonny's tedium and incites the inhabitants to throw all inhibitions to the oncoming winds.

Miraculously, Mahagonny is spared the catastrophe, while nearby Pensacola and other towns are wiped out. Mahagonny becomes a freshly libertine place of unrestrained sex, drinking, gluttony and prizefighting; the phrase DO IT is projected over the stage or declaimed by Jimmy Mahoney, and a year later Mahagonny is booming. A character named Jake eats himself to death to the applause of the population; in the boxing ring, Trinity Moses, one of the original three fugitives, kills Alaskawolf Joe, Jimmy's best friend, in a fight. (Parenthetically, JUST DO IT is now one of myriad similar advertising slogans for expensive sneakers and soda pop; corporate postmodernism encourages consumers to go all the way, be extreme, cut away from the crowd—by purchasing a particular beer, an enormous SUV, the slave-labor produced casualwear of a specific designer.)

While Trinity Moses is easily able to acquit himself of a manslaughter charge, Jimmy is arrested and put in chains because he cannot pay his bar tab. He is sentenced to death and executed, not for more serious crimes he finds himself accused of, but because he can't bribe his way out of his situation. In the third act God appears, condemning everyone to hell; the people of Mahagonny reply that they are already in hell, and always have been. Because of inflation, riots break out and the city of Mahagonny dies.

This loose plot could only work as the narrative pretext for a tapestry of musical drama. The shifting fortunes of a city over time can perhaps be accurately delineated only in a very long historical research or conveyed emotionally in a richly diverse piece of music. The complete history of the Chelsea Hotel, for example, where so much of the film was shot, may be a little bit like the history of the Mudd Club; as I told someone who proposed this to me as a book project, "If you can remember the Mudd Club clearly enough to write a book about it, obviously you were never there." But the Chelsea is a charmed place on the map of Manhattan—another one soon to be gone with the wind, evidently—and if the city outside its walls seemed to Harry Smith the epitome of soulless, money-grubbing Mahagonny, I suspect the hotel, and wherever he settled in the city later, was a site of reprieve where the excesses and extremes of the doomed metropolis were absolved or ignored by the judgment of God, or at least escaped the attention of a punishing deity, even though the Chelsea has hosted more extreme and transgressive behavior than most of the urban jumble around it.

The finished film *Mahagonny* is in many ways a more effective visualization of the Brecht-Weill opera than a quotidian stage production, because Smith's visuals—uncanny, startling, mesmerizing, freely shifting from the abstract to the concrete, rococo to minimalist, the "realistic" dailiness of people's faces and movements to magically animated Hindu gods and abstract animated blocks of colored matter—aren't eclipsed by Weill's music or Brecht's libretto, but "assisted" by it into an anarchy the opera itself never fully evokes, though it is one of the glories of the 20th-century musical theater, in a way that Harry Smith's film fails to be an important landmark of 20th-century cinema. Smith's work is too personal and fetishistic to truly engage the world that it pictures, and is more a beautiful mess than a legible work of art.

Weill knew his music would overwhelm Brecht's libretto. *Mahagonny*'s score, he wrote, "has a much more fundamental role than in purely story line opera, since I am replacing the earlier bravura aria with a new kind of popular song. As a result I can allay any fears that . . . this work is somehow derived from a spoken play. With great difficulty I have succeeded in getting Brecht to the point that he was actually challenged by the task of writing a text to suit musical requirements and I have examined every word with an eye to the demands of the opera stage. It is the first libretto in years that is fully dependent on music, indeed upon MY MUSIC."

As Smith's *Mahagonny* has a cruciform frame of four panels that often divide the image between two upper panels and two lower ones, and these images are often flopped or mirrored panning or static shots of the same image, collapsing into itself or spreading away from its center, when the upper and lower panels form a composite whole the effect is the creation of a cryptic sculptural object in the center of the frame; certain shots that move in the upper panels act as a proscenium for the lower ones, or a rising curtain that reveals them, or, vice-versa, movements of the lower images suggest footlights emphasizing the images above it; at times the frame itself is shattered into irregular fragments of imagery floating on black leader, and the image area again has the appearance of sculpture. I cannot be certain, but these passages suggest the element of mathematical analysis of Duchamp's *Large Glass* that Smith refers to in the full title of the film. I leave it for others to puzzle out this analysis, as math has never been my strong suit, and, as a spectator, I incline to favor Duchamp's own assertion that if we give the attributes of a medium to an artist, we must deny him the state of consciousness on the aesthetic plane about what he is doing or why he is doing it.

It may be true of *Mahagonny* what Duchamp said of the *Large Glass:* the ideas in the glass are more important than the actual visual realization. But we must leave that to film history to determine. Ideas have a longer reach than works of art; the historian's task is to determine what those ideas are, or were, and how successfully or not the work of art embodies them. The important thing for us, as the more or less contemporaneous spectators, is the film itself, a work of uncanny beauty that offers little to the analytical part of our attention, a synthesis of far-ranging references that nowhere produces Brecht's cherished "alienation" effect, except, arguably, in Smith's insistence that the film run the entire length of the recorded opera—that is, if, like me, you find yourself wishing the film to end at least an hour before it actually does. It's an artifact we can puzzle over interminably, yet celebrate for its suture of sound and image, its serendipitous surprises, and the sensory seductions Brecht hated in art, and we can find it exemplary too by considering its obvious refusals. *Mahagonny* is the product of infinite patience and aesthetic hermeticism, and the arduous job of making it on an erratic budget, over a span of time that causes it to lose its point as often as it finds it, knowing the results would have no commercial value, reflects an ethos of stubborn artistic opposition to disposable consumer art and easy answers to difficult questions that dominate most of our culture right now.

I don't wish to idealize the '70s or demonize the subsequent two decades of ever-more commodified cultural production. We would not want to return to that time any more than we want to live in this time. All periods of human history are disasters for our species even if they each contain some pockets of enlightenment and elements of humane progress.

Having known Harry Smith only through those who knew him, and through his films, I believe he was as tormented, self-doubting, disturbed and difficult, as complex and contradictory, inconsistent and self-destructive as many of the artists I've known in my life, or observed from a safe distance. An inner life that resembles a typhoon isn't required to make good art. Many of the most intriguing artists in every field battle to maintain focus without any help from neuroticism, to bring the invisible thing they conjure in their heads into the world as the thing by which they become known to others, and bring it into being at the same time that they are being ripped apart by demons of uncertainty, paranoia and abjection. Harry Smith seems to have been one of these, and *Mahagonny* is the perhaps too-assured, welcoming sprawl he rag-picked from his private hurricane.